CROSS SECTIONS
from a decade of change

ALSO BY ELIZABETH JANEWAY

FICTION

The Walsh Girls, 1943

Daisy Kenyon, 1945

The Question of Gregory, 1949

Leaving Home, 1953

The Third Choice, 1959

Accident, 1964

BOOKS FOR CHILDREN

The Vikings, 1951

The Early Days of the Automobile, 1956

Angry Kate, 1963

Ivanov Seven, 1967

NONFICTION

Man's World, Woman's Place: A Study in Social Mythology, 1971

Between Myth and Morning: Women Awakening, 1974

Powers of the Weak, 1980

EDITED BY ELIZABETH JANEWAY

Women: Their Changing Role, 1972

CROSS SECTIONS

from a decade of change

Elizabeth Janeway

WILLIAM MORROW AND COMPANY, INC.
New York *1982*

Library of Congress Cataloging in Publication Data

Janeway, Elizabeth.
    Cross sections from a decade of change.

    1. Women—United States—Social conditions.
I. Title.
HQ1426.J36   305.4'0973   82–3485
ISBN 0–688–01024–5   AACR2

Printed in the United States of America

First Edition

1 2 3 4 5 6 7 8 9 10

BOOK DESIGN BY BERNARD SCHLEIFER

Contents

CROSS SECTIONS

from a decade of change

Introduction:
Days, Images,
Memories, Hopes

IF, LIKE ME you were born in 1913, you should have acquired a sense of history one way or another, for history has been sneaking up behind you and banging you over the head ever since you arrived on this planet. Before I was a year old, six Serbian terrorist-patriots (choose which label you like) had managed among them, one June morning, to assassinate the heir to the Austro-Hungarian Empire and his morganatic wife and thus to set in motion the apocalyptic end of a very old order of life, shakier than it seemed but still functioning. Before I could read I followed the progress of the thunderous events that ensued by the size of the black headlines that marched across the breakfast-table newspaper. To a four-year-old, this density of ink reproduced faithfully the menace loose in the world; uncontrollable but not, alas, wholly unpredictable for no one afterward dared take its absence as certain. Security, comfort and love were contingent. They did not quite rest on bedrock.

The twenties tried to live as if they did, or most people tried, but contingency shadowed the margins of the solid world. New York was still a city of neighborhoods. Mine was complacent, respectable, and disapproving toward the noise and cooking smells of ethnic diversity, though we of the smug bourgeoisie could enjoy a season of romantic cosmopolitanism when incomers visited only briefly and kept their distance. We would stop to watch the West Indian cricket teams that sometimes took over the playgrounds nearby, whereas the sandlot baseball players were ignorable. My territory wasn't, thank God, as solid and close an enclave of middle-class unity as such neighborhoods had been in my parents' time; though even then there were surely obstinate dissidents. Earlier droves of daughters who ended by growing up dutiful must have felt a pull toward rebellion and daydreamed a future of impossible, heroic deeds. When I was nine I wanted to be

a pirate. Of course I knew such creatures didn't exist any more, but
it was in this rakish and no doubt sentimentalized image that the pull
of the margin came to me, as cowboy and vaquero and the bank-
robbing James brothers appealed to others. John Dillinger and "The
Bobbed-Hair Girl Bandit" inhabited headlines I could read. Earlier
I'd had a nurse who told me what she called "outside-the-world
stories," and I went on telling them to myself in a sort of personalized
science fiction mixed up with fairy tale. I was a dab hand at drawing
maps of nonexistent territory long before Tolkien sketched out Middle
Earth—for anyone but himself, that is.

There was a good deal of such romanticism around in the twenties,
in headlines and in fiction of all sorts of genres and values. Just as with
current Gothic romance, fantasy can serve both to comfort the mind
and syphon off the drive to act out one's urges and ambitions. But for
the girls of my generation, something was different and new. The dim
chance of effective rebellion was solidifying toward actuality even
while it still presented itself in the familiar fairy-tale style. As must
happen so often, change masked itself in ambiguity and possibilities
weren't easy to weigh. Perhaps my middle-class background was what
saved me from the illusion of total fantasy and Hollywood dreams—
they were "vulgar," though a sense of reality must also have pointed
out my utter lack of talent for stardom. I suspect such sense was at
least as common as illusion, for we who were resolved on getting out
didn't expect to escape into a golden dream but simply into the ordinary, active world.

That doesn't mean the golden dreams were useless. In the first
place they were available and familiar. We could stretch our ambitions
in fantasy because others had before us, and stretching is better for
aspiration than tranquillizers. Second, fantasy preserves an element of
play. To imagine oneself a pirate or an opera singer or a prima ballerina or a desperado could be passed off as a game, whereas becoming
a lawyer or a doctor or a scholar could not. Not only did these
occupations lack romantic glamor. More important, such realistic
goals had to be taken seriously. They demanded commitment, work
and strength. Of that we were wary; not out of laziness but out of
doubt of ourselves as trailblazers. We protected ourselves, therefore,
by betting against ourselves. Just the same, the old outside-the-world
stories let us exercise our hopes. They were masks for a growing real
strength as well as being distractions, and as time passed we used them
for the first purpose more than for the second. Our hopes and plans
grew within them like the chick within the egg.

As yet, however, the fact that the walls of tradition around woman's place had begun to crack was still so new that we dared not trust the news. Along with the rest of the world, we assumed that our personal histories would end as our mothers' had done, in the condition alluded to and never described in the fairy tales by the familiar ending, "And so they got married and lived happily ever after." It was a blank future after the wedding, no word on what living happily entailed, or felt like. Reality, of course, had something to tell us about *that,* and it was indeed the data of daily life in happily married families that motivated dream alternatives to the one orthodox, acceptable life history. For girls, *rational* alternatives didn't come into it, there were as yet none to imagine. Getting out, "breaking away," was as much a long shot as betting on the numbers, and logical planning as effective as rolling the dice. Rationality was irrational in our situation; better simply to hope, for reason would have to report how unlikely success would be. And if one was not ballerina or opera singer material, and too well brought up to suffer Hollywood dreams, hopes existed only in the masculine mode. I suppose we all knew a couple of girls whose mothers had enrolled them in what we called toe-dance classes or tied up their Saturday mornings with singing lessons, but for the rest of us, any alternative to "happily ever after" had to be based on male models and one sort (pirate) was as easy to turn to as another (president). We copied men in our dreams because there was no one else to copy.

The normal female alternative to "got married and lived happily ever after" was still "old maid." I had a family-full, both sides of it, mother's and father's sisters. They were talented, intelligent, daring within the limits of the possible (which did not include opera, films or ballet), respected by friends and acquaintances, and quite unable, any of them, to earn a living. Well, I daresay that's not entirely true. One of my father's sisters had trained as a nurse since her dream of becoming a doctor was a full-fledged outside-the-world story that affectionate parental concern was forced to deny her. All through the war whose headlines had smudged into my infant mind the presence and something of the meaning of terror and tragedy, she had nursed in a hospital in France. Was she paid for her work? Or did the Mother Superior, a lifelong friend thereafter, assume that this American woman was volunteering? I don't know, but I assume that was the way of it.

Then there was my mother's sister who painted miniature portraits and certainly was paid for them; but who knows how much?

Under pressure, she would doubtless have tried to turn it from an accomplishment into a professional skill and she might have succeeded, for the ones I have are charming and good likenesses. But she was also engaged in (employed in?) keeping house for her widowed mother, my bossy old matriarch of a grandmother, her bachelor brother, the family breadwinner, and her younger sister, another old maid, much loved by children and just a little flighty. Certainly that energy and effort could have earned income, but the pressure didn't come. The bit of inherited money, the brotherly support sufficed—just—to spare my aunts the coarsening, strengthening struggle to keep themselves. They were taken care of, and they cut their lives to fit.

I loved them too much to be really frightened of their fate. I didn't want it, but the occupations and interests they had contrived to cultivate prevented their lives from terrifying me. It was a friend of my mother's who managed to do that. I was taken to visit one day, the ladies settled to tea and chat, and I retreated behind the sofa and began, not very hopefully, to pull books out of the shelves there, hoping to find some volume into which I could retreat and not succeeding. "I never get up in the morning until ten o'clock," said my mother's friend. "It makes the days shorter." Behind the sofa, a *frisson,* a chill of the spine.

But the cracks in the walls were widening to let in rumors of possible action and even fame, though the latter was never entirely secure or free from the risk of notoriety. It took one or the other to get a woman's name in the paper at all, except for the society pages or the Sunday rotogravure, where debutantes and their socially prominent do-gooding mothers gazed forth. *They* held no interest for me, but rumors of action brought another sort of frisson to someone who believed that she could, in a pinch, put words together acceptably. This was a family talent, like having an ear for music in some lineages. My father's side, the Halls, commanded a knack for writing in the same way that some clans can always produce a pickup orchestra of siblings, cousins and uncles. And the twenties were rich in known writers. The poets were romantic; not exactly notorious but tinged with the atmosphere of Bohemia or at least Greenwich Village. Edna Millay and Elinor Wylie had certainly had AFFAIRS. The solid successful novelists, Willa Cather and Ellen Glasgow, were not publicly attached to any such goings-on by the press, but they were present, they were there and reported on. And there were the journalists and wits like Dorothy Parker—

Yes, I know, I said we had no female role models and, in spite of this list of achievers, it's true. Their existence did establish the fact that females could get published, find places in magazines and on bookstore shelves, but we who were young had still to move them into our dreams. There were difficulties. For one thing, Famous Women Writers were still rare enough to carry the element of luck with them, not the quality of reasoned, purposeful work arriving at a planned goal. On the other hand, those to whom such sober characteristics could be applied were, in turn, not fantastic enough. We had so far to go, said all the paraphernalia of everyday life. We could envision the hard work of a public career with our minds cognitively, so to speak, but experientially cognition was not supported by enough data to reinforce it. It seems to me we needed that atmosphere of fairy-tale, gambling and miraculous luck to sustain us. I believe we wanted to have to depend on the Goddess Fortuna because we were still so unsure of ourselves.

What we were attempting after all was a total reversal not only of history and its public traditions but also of the daily life in which we were immersed. For that we needed super-female strength, the courage to face the size of the task and the minute-to-minute persistence to do it over and over and over again in the face of threats and beseechings and naggings and clear statements of the impossibility of the whole undertaking, which after all have not ceased yet. We needed heroines and saints, not just role models. The existence of some women writers was important, it did establish that such a way of getting out could work, and in my case it was one I might dredge up the elementary skills to try. But though I wanted to do their work, I don't remember ever wanting to live their lives. Some seemed too respectable, some seemed too disastrously, familiarly feminine, but one way or another they all seemed limited. Yes, there were women writers, but I wanted to hitch my wagon to a genius—where was *she*? Oh, I didn't think I *was* one, but I needed the pull, the height, to tie ambitions to. It wasn't Millay I wanted to copy, it was Keats; it wasn't Cather, it was Dickens or Dreiser, esteemed a genius in those days.

How much did it hurt us that we felt bereft of stars and geniuses to copy? God knows. Human nature is flexible, and the fact that my generation of girls had to deny so much of our femininity was really not so destructive as it may sound, given the definition of femininity then current. What we suffered, I think, was not so much a split in the self as it was finding that self isolated and choosing isolation. Since we could not dream ourselves into intimacies with female models, since we had to turn to men as patterns, we adopted many of the attitudes that went with the patterns. That cut us off from most other women. We thought they were silly, limited and ignorant: "dumb blondes" who wanted only to date and be popular. (We had hours of envy when we wanted that very much too.) But our assumption that prom queens desired only to settle down in the prison cell from which we wanted so desperately to escape reinforced our condescension. We saw them as agreeing eagerly to a life we couldn't accept, a life we knew as a dead end, a trap, a betrayal of possibility.

Did we, I wonder, persuade ourselves there was something new about our feelings of being special and chosen as a way of preserving the impetus to change? If so, we were wrong factually and right emotionally. There wasn't anything special in us except an awareness that external change was beginning. But it was very much man's world still. If we acknowledged that behind us stood long lines of angry, grieving, desperate women, we also had to acknowledge that they had failed. That admission would sap the strength we were beginning to possess, for it would tell us again how likely it was that we would fail too, and fantasy or not, we needed to think we could win. Because we were not secure in our judgment of the outside world, we transferred the sense of change to our own identities, not out of egotism but in order to strengthen the hope that change allowed us to nourish. Without it we would have had to give up and prepare ourselves to accept the common end of woman as being forever "got married and lived happily ever after." Which isn't to say that we opposed marriage in principle. What scared us were those long, repetitious, narrow existences in which (we thought we had evidence) the lives of our mothers were laid. We were ignorant out of fright, we chose isolation because that seemed the only way to save ourselves, to get out.

Well, some of us did get out, and many of those who did had help from the citizens of the past, which we were so busy rejecting. It was the aunts who helped my sister and me. She went off to Wellesley in the twenties, first girl in the family to get to college, when "Bible" was still a required course, Greek favored by intellectuals, black stockings and bloomers worn at gym. Part of the money to send her was skimped out of those small funds the aunts guarded so carefully. The new venture was also empowered and seconded by my father's large opinion of his daughters' possibilities and surely endorsed by his awareness of the loss inherent in the lives of his sisters. On the face of it, nothing remarkable happened. My sister and I too, later on, were simply being offered an education, and by the time we got it, decades had passed since the first young women had drunk from the Pierian spring of higher learning. But in fact we were part of a reversal of history, an absolute shift in the quality of reality. For us, being taken care of was over. We were pioneers. We were going to college without any pretence that it was a way to acquire some female accomplishments or to widen our ability to raise a family of cultivated children. We were going so that we could learn how to earn our livings. In France, Simone de Beauvoir, of much the same generation, was undergoing much the same experience. The economics of family life was a basic cause: I grew up knowing exactly what "shabby genteel" means. But the response of the family to that pressure was new. Where economic problems would have set earlier parents to thinking of advantageous marriages for the girls, we were, astoundingly, treated as if we had been our brothers. We were offered the chance of a career.

More history had manifested itself by the time I got to Barnard in the thirties. There were menacing headlines again marching across the top of the morning paper and speaking of bad times, terrible times, uncontrollable, predictable only by being there forever, it seemed. And not only headlines. There were bread lines and soup lines in the streets and shantytowns (Hoovervilles) on the Jersey flats by the railroad tracks. History professors played us radio broadcasts of Hitler's rhetoric. I worked summers and Saturdays in a department store for pocket money and clothes money, and one winter when nothing would stretch to keep me at college, I wrote advertising copy for the bargain basement there. True, my sister pulled strings to get me taken on, and so I suppose there was arguably an element of "being taken care of " still present; but I worked for my money, banging out ads for elegant $3.95 dresses and "seconds" on tablecloths or pillowcases with my built-in facility at words functioning as a craft-skill. There were a lot of hard-pressed ambitious young around, and we looked up at the dark skies and had fun under them, like gypsies sheltering under a tree as a thunderstorm gathered. If the air crackled with doom-lightning, there were messages of defiance too. If the thunder growled, we were no longer immobilized, shackled by protection. This was the large world. I had somehow got out and never, never, never, whatever the thunder said or lightning showed, *never* would I have to go back to the dependence of being cared for at the price of losing my mind and my judgment and my freedom and my right to question and judge events and act on that judgment myself.

I don't put this down because the experience was unique but because it wasn't. The trouble is that while it all seems like yesterday to me, still vivid and meaningful, still presenting the alternative to dependence and all the mean bargains it demanded, it hardly exists for those who didn't live through it or something like it. That's not the fault of the young; it's the result of Respectable Thinking and Writing and Recording and Defining by all the Respectable Dealers in Power and the Respectable Philosophers and Historians who tidy up their gardens for them. You can call it the Establishment, but it's really too nice a name. William Cobbett, British journalist and radical reformer, labeled it "The Thing." I think of him glancing back at the smoke of early nineteenth-century London, on one of his famous rural rides, and trying to sum up in a word the frustrated anger he felt at the heavy weight of bureaucratic stubbornness, aristocratic greed, political sham and complacent corruption that he saw there; and there wasn't any one word heavy enough, condemnatory enough, *complete* enough to cover the system that blindly, blandly, shut its eyes and its ears against any effort to save itself by reforming itself in its own interest—and so he named it The Thing.

And it's still with us. The Thing sits there solidly and says to rebels and reformers now, as it did two hundred years ago: Why make such a fuss? What can't be cured must be endured. Whoever said life was fair? And because life is not fair, The Thing grunts and chuckles and labors to make it less fair. Women have got out, desperation and determination supported us as we tunneled and fought our way through or under or over the walls; we are here in the ordinary world—but why, asks The Thing, should we be encouraged in any way to feel that accomplishment as a prize or a pleasure? The Thing will do its obstinate best to make sure that we find as little cause for rejoicing, and as much guilt, as possible in our escape to the human condition. In order to dampen our joy, it will also do all that it can to make sure we don't remember the forced and narrow compromises we left behind. Why should you remember your victimization, it asks—as if we ourselves had chosen that state and recalled it now in masochistic delight. But if we forget, we forget not only what we left behind but the fact that we left it; we forget both victimization and the strength that overcame it. Let us not forget the limits on thought and action that fenced in the genteel middle class lest we cease to behave like "ladies," anymore than we forget the mean servitude and drudgery and denial required from the less fortunate. If the circumstances of repression differed with class, the anger they inspired was the same, and so was the silencing of anger and its forced conversion into apathy or craziness or misdirected violence. Let us not forget how these differences were used to separate us from each other and disguise the similarity of our destiny behind hatred and fear and envy of woman for woman.

No, what the generations of women before mine but culminating in mine as an opening advance guard for the activists of the sixties and seventies—what we lived through was an epic, a revolution, never before experienced. It was the first step beyond fantasy and tokenism toward the real public presence of women as equals and free agents— *and nobody says so.* We're asked to take it for granted, as if real life, felt and done and chosen and dared, was a story projected on the screen contrived and forgettable, a miniseries to be interrupted by commercials when necessary. If we think about history at all, we're invited to see it as inevitable and complete: "You've come a long way, Baby!" But if it's complete, no more can or should be done. And if it was inevitable, then our own efforts had little or nothing to do with it. The whole thing must have been easy, hardly an achievement at all. But if it was easy, it hardly matters; it simply comes down jokily to getting out of long skirts and corsets and being allowed to smoke. So says The Thing. But it was not easy or inevitable or unimportant.

Until we understand that, we won't know what we have made and what has happened to us and to the world because of our own making. No doubt social change has always been present. It has been graver and more fundamental in the last century than perhaps ever before, and women were not the primal factors in the beginning. But our response to change has been neither timid nor uncreative. Unasked and often unappreciated, we have struggled with social disruption in the interest of maintaining the bonds of community and family. And not because we wanted, or expected, to be taken care of; the taking-care-of has been rather the other way. Let us remember it. If we don't we'll forget our own strength and put our trust in the mutterings of The Thing. "I don't want equality," said a woman to me last spring, "I want to be taken care of." Perhaps she was only tired, but she sounded (and looked) as if she didn't have much to worry about and was trying on the Cinderella Complex as if it were a modish new dress instead of a fusty old hand-me-down. I didn't know what to say to her. "You don't know what you're talking about" would have been true, I expect, and also unpersuasive. She *didn't* know what she was talking about, which she can't be blamed for. But she sounded proud of her ignorance.

That shook me. She's an omen. Oh, not a new one, but an omen just the same, and a sign we shouldn't forget. She says to me that the rest of us need to hang onto our new knowledge of our old, old history and of the dramatic change that some of us alive today have witnessed ourselves. If we forget where we came from, we may find ourselves back where we used to be, living on an island of the present and looking at a future we can't plan for because we have no knowledge of the past, no living awareness of process and change, of continuity and causality in which we can take a hand because we know we have done so already. Then The Thing can lurch up and present its self-serving arguments as if they were facts, and we won't have any grounds for disbelief.

I don't mean to scold—women have been scolded enough; and I know, too, why we tend to turn our backs on the past. It *has* been a history of victimization. It has also been private; not *real* history but just what happened to us. And there seemed for so long to be so little change in our lives, so much repetition (though how can we be sure of that if we don't try to remember what happened?). Private and painful, repetitive, inescapable—and unimportant, too, for that's what we've been taught till what seems like only the other day. Those are passive reasons for refusing to look back. There's another, a positive, active reason in that we grew up desperately wanting to get out, into the future, not to repeat the past, not to live our mothers' lives. We were *disgusted* with history, we were aching for change, we felt as if looking back could only turn us, like Lot's wife, to a dead forest of pillars of salt. For centuries, for millennia, had not millions and millions of us relived our mothers' lives thousands and thousands of times? How could such history do us any good? No wonder we chose fantasy instead. When our private histories ended "And so they got married and lived happily ever after," why should we want to study their myriad retellings? The only other stories for our imaginings were fantasies in the male mode that began "If I were my brother, I would —" Since we weren't our brothers, these were not empirically useful; but at least they were pleasant.

Now, at last, we have something to remember that is both good and real, the beginning of a testament in which we've got as far as the Book of Exodus, on Getting Out. We have still to map new territory and settle the land and work out the human laws for living there together, but we do have a store of information that can be put together into a structure of knowledge and, when we get enough, distilled into the essence that is wisdom. Let us not forget it in favor of fantasy.

Fantasy is not confined to women; men use it too, both aggressively and defensively. The powerful have always been willing to help the weak dream unproductively instead of thinking forward toward action. But when we say "men too," we should still take note of a difference, and that is the difference between "some" and "none." Yes, many men have been kept in bondage, removed from power, as women have been—but they have been kept there by other men. If most men have been powerless, a few have not.

It astonishes me that the difference between "some," a "few" and "none" makes so little difference in our thinking. How unambitious women still are! We say to ourselves, "Most men are not powerful, their lives are almost as limited as those of women, so why should we complain?" But the difference between "a few" and "none at all" isn't small, it isn't unimportant. It's the difference between the possibility of achieving independence by your own actions and efforts in the real world and being debarred from the start, being offered no chance at all. If no chance is possible, who would break her heart trying? Some men have found themselves in that position too and have withdrawn and given up. We who were once inevitably labeled weak and born into dependence share a lot, and what we share begins with the denial of hope. But never have *all* men been denied the right to hope and dare and plan their way to successful rebellion. Women were denied that right, and so the equality of dependence that most of us shared was never entirely equal. Men could hope when we could not, and all of us knew it. The knowledge separated us from each other, even in our status of dependence. Because women were there forever (properly, said The Thing), men could only suffer if they allied themselves with us.

Well, preventing alliances by emphasizing difference and division is a familiar tactic of a dominant elite. The rest of us will overcome our sense of difference from each other best, I think, as we work and act in concert toward common goals, and though that has begun, we haven't got far yet. Recognition of human likeness lies ahead in a future that has still to be imagined and made operative. At any rate, history in the large has finally noted that women are working and hoping for change and taking such work seriously instead of draining emotions into fantasy, knitting our own double binds and accepting the role of victim, martyr and long-suffering secret agent of vengeance because direct action for oneself could not be envisioned.

Even now our self-esteem is fragile. To describe the process of victimization can be taken all too easily as an exercise in "blaming the victims." But we need very much to examine and understand how the assent to victimization can be elicited. It's done by turning the mind of the victim against the victim's own interests. Women who "want to be taken care of" have been convinced that they can't take care of themselves. Naturally they fear to try and resent those who tell them they could actually manage if they did try. They feel as if they were being given a pair of skis and directed to the ski jump without benefit of lessons. Telling them to go ahead, they *can* do it, only makes them feel worse: It seems to condemn them for timidity as well as ineptitude. It discounts sincere, and crippling, emotions. But those emotions are neither inevitable nor permanent. The challenge of changed reality can in itself bring about a positive response. Some women, forced to jump by circumstances, will rejoice to find themselves coping quite well thereafter. Others learn from each other and move forward together. In any case, we need our recent history and its examples of women who did break patterns, survived and prevailed. Case histories and role models diminish the force of orthodox arguments asserting the inevitability of feminine weakness.

Perhaps this sounds like that familiar and discouraging statement, less heard now than it was a few years ago but still with us, "I did it, why can't you do it too?" If it does, I apologize. I think that many of us who did get out when the going was harder had to do it in ways that hurt, and we came to accept more traditional ideas than was truly necessary. If there are role models in my generation, I hope they will be temporary expedients, not permanent heroines. We did have to cut ourselves off from most other women and condemn their passivity; we did have to break with the old role in the bitter, personal fashion that often turned us against our mothers in order to fight free of the victim's part, which we were rejecting. We were choosing to try to become human beings instead of women; we believed that there was not enough for us in woman's place, and we were right. There isn't. But our rejection of the female role was colored by the fact that we had to turn to male models for our apprenticeship. I suspect we rejected too much of the one and accepted too much of the other.

For my generation, then, the second wave of feminism that began to rise in the sixties involved a new process of learning. We who had to take our measure from male mentors when we were young now have a chance to discover some old errors of thought and patches of blindness as we find teachers in those who would ordinarily be protégés. Perhaps this is one reason for the absence of age discrimination in the women's movement. Young and old and in-between, we often find ourselves thinking together, not by fiat but because our experience is still one of discovery, communication and evaluation. When I urge that we remember the past, it's not because I think that the past is something to be copied reverently but because the roots of the learning process on which we're still engaged lie there. We don't want to forget the noble and selfless discoverers and founders, but we don't want, either, to forget the blunders and patched-together solutions that limited us while they kept us alive.

There are various strands that run through the thinking and the expression of ideas and reactions that make up this book, but the central one is an urgent insistence on the need to understand *process* as a first step toward managing change. The conscious and the hidden mythologies, alive in any and all societies, which present themselves as ways to understand the world *and* to behave in a way that will bring rewards in that world, tend to be static. They set up First Principles, axioms of belief, roles to be learned that will lead to success in relation-ships guaranteed to be desirable—that is, they instruct us how to find a Happy Ending, to "get married and live happily ever after." In slow-moving, stable circumstances, they may work fairly well fairly often. What they leave out is change, and in our time change has become as omnipresent as any static First Principle of the past. This is not to deny the value of principles as goals; but how do we get there? When women aspire to an equal chance to influence our futures and have a say in the way the world works, we need to understand the way one circumstance leads to another, how decisions are both made and implemented, that cause and effect aren't automatic but have to be worked at.

Now, in the private, domestic sphere so long made our territory, we know all that. We have had a great deal of experience in studying the way process works in terms of personal relations, family politics, sexual démarches, power plays and alliances within the shifting groups that deal with everyday life. One profoundly enlightening opportunity for watching process comes with raising children and following their growth; another exists in the responsibilities of caring for aging parents. Our problem lies in applying this fund of useful knowledge to the Great World of Respectable Thinking and Proper Behavior, where The Thing presides. For that we need intellectual daring and enjoyment in action, the opposite of the impulse to relax and be taken care of. Intellectual daring, however, can turn into self-defeating theatrics if it forgets the daily data of living and available change in the treasury of the past.

Not much of that history is written down. Some of it gets into fiction, but mostly we tell it to each other in hundreds of thousands of conversations, full of reminiscences and comparisons. It often sounds like high-school chat, with its self-mockery and appeals for sympathy over the teller's ridiculous reactions to situations she should have understood. In adopting that mode of discourse, that mimicked juvenility, there is a concealed strength. We are returning to a period of possibility, before the constraints of adult roles were accepted; before the male-female central relationship, which is still culturally prescribed and still defined as most important, overrode other intimacies and playful friendships. Play is not only fantasy; it is also a place to test one's abilities and try on roles and behaviors. Significant things can be said then just because they do not have to provoke significant reactions: Dealing with each other can be tested too. So, talking together "like girls," recreating an old and free experience of sharing emotions and knowledge, women make clear to each other much of their lives that isn't juvenile or trivial at all, much of what we learn from the dailyness where actions and repetitions hold our lives in place.

It's true there are demerits in "girl talk." Using it, we still sound like victims. But we don't, in fact, *think* as victims when we call up once again the defensive self-mockery of adolescence. It is a defense behind which our courage rises. Though one wave may not run as far up the beach, the line of furthest reach goes steadily higher. But we must look at the rising line, not just at the advance from one wave to the next, and that means hanging on to our knowledge of the past. Thus we see the extent of change and will not be baffled by moments that seem like retreat but are in fact consolidations of progress. For women today, history isn't abstract and detached—it's very personal. Knowing how far we've come and what we have overcome is a profound source of strength.

History is public too. Many contemporary arguments against women's advance toward full humanity, and so toward establishing, in time, the full humanity of men too, are based on a denial of the possibility of change. The whole school of thought that has seized on the idea that human behavior is genetically determined works actively to contradict the possibility of meaningful historical shifts in human existence. I don't suppose that most of its devotees are fully aware of this effect, and some who are aware of it probably regret the "realism" that declares that social evolution is a mirage and that we human creatures are programmed by the adjustments of our genes to physiological evolution, so that the events and responses of three or four million years ago control and direct the vital ingredients of our existence today. But the product of this interpretation of life is a kind of specious eternity of the present, as if nothing ever changed underneath and so all the unmistakable changes that we have witnessed in the last few years are not really there, or at least are quite unimportant.

A century ago this kind of sham scientific thinking was largely concerned with justifying the existence of class and race differences. Gender difference was so thoroughly taken for granted that the question hardly arose. Nineteenth-century biologists spent their time figuring out the primitiveness of the Negro race vis-à-vis the Mongolian and how far each had evolved along the path from the ape toward the high ground occupied (appropriately) by Caucasians. We aren't yet rid of all efforts to shove blacks off the contour line, but today it is the inevitability of gene-directed gender roles that holds center stage. "Man and Woman created He them," say these pundits, as if the advocates of teaching Creationism had already won the day.

It is our sense of history, the record of change, and our awareness that process occurs, that one thing leads to another and some advances become irreversible, that life not only feels different but is lived differently, which can alone refute the spurious, eternal present offered by such theories. They are another form of "lived happily ever after," though the "happily" is not emphasized. Nothing is static, though some periods move more slowly than others. Humanity today is on a journey, as it always has been, but the pace has picked up and our rate of advance demands more attention and calls for more decisions. In order to make sensible choices about present actions and their effects in the future we have to be able to track the road we have been following. When we look back, we observe unmistakably that women's lives have changed more than have those of men. That appears to me to give us a stock of experience of inestimable value—if we will just hang onto it, turn it over in our minds and share it, both in personal chat and in more public objective discussion.

The changes in women's lives do not promise either a happy ending or yet an apocalyptic disaster. Cause and effect are seldom straightforward. I regret that the first Presidential election I can remember, which was the first in which women voted, sent Warren Gamaliel Harding to the White House, and that a sixty-years-later echo gave us his objective correlative in Ronald Reagan. If that was all history had to say we might as well forget it. But of course it isn't all that history has to say, anymore than recent attempts to persuade us that women do too want to be taken care of provide my generation with anything but the occasion for a horse laugh. We were born there, thanks, and we know better. We want to see no more frustrated old maids and no more supportive sons and brothers sentenced to official celibacy in order to take care of capable women. And oddly enough, if you look around, you don't see any more of them, do you?

Some of the essays in this book deal substantively with history and change. Some of them take off from another starting point, often literary, but the criticism included here is also involved with the reflections of outer, shifting events and processes. Most of them were written to order in the sense that a particular question or a central theme was to be addressed; but reading them over I feel a constant thread running through them that is less a conscious exercise than a consistent response to aspects of our lives today. I see the coming together of women as a necessary reaction to events in the external world; but it is not just a necessary response—it is a highly creative one. More consciously than any other group of human beings who are moving away from the territory of the governed and the so-called weak, we are reflecting on what we have to bring with us from our earlier way of life, not only on what we must unlearn and leave behind. We know we bring modes of seeing and styles of intervening in the processes of power that have been downgraded under the universal rule of The Thing but that we believe have great value not only for survival but for the re-creation of a community of existence and of the spirit. I believe that there can be found, in our experience, alternative approaches to current ways of managing the politics of the public sphere and the psychology of personal life, ways that are becoming increasingly destructive. Reform will be a long task. Choosing trust instead of hostility, commonality instead of polarization, searching for the overlap of humanity that diverse individuals share, will not be easy. But what we have to mine and to study are the hitherto over-looked lives of a majority of this species.

We don't want to hang onto history as a set of totems but as a field of study. It's a rich one, both in data and in structure. It has a lot to tell us even, perhaps especially, when it hits us over the head in order to make its point. But all the time what it has to say is not merely interesting—it points ahead to future action, which will be both prac-tical and hopeful.

My hope is that some of these cross sections of observation from recent years can be practical for others beside myself.

HISTORY

INDIFFERENCE TO HISTORY is so pervasive and widespread that it can infect anyone, even those who repeat to themselves that change is always with us and that our memories of the past illuminate the present. That includes myself. My memories of the twenties are childish, subjective and limited, though I think my "smell" of the decade is accurate enough. Even for me, however, it was an eye-opener to read and review a collection of reminiscences, written and published at the time, by women who had broken out of the barrier around woman's place. In 1978 The Feminist Press reissued a series of brief memoirs that had appeared half a century earlier in the pages of *The Nation*. They were published anonymously then. Even Freda Kirchwey, feminist editor of a liberal magazine, was not going to ask contemporary "women achievers" to identify themselves. One change in the context of our daily lives is clearly the entitlement society now allows women to talk about our private lives as fact, without turning to the resources of fiction as a necessary disguise. Now we know the names of all the contributors but one, which expresses another bit of fact: the inevitable invisibility of women in the past.

Very arresting is the diversity of the limitations that these writers tell about. Wealth was a barrier to getting out, just as poverty was. So was affection with its insistence on the family's need to care for a girl, different in kind from neglect but effective too. Whatever might be the circumstances of women's lives, they could all serve as limits to growth and soporifics to ambition.

Another more recent review takes us back to a setting and a period closer to Cobbett's Thing, that self-satisfied monster of moralistic hypocrisy that stretched like a somnolent dragon across the road to equality, drowsy but always ready to stir from its doze. Judith Walko·

witz's study titled *Prostitution and Victorian Society* is notable for its detailed information on how the repression of poor women was implemented and justified in nineteenth-century England and how alliances were first built across class line in the teeth of scandalized shock plus an obbligato of mockery.

Here also is the introduction to a collection of essays discussing still lively issues raised by changes in views of women's education and its purposes over the last decade, published originally in *Change,* a magazine devoted to topics of concern to educators and now, sadly, defunct. 1974, the year in which this paper was written, is now itself receding into history—but one wonders how fast. The comparisons I was making here between the vision of women's education held during the seventies and that typical of the fifties may be even more revealing now than they were when first advanced. Backward looks grow increasingly pertinent when advocacy of return to the past becomes more insistent. More than ever we need accurate knowledge of what the past was like so that we can judge the truth of what's presented to us under the label of "the good old days" or "traditional family values." There were indeed elements of good in the old days and some traditions certainly were valuable; but which ones? What costs were exacted in exchange?

Today the emotional force of nostalgia (and we are all vulnerable to the dream of a golden age) is being used to justify a return to conditions of inequality for women and for minorities in a way that's morally offensive. It's intellectually offensive too, because the descriptions of life in the past that accompany it are as full of lies as a plum pudding is of plums. These descriptions are in fact prescriptions for behavior, behavior pleasing and convenient for our contemporary dozy dragon. Not only dozy but stupid too, inattentive as ever to the pragmatics of life today. The prescribed behavior is no more going to resolve our present difficulties than does the "history" it invokes supply accurate data. A resurrected inequality will be no more viable the second time around than it was before. My own pragmatic nature actively resents the need to disprove, over and over, the thesis that it's possible to repress rebellion successfully by shoving people back down to the status they occupied before they rebelled. It isn't possible. No apparent success will last. People who have rebelled once will do it again sooner or later and then again if they have to, and meanwhile they will have learned some useful lessons from their earlier efforts; that is, from history. Which points to another reason to hang onto our awareness of the past and the information available there for doing it again if we have to—usually with increased bitterness. Have the Irish forgotten their past? Have the Israelis? Have black people, whose advance is being threatened even before it had got far?

Unfortunately if efforts to turn the clock back don't work in the end, they can make a lot of trouble first, while men and women of good will emulate the sleepy Thing and give the attempt the benefit of the doubt. These days I find myself entertaining more and more often a childhood memory from the twenties: reading *The Wizard of Oz.* Is it possible that the array of philosophers lecturing each other in the think tanks of the right wing started to read that book but never finished it? Sixty years later a sensation of *déjà vu* haunts me now and then, suggesting that we are witnessing a replay of the sleight-of-hand techniques that kept the citizens of the Emerald City in order by clever hocus-pocus that was aided, to be sure, by their own determination to suspend their understanding of reality, causality, and all the every-day operations of the processes of existence. In the end, we all remember, the Wizard's power was exposed for the trickery it was, exposed by a small dedicated band of activists who had given up on being taken care of and who learned, reluctantly, the usefulness of courage. Sometimes in the watches of the night I try casting familiar characters from the current political scene into the roles of those reluctant heroes. Tip O'Neill could play the Cowardly Lion without any makeup, under-studied by Teddy Kennedy. Imaginative casting would surely offer Senator Alan Cranston the part of the Tin Woodman. The ragged overalls of the Scarecrow would serve as an appropriate costume for many possible representatives of the people at the bottom of the ladder who have been neither appeased nor made whole by being labeled "truly needy." But where, oh where, is Dorothy? Can we hope for a Kansas tornado to blow her in? Or must we Munchkins set to work and save ourselves?

These Modern Women: Autobiographical Essays from the Twenties (Review)

Half a century ago Frieda Kirchwey, editor of *The Nation,* invited seventeen feminist women to contribute anonymous autobiographical essays that might offer clues to the origin of their beliefs and report on the ways that life had tested a dedication to equality. They were published in 1926 and 1927, followed by comments from three well-known psychologists on the validity, direction and significance of the feminist force. Now The Feminist Press has reissued the series, with an illuminating introduction by Elaine Showalter and biographical sketches of the sixteen women who could be identified; one appears to be totally lost. It's an exciting book, painful and exhilarating too.

Fifty years ago, as today, the range of women who thought of themselves as feminists was wide and few generalizations fit them all. Naturally these reports reflect a country very different from ours. Many of the writers grew up on backwoods farms, more were daughters of clerical families than we'd be likely to find today, black women were not included, nor Native Americans, and indeed only artist and writer Wanda Gag came from ethnic stock that was not WASP. But if their backgrounds were not as diverse as they would be now, their activities were varied enough: lawyers, social workers, writers, journalists, professors, a cartoonist, a poet, a trade-union activist, a child psychologist and a political militant who married a liberal Republican governor. True, they represent a small, successful elite of professional women able to keep themselves: The circumstances of their choice dictated that. But they certainly got there by their own efforts, almost always unaided and frequently against great odds.

What do they have to tell us, these letters from the feminist attic? Why republish them now, when both theory and experience would seem to make the problems of this struggling generation obsolete? For a number of reasons. First, experience is not all that different. These essays record the continuing effort necessary if women are to become the human creatures they want to be. Conditions change a bit but not totally. These women fought their way out of traps set by affectionate families, patriarchal demands were stronger perhaps, furious drunken fathers kept mothers in economic servitude, families were larger; but there were also fathers who respected their daughters' minds and wills and capable mothers, active themselves, who encouraged involvement with life. Sharper then but still abundantly with us was the public assumption that what these women wanted they could never have, that their ambitions were ridiculous and their judgments deviant.

Attitudes toward sex were different for many born in the nineteenth century and raised in Puritan style; they were also influenced by the struggles of their mothers to manage large families, backbreaking work and sometimes the shiftlessness of their husbands. The new psychology stemming from Freud, Jung and Adler was liberating; and yet, the writers knew that freedom to enjoy their own sexuality in no way brought them easy equality and the chance to enjoy both career and parenthood. Most of them married, only five had children; and marriage too could be a trap. Housework was women's work, career or not; and husbands were known to call on their talented wives to rewrite or even write the work they published as their own.

Most significant is a note echoing here that only now is coming to the fore in research and study: the significance of the relationship between mother and daughter. Women poets and novelists, theorists like Adrienne Rich and Dorothy Dinnerstein, are exploring this hidden, secret, dangerous question in search of a new understanding of the bond that has had to be broken and denied. And so were the modern women of the twenties who adored or raged against, pitied or rejected, the women who'd raised them. We are still uncertain of our female heritage. How was it with you? We want to ask our own mothers, and fear to. How was it with you? We wonder about our grandmothers. Well, here is a book to tell us something. Not all, but what it tells is true.

Elaine Showalter's introduction is a brilliant consolidation and response to material so full of social history and of ideas. Of the three contemporary analysts, only Beatrice Hinkle, a Jungian, sees more than her own theories. Behaviorist John B. Watson and neurologist Joseph Collins inspire little more than the reaction: Read them and weep for all the women (men too) who may have had the misfortune to come to them for guidance. As for the book itself, read it for wisdom.

Prostitution and Victorian Society By Judith R. Walkowitz (Review)

J UDITH WALKOWITZ HAS written a classic of social history, full of vivid experience bound together by a profound understanding of the social ideology and moral myth of Victorian England. But since this is a tale of an attempt to legislate morality (and of its failure) it also carries a message for today, one that is easily summarized: The road to hell is paved with good intentions.

Mid-Victorian England was a country of optimism, prosperity, complacent piety, and rigid class distinctions, of rising production at home and empire building abroad, whose aspirant middle class still worshiped the icons of a landed aristocracy. Varnished with ostentatious comfort on the surface, tremors from below could still be felt. It was not simply the poverty of the "Have-nots" that menaced the "Haves," however; it was a sense of their moral obliquity, of the existence of pervasive social evils that did not yield to the authority of evangelistic do-gooders. How could a bustling empire maintain itself if the lower classes persistently contravened the spirit of respectability and order, of moral as well as physical health? The progress of industrial technology combined with scientific and medical advance to bring a new element into charitable concerns, an element of potential cure. The poor, perhaps, might not always have to be with us—if they would just listen to their betters. Victorian crusaders were determined to cure social ills not just by moral force—that was taken for granted—but by methods of social control and enforced sanitary measures, which would make every worker a healthy worker, every woman a virtuous adornment of the home—her own home if her income allowed, but someone else's if need be. "The end of Government," pontificated Dr. C. W. Shirley Deakin, "is the Good of Mankind," and to that end he posited a Ministry of Health whose large staff of "medical officers" and "sanitary police" would not only look after the nation's health but also suppress "public nuisances, obscene literature, and demoralizing exhibitions of every kind."

As might be surmised, Dr. Deakin's vision derived from an uneasy suspicion that health, order and respectability were more hopes than actuality. Dr. Walkowitz's tale of the crusade that failed opens with a horrid discovery concerning the health of the armed forces. Consequent to the revelations of brutal inefficiency in the Army's medical service, made during the Crimean War through the work of Florence Nightingale, supervision and reporting had been tightened. In the 1860s it became clear that much remained to be done. Attention centered on the spot where, to the Victorian mind, physical and moral health coincided: venereal disease. The figures were disastrous. Among troops returning from India, nearly three men in ten went to hospital for this reason. The Navy showed more than one in ten.

This was worse than a public nuisance: It was evidence (said a letter to *The Times*) of "one of those foul streams running through humanity in the mass which proves its tendency to moral decay." Clearly something had to be done to arrest this hideous social evil at its source. Wellington might have been willing to lead an army he described as "the scum of the earth" but the Duke was dead and times had changed. So in 1864 Parliament passed the first Contagious Diseases Act. In eleven garrison towns in southern England and Ireland, police were empowered to round up any woman they could identify as a prostitute, examine her either with her assent but under a court order if necessary, and commit her to a locked hospital for as long as three months if the medical examiner diagnosed disease. A later act added that any woman who had got onto the police list could be examined at regular two-week intervals, presumably forever. Though it was the health of the troops that was central, they were not to be subjected to inspection, lest it lower morale.

The Victorians were not all authoritarian bigots devoted to curing ills as they saw them by means they alone could prescribe. There was resistance to the acts from the beginning. Stalwart civil libertarians joined nascent feminists and working-class unionist men to condemn this coercion of any "identified" woman. Victorian morality itself declared that the authorities were in fact "licensing vice" by accepting the encounters between the troops and these "fallen women." Not only feminists deplored the double standard exhibited in the harassment of women and the exemption of men. The examination itself (and it was certainly done brutally) gave rise to particular horror: "instrumental rape," it was named.

The upholders of the acts, in turn, declared their sensible scientific purposes: to regulate what could not be halted. And indeed, it could not be. For its own reasons, the military establishment did not permit enlisted men to marry, preferring an army of easily portable bachelors to those who had family ties. A backlash of hostility to the movement to repeal the acts was not long in condemning such support for the undeserving, unrespectable poor. A special target was found in the brazen women who actually appeared before public audiences of mixed sexes to speak for repeal, to plead the cause of the harassed and shamelessly demonstrate the implements by which examinations were made on the "miserable creatures who were masses of rottenness and vehicles of disease." Far more dangerous than the prostitutes themselves was the "shrieking sisterhood," which attacked the roots of Victorian sensibility by defying not only class restrictions but the image of delicate feminity itself.

In the end, after twenty years, the acts were repealed. Nothing much had changed, insofar as the well-being of the armed forces was concerned; and nothing much did till better diagnosis and the invention of salvarsan provided an effective cure for syphilis, but that was in the twentieth century. No improvement in economic well-being offered the "unskilled daughters of the unskilled poor" opportunities of employment that were clearly preferable to a life on the streets. For them, the only change was a professionalization of prostitution. Where once it had been a transitional, seasonal means to keep body and soul together at a slightly greater return than that offered a domestic slavey or an underpaid seamstress, it had become a trade defined by authority and now hard to leave. Women "known to the police" were not welcomed by landlords and could be summoned for regular examination. They had been free agents, grouping together in threes or fours for support and friendship. Now they needed "protectors" and most of them were provided with "bullies"—or pimps, as we would say. A social isolation imposed from above cut these women off from their working-class origins and prevented easy absorption back into a neighborhood. Perhaps the most important result of the acts was the training given to protofeminists, training that could be seen in the discipline and in the hostility to "male vice" and the hypocrisy of the double standard later shown by the militant suffragettes. Coercion of the unrespectable poor had simply hardened class and gender lines.

A work of impeccable scholarship; a parable for today; yes, both of these. But let the reviewer not founder in her own morality. This is also a book that abounds with lusty life and exceptional characters. Here is Josephine Baker, a true heroine, leader of the women's part of the repeal effort, as sensible and humanistic as she was charismatic. Police Inspector Anniss of Plymouth dodges in and out tantalizingly, a cold and indefatigable bureaucrat, hunting down suspected women as he had once hunted down deserters from the Navy, a character who should have been memorialized by George Bernard Shaw or Brecht. Stalwart Quakers and Non-conformists, men and women alike, dared harassment and presented their arguments for civil liberties. An aristocratic old gentleman invited the House of Lords to uphold the acts and resist the drive to lift the age of consent from thirteen to sixteen on the grounds that "very few of their Lordships . . . had not when young men been guilty of immorality. He hoped they would pause before passing a clause within the range of which their sons might come."

Nor are the voices of the women at risk absent. Caught in the turmoil of an age of change, forced off impoverished farms, following emigrating men into the cities, with no comfortable bourgeois papa to look after them, it was perhaps the most independent and daring who went on the streets in defiance of morality and proper womanhood. Treated as pawns, described as miserable creatures, as carriers of corruption, their voices across a century remind us of their humanity. One was asked why she objected so to forced examination, since she was ready to expose herself to any man. She answered, "I should have thought you'd have known better nor that. Ain't one in the way of natur', and the other ain't natur' at all. Ain't it a different thing what a woman's obliged to do for a living because she has to keep body and soul together, and going up there to be pulled about by a man as if you was cattle and hadn't no feeling, and to have an instrument pushed up you, not to make you well (because you ain't ill) but just that men may come to you and use you to thersils (sic)." Said another, asked whether she had been bribed to testify for an agent of the repeal movement who had tried to help her, "I think we are allowed to know our own feelings: we are not beasts of the field."

That is the voice of humanity speaking, out of the unrespectable poor. Perhaps it addresses itself as pertinently today as it did then to those who feel called on to succor in their wisdom only those approved and deserving, only the "truly needy."

Women and
Their Education

I<small>F YOU WANT A</small> measure of the social change of our times, join me for a moment in speculating on what that title would have suggested a scant twenty years ago, when presidents of women's colleges were peering into the clouded crystal ball of the fifties in the hope of discovering a cure for the strange malaise that was overtaking the brightest and best of their alumnae. "What am I doing here?" graduates of the Seven Sisters were asking themselves as they sorted the laundry or put the vacuum cleaner together to give the venetian blinds a thorough going-over. Perhaps even more often the question was "What was I doing there—listening to lectures on Seventeenth-Century French Poetry, Organic Chemistry, and Money and Banking—when I was fated by the Destiny of Anatomy to end up here?" For the decade of the fifties was not one in which the graduates of even the most prestigious women's colleges easily contemplated a change in their fate, their status or their occupation. Married they must aspire to be; housewives they must expect to become.

What that meant is thoroughly documented. To take an accessible source, in June of 1949 the *New York Times* published a survey of responses to a questionnaire sent by the Seven Sister colleges to graduates of the class of 1934. Eighty-two percent of my classmates (as they were until the Great Depression constrained me to become a premature dropout) reported that they were married, "and happily too." At least less than 7 percent had been divorced and half of those had remarried. Of the married graduates 88 percent had children; in 1949 the unmarried presumably were not asked. "Socially life for '34 revolves around the home, the bridge table and her clubs," the *Times* reported, though it did mention replies from a few "individualists,"

39

one of whom "gets most pleasure from telephoning, one from television, and three from drinking."

And what did our alumnae think of their education? Well, almost all of them would have gone to college again, though only 30 percent were certain that they were going to send their daughters. Nonetheless, one in five was critical enough of her college experience to feel that changes should be made. "College," they said over and over, "prepared me for something I'm not; to be a professor, and not for the life I lead; for something better than the monotonies of dusting, sweeping, cooking and mending." And what was the remedy proposed? To change—not the world—but the curriculum. "More practical training . . . courses in cooking, dressmaking, household management, child care and psychology, even in entertaining and 'how to have a dinner party,' are among the suggestions."

Let us not think that such a program of Women's Studies was anathema to educators. The retiring head of Wellesley, addressing herself to this group of alumnae, declared, "College failed to teach these women that most people accomplish most in the world by working through established social institutions, and that the family is entirely respectable as a sphere of activity." A contemporary head of my own Seventh Sister was convinced that women's education should not parallel that of men but relate to their expected future lives, which meant an expected career as a housewife. As for any other possible career, it was conceived as being a stopgap between graduation and marriage or a kind of insurance against the bad luck of spinsterhood. George Schuster, President of Hunter College, declared in 1952, "The country wants young ladies who can graduate from college, can type, spell and take a job as a secretary." In 1956 a *New York Times* story on Radcliffe women holding doctorates was headlined "Even a Ph.D. Can't Escape the Kitchen." And in 1957 David Reisman was reported as offering the American Association of University Women his condolences on the fact that "in spite of 'good statistical evidence' that women can earn their degrees and still find a husband, a third or more drop out after the Freshman year. The social scientist expressed confidence that an education could be given women that would prepare them for the highest and best eventualities of marriage and career."

Please do not imagine that this brief historical review is intended to evoke an attack of the Virginia Slims Syndrome: "We've come a long way, Baby, and so we can stop right here and relax." On the contrary, the evidence that we have made some progress suggests to me that we should redouble our efforts, for once the Old Ark's A-Movering, it's wise to keep on pushing. I do think, however, that we are entitled to take some cheer from the evidence cited above of how entirely wrongheaded were the agitations of the fifties; for if academic respectability was arrantly mistaken two decades ago, it may be just as off-base today, its assumptions as false, its conclusions as dotty. To take an example to hand: The idea that affirmative action to increase employment of women and minority members will somehow subvert an existing process, by which promotion and tenure are now granted on the grounds of merit, is patently ridiculous. Academia has been getting on without half the research talent and teaching skill it might have laid claim to just by ignoring women. Add in the overlooked male moiety of the minorities, and the store of neglected merit and ability climbs still further. How the Establishment can suppose that restricting its talent pool to 30 percent to 40 percent of the population should be labeled "a search for excellence" or "promotion for merit" is—well, beyond me. The Elite has its reasons, shall we say, that Reason knows not of.

No, I have offered my bit of history from the fifties not in order to justify appeasement but rather to reassure those who are worried about disagreeing with today's learned men on today's issues. Many of these sages were happily, convincedly wrong twenty years ago, just as wrong as any human being (always including ourselves) may be. They turned their analytic and sapient gaze on the world and perceived that the education given women "did not prepare them for life." Clearly, then, this education had to be changed or women's lives would be swamped and flooded by frustration and anger. And while they pondered this deep question, women's lives started to change; the alteration picked up speed; frustration and anger supplied the motivation for women to meet the challenges of reality and cope with the world that was demanding that they find economically valuable work that would engage their capabilities—and in the twinkling of an eye, all that fuss about how to educate our daughters blew out of our minds and vanished in thin air. "Women and Their Education" has ceased to mean "cooking, dressmaking, household management, child care and entertaining," and now denotes an ever-widening range of topics, a new field: Women's Studies, and the influence of women's interests on the traditional curriculum. Let me summarize the questions raised in the book which this essay introduced:

I repeat, the progress we have made does not mean that we have reached our goals or even an acceptable place for a rest halt. Equality of opportunity on campus is still a hopeful dream. But the stock-taking that these articles offer us is a valuable enterprise. Not only does it indicate those areas where advance has taken place—or not taken place. It also directs our attention to some problems, and some possibilities, that are frequently overlooked in discussions of the obvious issues. Let's look at a few. That there is opposition to the promotion of women among older male professors is a commonplace. Back in 1969, when affirmative action programs were still sleeping underground, Ruth Hawkins described *The Odds Against Women.* It is an interesting and still useful report of the actual situation; but its analysis of the psychological background to the situation is even more telling.

Thus, says Hawkins, the male Mandarinate of Academia prefers to teach graduate rather than undergraduate students. It rates research above teaching in its hierarchy of values. And it uses, as its measure of accomplishment, the record of publication of aspirant faculty members. Any academic who questions this complex of attitudes and beliefs is clearly at a disadvantage in seeking to rise in her/his profession. Members of both sexes do so question the complex; but women, feminist women most of all, question these values with special seriousness. No doubt this questioning is based in part on experience. Women publish less than men, having less time to write and to research, since they habitually add the job of housekeeping to that of professor. In the past they have been steered toward teaching rather than research—and to teaching at the undergraduate level. But experience is not the only reason they question the traditional standards by which research, publication and teaching of candidates for higher degrees are assumed to be the most valuable occupations in the university. The broadening base of the student body and the increasing need for teaching that is involved and responsive require rather different standards, standards that are more flexibly adaptable to changing conditions on campus. These changes in themselves validate the challenge that women have mounted to the traditional professorial icon.

Elaine Hopkins's report on her years of wrestling with the red tape of departmental standards and requirements for employment carries the story forward from 1969 to 1973. It is the same story of self-defeating rigidity. Hopkins, a competent teacher of undergraduate English courses, was recurrently threatened with dismissal from a Midwestern state university because she had not made "adequate progress" toward a doctorate. Fair enough, by the Old Boys' standard.

But when Hopkins did find a good and stimulating doctoral program that emphasized the teaching of composition and literature at the undergraduate level, which was exactly what she was doing and apparently what her department needed done, it was *disapproved* on the stunning grounds that, once she got her doctorate, she would have nothing to teach! And why not? Because "everyone knows" that holders of Ph.Ds. don't want to teach literature and composition to undergraduates, they want to specialize, do research and publish. "Having originated in the medieval monastery, the modern university is a world of credentialed scholars competing for status," writes Hopkins. I would like to modify her definition only slightly. That's what the educational establishment *thinks* the university is and will remain. Can they keep it so, in the face of a changing student body and changing social demands?

Other articles collected here pay special attention to one component of the changing student body that will certainly grow in importance and is already present in greater force than is realized by the Establishment. These are returning or continuing students, women who are getting ready to enter the labor force as their children grow older (and inflation grows sharper) or middle-aged individuals, already working, who want to change or upgrade their careers. It is women who are the subject of the two analyses included here, one personal and experiential, and one based on a statistical study; but some investigation of my own for a paper on continuing education as a whole, indicates that the trend is not confined to women. This suggests once more that the experience of women, who are responding to social change with exceptional sensitivity, should be seen as instructive for all. The return of women to college portends an increasing participation of older people in education, both sexes of them, and at all levels.

Which brings us again to a consideration of the value of flexibility in the outlook of institutions of higher learning and of their faculties. In an analysis of *Why Women Go Back to College,* Pat Durcholz and Janet O'Connor note, "In some publicly supported colleges, these women make up as much as 10 percent of the student body." A 10 percent increase in possible students would certainly be a boon to many an institution that is looking at a decline in applications, though we mustn't assume, of course, that such an increase is everywhere available. On the other hand, we shouldn't imagine that the women who have got themselves back to college have whimsically wandered in off the street, in response to a selling campaign. On the contrary, older students represent a real potential because so many have had to get themselves on campus under their own steam. Few indeed are the imaginative and innovative institutions that have gone out looking for them, have set up useful guidance programs to help them over the culture shock of entry and acculturation on campus, and have tailored curricula and hours to suit their needs and special demands. In short, what's there is solid.

Once there, what they want is not just to amuse themselves, though certainly some well-to-do women are enriching their lives and stretching their minds by studying "for fun." (So are some men.) But the result of a questionnaire circulated by Durcholz and O'Connor to a random sample of 245 women on two campuses in the Cincinnati area breaks down as follows: 35.4 percent are preparing for employment; 30.3 percent are responding to a need or desire for education or achievement; 25.3 percent are seeking personal growth; 4.5 percent believe further education will promote independence; and 4.5 percent are looking for stimulation. (I should add that my own look at the field indicates that most women returning to college are doing so for a mix of purposes; and often those who go back originally for "stimulation" or "personal growth" end up in demanding degree programs or preparation for professional careers. They tend to get hooked on ideas, and more and more they enjoy success instead of fearing it.) Records show that the returning women studying at the University of Cincinnati earn excellent grades, with both full- and part-time students achieving B averages. My own findings agree.

This is good news for students and colleges. What about the bad news? There's plenty. Too many students head for training in traditional areas of "women's work." These areas are often oversupplied and almost always low-paying. Teaching from elementary to college level is not a growth area at the moment, but more than half of the sample Durcholz and O'Connor reached were preparing to teach. That indicates a serious lack of career guidance, and that, in turn, indicates a fundamental inability on the part of the institution to take returning students seriously. In addition, not many colleges welcome part-time candidates for a professional degree; and rarer still is the campus that offers adequate child care—or any child care, for that matter. This inattention to their needs puts a kind of social limit on the women returning to college. They almost all have supportive husbands; they have to. "76.3 percent of our respondents replied that their husbands' attitudes were either favorable or very favorable," say

Durcholz and O'Connor. But, as the authors then go on to ask, what happens to the women who run into opposition from their husbands? Answer: They stay home. Not only will they get no support in doing two jobs, studying and running a house. If their husbands refuse to share incomes or to sign a student loan application, the woman can't make it on her own, for her husband's earnings will make her ineligible for student financial aid.

And what, it may be asked, could or should universities do about that? Isn't any dispute between husband and wife over her desire to move outside the traditional family role a purely personal matter? Why should any institution intervene in such a situation? What has it got to do with education?

There are two answers; one from the women's point of view, and one concerned with the interest of the institution of learning. For women, the *privatization* of their needs and ambitions isolates them from help. "That's your problem," says Society or its representative organization, in this case the college. "Cope with it by yourself, each one of you." To a Depression dropout who remembers the 1930s well, this response is hauntingly familiar. It was what Washington told the unemployed during the Hoover administration. The administration was distressed about the problem, but it didn't see what it could do to help. Unemployment was a private matter, between a worker and his employer. Result: The Hoover administration rapidly found itself removed from office and replaced by a Roosevelt team that was at least willing to try to cope. For the first time, unemployment was seen as a public, governmental problem. Solutions were still hard to come by, but someone was finally asking the right questions. Hoover's failure was not one of morals but of perception.

It is that kind of failure that is haunting today's institutions of higher learning: lack of perception, lack of imagination. This may seem an odd and even an unjustified criticism today, at a time when superior male universities and colleges have accepted women as students, when their presence and that of applicants from minority groups is growing in professional schools, and when experimental programs and new branches of study are being undertaken. The trouble is that all too often these changes are made perforce, against the grain; and because they are entered upon in a spirit of sullen indifference and even resentment, the great potential benefit of such changes for all segments of Academia is not recognized. A chance for real profit is deferred and perhaps lost. Women, minority males and experimenters have something important to say to their colleagues. They look at the universe of teaching and learning from a new angle. They have special knowledge of the World Out There, beyond the gates of the institution. Consequently they bring more than a quantitative addition of bodies to the talent pool. They bring also a qualitative increase in what is known, what it is significant to communicate to coming generations. By definition, since it has not been publicly recognized before, this knowledge comes out of private experience. But to dismiss it on such grounds is willfully to choose ignorance.

Fifteen years ago, the black experience was still being dismissed in this way. Ghettoes are very private, those who move outside them become "invisible men." But who today would want to minimize the effect and extent of the waves of knowledge that have broken through the ghetto walls and made us look, not just at black history but at urban culture, at the experience of poverty, at all of *white* economic and cultural history in this country, with new eyes? When black knowledge ceased to be private, it set in motion a fundamental reassessment of the whole social mythology of our civilization.

There is no doubt that women's experience will also produce a profound effect. Even those twenty-year-old efforts to adapt the college curriculum to women's needs, as then perceived, pointed to *something* in women's lives that demanded attention. The effort to deal with the problem by making education for women more special and private proved to be exactly wrong; but it was evidence that some disturbance was being felt. The compass is swinging round now, but it will go still further before it completes its course. Today women are allowed to study the full, traditional male curriculum and to teach it as and where they can. What has not yet taken place is the process of input through which they will refresh and extend the curriculum out of the substance of their lives, past, present and to come.

The "privatization" of women, then, is not a private matter. Rather it lies at the heart of the difficulty that the Establishment feels about incorporating them into itself. (And not only the Establishment. Kate Millett's report on how the Peace Strike came to Smith and Vassar makes clear that the revolutionary male is no readier than his middle-class mentors to see his revolutionary sister as a full-fledged comrade.) Articles collected here note how women in professional organizations of scholars have been welcomed as dues payers and passed over as possible officers. The field of women's studies is often regarded with suspicion and distaste or shrugged off as a ridiculous boondoggle.

Catharine Stimpson's report on its birth and growth is thoroughly realistic about the intellectual and financial opposition these programs face and the hesitancy that still hampers their proponents, who are largely untenured and thus badly equipped to be crusaders. (I note with pleasure, however, that the University of Chicago Press has just asked Professor Stimpson to edit a new journal that will deal with scholarship in the woman's field; certainly an influential vote for the solidity of the discipline.)*

In general, the position of the Establishment is a grudging acceptance of the presence of women, an acceptance enforced to some extent by government antidiscrimination orders, but certainly not a warm and welcoming hospitality. Lafayette, we are there—but they wish we weren't. There are a number of reasons for this aversion, and if we are to deal with it successfully, they are worth looking at. The Mandarins don't want us, in the first place, because they are comfortable, and if you are comfortable, why should you desire change? Then the change they're confronted with is wide-ranging enough to be disturbing. Affirmative action, in itself, means shifting habits of promotion and of procurement of apprentices and protégés, inviting people in whom one doesn't know. In addition, the presence of women on a professional level of equality forces a rethinking of one's opinions on sex roles and functions, and these tend to run fairly deep. As Ruth Hawkins notes, the male tenured professors who must evaluate women candidates for employment or promotion often suffer "an inability to distinguish between these women and their homemaker wives." Pointing this out is not to downgrade the value of the work of homemakers but to indicate that they necessarily stand in a different relation to their husbands than do their husbands' colleagues: a *private* relation, please note, which once again reinforces the pervasive view of woman as a private creature unfitted for public activity.

This archaic but still widespread assumption not only hampers women as individuals, it also works to discredit their ideas: Vide the reaction to women's studies. Women today, including many women who do not count themselves as actual members of the women's movement but simply as professionals who expect rational treatment from others in their profession, confront the academic establishment with the need to change more than recruitment programs. They are declaring that the whole conceptual structure of reality, and therefore

---

* Seven years later the journal mentioned here, *Signs,* is alive and well and an indispensable compendium of research in many disciplines.

of what should be taught about reality, is changing. Now the Establishment tends to believe that there is in existence a concrete body of knowledge, already pretty well organized, that our society should communicate to its progeny. Changes in it, additions to it, may be necessary from time to time—but how can *women* (for so long private creatures) have anything serious or considerable to add? What's more, they often are drawn to new teaching techniques; and they react with too easy an approval to those odd figures, distressing to all Mandarins, not only maverick academics but laypersons, fanatics and rebels, totally uncertificated by the laying on of professorial hands, who want to shake up the standard body of knowledge as if it were a cocktail. The hierarchy is being told to change both its habits and its definitions, its understanding of how the world is put together; and making these demands are the untenured, the uncredentialed, the unfrocked, whom it can only regard with emotions that it would be too kind to call mixed.

What can academic women do about this situation? I think they had better go on doing what they're already doing, firmly, ardently, unshakably. While I can sympathize with the reactions of the academic establishment and realize that these emotions will have to be taken into practical account, it is my considered opinion that the judgment of the Establishment is seriously at fault. Its members are overlooking major changes that have taken place in society and that affect both the student body and the body of knowledge that it's important—yes, let's use the hated word, that it's *relevant* for the students to learn. These changes, therefore, can be ignored by the research institutions and the teaching profession only at their peril. Let me offer an example. I take it deliberately, for the comfort of the males in Academia, from a male and from a source that can in no way be associated with women's influence or with radical thinking: namely, from the August 1974 issue of *The Scientific American*. Urie Bronfenbrenner, professor of human development and family studies and of psychology at Cornell University, has contributed an article, "The Origins of Alienation." I quote its opening:

> Profound changes are taking place in the lives of America's children and young people. The institution that is at the center of these changes and that itself shows the most rapid and radical transformation is the American family, the major context in which a person grows up. The primary causes and consequences of change, however, lie outside the

home. The causes are to be found in such unlikely quarters as business, urban planning and transportation systems; the ultimate effects of change are seen most frequently in American schools and—not as often but more disturbingly—in the courts, clinics and mental and penal institutions. The direction of change is one of disorganization rather than constructive development.

I shall not go on to summarize Dr. Bronfenbrenner's data and conclusions, but simply point out that these profound changes in the basic structure of family life, "the major context in which a person grows up," and which come from *outside* the family, are the very stuff of day-to-day living for women in America and have been for years. They concern us at every level, from that of practical coping to that of steady philosophic thought, and on to distressed anxiety. We know about them because dealing with them has been assigned to us as our duty and, be it noted, almost always as our *private* duty. Managing details of daily living are held to be chores with which women can be trusted—and raising children who can live successfully as mature adults in this changing and challenging society of ours has automatically been included in our duties, without conscious determination.

For years now we have been talking about the difficulty of fulfilling this demanding obligation without assistance from the community, without support from other institutions, individuals or groups. In reply we have been told that we are selfishly making a fuss over doing something so easy that our grandmothers and greatgrandmothers managed it with little hardship and no formal training. We have certainly been blamed when we failed, but we get no credit for suggesting that failure is possible. Instead, it's been judged as private failure, probably due to selfish reasons. We could do better if we tried.

Against this background it is indeed a pleasure to discover Professor Bronfenbrenner stating flatly that changes affecting the family are major, are public, and desperately need to receive the consideration of the scientifically minded community. No woman, I am sure, would take any pleasure in saying "I told you so," for we take no pleasure in having become aware of these problems long ago. But we *have* been saying so; and it should be recorded without recrimination, just as evidence of the sort of knowledge of social phenomena, in the real world, that women do know about and that deserve the attention of all of us.

The crucial point lies just here. These profound social changes, profound enough to have affected the least reachable element of soci-

ety, the family, are not simply the business of the women who have
been trying to deal with them. As Dr. Bronfenbrenner points out, they
affect the children of our society and, through them, other institutions.
*It is no longer possible to see the problems of women as isolated and
personal; beyond this, it is no longer possible to see the problems as
pertaining only to women.* They derive from technological change,
from scientific and medical advances, from new styles of living and,
above all, from the economic restructuring of society, which have
together altered the ways men and women live with each other and
raise the next generation. The special knowledge of women, summarized in their current demands and aspirations, can be taken as a
portent of social needs that affect the whole community. Just as the
shocking rise in unemployment during the Depression years signaled
a major change in American society, so the experience of women over
the last generation, culminating in the protests and reactions of the
seventies, points to an alteration of earthquake proportions in our
institutions.

If the institutions of learning are going to retain their usefulness
and endure, they will sooner or later find themselves forced to take
account of the advances, vicissitudes and shifting needs of the rest of
us. The institutions are not immune from these needs, which affect all
American society, top as well as bottom. Minority members, the
unconsidered poor and women in enormous numbers are not only
sufferers from today's social convulsions, we are also pioneers in coping with them. We are in a position to instruct our instructors out of
the grind and surge of our everyday lives; and what we have to tell
them is vital and unique.

Let us return for a moment to Elaine Hopkins's comparison of the
modern university with the medieval monastery. Hopkins means the
analogy harshly, for she sees the monastery as a bastion of tradition
and orthodoxy, turning its back on the world of reality and confining
its membership to a chosen few. That is part of the history of the
monasteries, but it is only part, for they did not always symbolize
intractable rigidity. True, they were formed originally by men (and
women) in retreat from a world of violence and chaos, but as time
passed they came to perform functions quite different from those of
a safe haven for the frightened. They not only preserved ancient
knowledge, they welcomed new information even when it came from
a different culture, as with Arab mathematics. They pioneered new
agricultural methods and experimented with land use. They served as
entrepots of trade for whole districts. They sent advisers to rulers,

from local barons to Charlemagne himself. When it seemed necessary, they did not hesitate to inveigh against these rulers. In short, the monasteries were, at various times and in various places, open, listening and flexible; and above all, in touch with reality.

So we should not, I believe, despair of their present descendants. Women have both history and reality on their side. Our knowledge of the world as it is is really quite formidable, broadly based, aware of detail, and not afraid to make connections between areas that the traditionally minded see as separate. Our experience makes us interdisciplinary. Well, this is a most useful and needed ability in a fragmented society and particularly in an educational system where the trend for years has been to know more and more about less and less. Research is valuable—if it is used; and to be used, it must be allowed to connect with other research and, even more, with everyday life. In contemplating women and their education, therefore, let us not ask merely what the educational institutions can do for us (they can surely do more than they are). Let us ask also what we can do for them. We can do a great deal by supplying not only talent but wisdom; and the institutions that first realize that (as some already do) will be the ones best fitted to manage present problems and confront the future boldly.

One particular stretch of history is treated in the following account, and it seems to demand its own brief introductory note, because it has a history of its own. Twice now I have contributed an article on the women's movement to a massive medical text—A Comprehensive Textbook on Psychiatry *edited by Drs. Kaplan, Freedman and Sadock, and I included the first version of this chapter in an earlier collection of my own,* Between Myth and Morning. *Here, now, is the second version. Well, it may be asked, isn't that pretty repetitious? Do you really want to run it again? I do, and the reason is this: Faced with a request to "update" the history of the women's movement after a gap of five years, I found it impossible. The only recourse was to start from the beginning and write it all over again. So much had happened and, even more important, so much had changed in the way that I and other women thought about our position and our progress, past and future, that any evaluation of the movement had to be rethought, start to finish. So the two versions of this study can be taken as benchmarks in a shift of what French historians call* mentalité, *and it may be useful for readers to have them both for purposes of comparison between a vision from the mid-1970s and one that dates from the end of the decade.*

The Women's Movement

WHAT IS THE WOMEN'S MOVE-MENT? It is, first of all, a *movement*; that is, a process involving change, and change at many levels. It is also, of course, a movement taking place within society and thus interacting in a diversity of ways with individual women and men, with other social trends, with political groupings, with intellectual concepts and with accepted norms of behavior. For students of psychiatry its impact on these behavior expectations may well be its most obvious aspect. But changes in behavior are embodied and embedded in lived experience. They are the product of shifts in the underlying texture of life. The extent of contemporary change goes far beyond the lives of women; but the fact that women's lives have been shaken so profoundly points up the significance and the depth of these shifts in our ways of living. Not only are relations between women and men undergoing alteration. The structure of the family has been altered by external economic and social pressure until traditional estimates can no longer be taken as valid. The women's movement or, as it has been called, the "rebirth of feminism" in the 1960s, originated as a response to major changes in society, changes that had long been under way but that were becoming too demanding to be ignored. Since the rise of a conscious sensitivity to these demands among women, and a number of men as well, a diverse reassessment of personal and social relationships between the sexes has been taking place. Future practitioners of psychiatry must expect to find some conventional assumptions about "normal" masculinity and femininity challenged not only by behavior but theoretically as well. For adventurous thinkers this can be a most exciting opportunity for revaluation.

To take a simple and familiar example: If women today are able to look realistically at a wider range of potential occupations while accepting an increased need to work for pay outside the home setting, our current definition of what is psychologically normal in female aspirations must widen far beyond the traditional view of woman's role, which sees her as centered in home and family. Economic and social changes that now require more women to earn and (to some extent) permit them to work in new fields thus assign new meaning to patterns of behavior; what was once odd, even deviant, is now frequent and average. While this is true of all transforming trends within society, it is of great, perhaps greatest, significance in the case of shifts in gender behavior. Modern psychiatric theory sees the development of sexual identity, properly expressed, as central to human maturation, and its frustration or distortion as pathogenic. Today, however, the expression of masculinity and femininity does not always jibe with conventional definitions. When reality challenges theory, it would seem that some rethinking is due, if only to re-establish the value of the tested theory under new conditions.

Historical Changes in Women's Position

The contemporary shift in women's activities and perceptions of their role is not unique. In earlier times not only women but most men pursued their occupations within family settings and included membership in a family or clan as part of a felt identity and social status. Much productive work was undertaken by family teams, both on the farm and in small business enterprises. Two excellent sources of information on work done by women in this country are now available in Dr. Gerda Lerner's *The Female Experience: An American Documen-*

tary (Indianapolis: Bobbs-Merrill, 1977) and Dr. Barbara Mayer Wertheimer's *We Were There: The Story of Working Women in America* (New York: Pantheon Books, 1977). Both books document the wide range of occupations and the remarkable technical skills of women in pre-industrial America and record their reactions to their lives; in Dr. Lerner's book, in their own words. Dr. Wertheimer notes that beyond the daylong tasks of Colonial American women, which provided almost everything that their families ate and wore, plus lighting (candles), soap for laundry, quilts for bedding and medicinal herbs, many women also assisted husbands or brothers in business enterprises conducted at home or on the property. Some of them grew skilled enough to run their own businesses, and we have lists of female silversmiths and pewterers, shipwrights, gunsmiths, blacksmiths, butchers, pumpmakers and millers. Farm women too expected to work outside the house. Dr. Lerner includes an article, which appeared as late as 1905, describing the life of an Illinois farmer's wife. Aside from the chores of homemaking, she fed and tended cows, a horse, sheep, hogs and chickens, planted and weeded a vegetable garden (plus a bed of flowers for her own pleasure) and kept an eye on her children. One pleasure she mentioned: During the half hour to three hours she spent operating an "old-fashioned" churn, she was able to read!

Aside from the historical shifts in the work roles of women, we should also note early changes in family structure. True, the length of time in which nuclear families consisting only of parents and children without members of a third generation present have been the general rule is still unsettled and a matter of lively debate among social historians and demographers. (See Aries, Laslett, Shorter, Stone.) There is general agreement, however, that the rise of modern political institutions displaced and weakened earlier kinship networks, so that parent-child relationships increased in emotional importance as links to larger kin or community groups became less important economically and socially. Literary references support the view that our contemporary idea of "home" as a haven of emotional warmth and personal gratification cannot be dated back past the eighteenth century. (See Janeway, *Man's World, Woman's Place.*) In addition, a factor often overlooked that affected the nature and the duration of any family structure was the high mortality rate among young adults as well as children, so tragically common in the past. Many marriages were remarriages, many children were orphaned, and many families were "hybrids" of parents and stepparents, siblings, half-siblings and stepsiblings, plus the occasional niece or nephew. (See Stone, 1977.) In short, contemporary changes in marriage and family patterns are indeed extensive and influential, but not the first to have happened. We should not imagine that an idealized nineteenth-century middle-class family structure (whose "normality" appears to underlie a good deal of sociological thought as well as psychiatric theory) was either universal or of long duration.

A division of labor between the sexes *is* of long duration, and it has always played a part in the value assigned to the occupations of women, to their independent connection with a world beyond the family setting, to their self-esteem, and to the expected behavioral female role. The lines along which work is divided, however, have varied widely. The description of women's work in pre-industrial America points to a situation in which the labor of both sexes, while long and hard, was reasonably similar in locus and estimated value, at least for the poor who made up the great majority of the population. During the next two centuries, however, productive work moved steadily away from the home, particularly work that brought a cash return. As fewer goods were produced at home, cash income increased in importance, enhancing the value of what was becoming both work mainly done by men and the main work of men. Those who stayed at home became more isolated and dependent, economically and psychologically. A decline in the birth rate during the nineteenth century, combined with growing urbanization, suggests that family structures were already under pressure to adapt once again to new environments, new goals and new roles. A pattern developed in which a male bread-winner headed the family, while the central occupation of married women was seen as wife, mother and homemaker. That this was the normative situation in Europe and America by the end of the nine-teenth century is of course evident in Freud's work, while fifty years later the American sociologist Talcott Parsons still took it as basic to his well-known analysis of the process of socialization.

When in 1955 Parsons defined the role of the husband-father as "instrumental" in performing the essential function of earning the family's sole or chief income and thus defining its place in the outer world and directing its "style of life," he was able to assure his readers that the adult feminine role was still anchored primarily in the internal affairs of the family despite the presence of women in the labor force. This wife-mother role was "expressive"; that is, it had to do with the maintenance of personal relations, the regulation of tensions and the socialization of children by emotional connections, not—as in the past—by shared family labor. But the family, as Parson says, is not a system complete in itself. It is a subsystem of society; and for women's chief role to be played out there requires that she be confined within a distinctly limited area. Parsons is concerned lest the socializing agents of the family, that is, the parents, should be too completely immersed in family ties and urges that they play a part in wider community activities. At the same time, however, he regards the occupational role of the husband-father as the most important tie to the outer world and the only one with a clear and necessary public function. It follows that any external role played by the mother is implicitly of less value and, since it is not functionally necessary, it must be improvised. (See Parsons and Bales, 1955.)

We are all indebted to Dr. Parsons for his analysis of the function and structure of what was perceived in 1955 to be the normal American family and the expected gender roles. Even now there exists a fairly widespread assumption that these roles are desirable, even if less frequently adhered to. It is just here, however, that the economic and social changes that produced the women's movement demand attention, for they have shifted the external circumstances of life so dramatically that Parsons's distinction between "instrumental" and "expressive" roles has become remarkably difficult to validate or maintain.

Thus today, far from there being (as Parsons believed) "no serious tendency" toward "symmetry between the sexes," the instrumental work role of women has once again grown more similar to that of men, while men have found themselves somewhat more involved in the expressive side of parenting through active child care. A working mother is now as normal and average as one who does not hold a job outside the home, and the greatest influx into the labor force recently has been that of mothers with children under the age of six. The once average family of four (both parents present) where only the father works has shrunk to an unprecedented low: in 1976 a mere 7 percent of all families. At the same date, nearly 20 percent of American families were headed by women. The average pattern, in fact, is now that of two working parents. It is from this widespread experience of life-as-different-from-expectations that the women's movement emerged—or, better, re-emerged—in the 1960s. One of the things it discovered was its history.

History of the Movement

While individual protests by women against restrictions placed on them run back (in America) at least to the "heretical teachings" of Anne Hutchinson who was tried in Boston in 1637, we can best date the organized start of a women's movement to the well-known convention held in Seneca Falls, New York, in 1848, under the leadership of Lucretia Mott and Elizabeth Cady Stanton. This was, of course, a year of revolutionary uprisings in Europe, and the Seneca Falls convention issued a Declaration of Sentiments and Resolutions that rewrote the Declaration of Independence by holding that "all men *and women* are created equal." Early feminist activity concentrated on removing legal disabilities from women and obtaining for them such rights as that of married women to hold property in their own names, to sue for divorce, to gain educations on a par with those of men and, as a major and central goal, to vote. Many of these goals were reached during the nineteenth century, but the prize of national suffrage for women had to wait until the Nineteenth Amendment to the Constitution was ratified in 1920. During these years the low status of women was being challenged both in practice and in theory. Educational opportunities increased as women's colleges were founded and, after a grudging start, newly established state universities set up programs of coeducation. Entrance into professional schools was more difficult, but some women did succeed in training for medicine and the law. Meanwhile, at a lower level of economic return, poor women, including many immigrant women, worked in factories and mills out of sheer need or became domestic servants. The movement reached out toward employed women through the Women's Trade Union League; but organizations of women were not warmly welcomed by the American Federation of Labor, and the textile and garment workers, where women's participation was high, ended by forming independent unions; even there, women have not played leadership roles.

After the vote was won, the first wave of feminist activity largely died away, although women continued to move into professional careers during the twenties and the thirties. Many of them, however, remained single, or if they married did not have children so that a choice was obviously felt to exist between marriage-and-motherhood and the pursuit of a full-time career. A major experiential change came with World War II when women entered the labor force to do war work in unprecedented numbers, undertaking jobs in heavy industry that had previously been reserved for men. But, again, no organized movement protected their interests or spoke for their rights, though some special needs were perceived: Witness the provision of federally funded child care. Most unions then, however, were uninterested in sponsoring efforts to gain equal opportunities for women workers as many still are today; indeed recent statistics indicate an actual decline in the proportions of union membership among women (from 12½ percent in 1972 to 11 percent in 1976) even as the number of women at work rose.

When men returned to the civilian work force at the end of World War II and war work per se largely ended (along with funded child care), many women returned to the traditional feminine tasks within the family. The atmosphere of the forties and fifties was one of "togetherness," celebrating the large family. The birth rate rose significantly, though some of the "baby boom" was due to a catch-up in births that had been delayed by the economic depression of the thirties and the absence of men during the war years. A classic expression of approved feminine behavior in this period can be found in *Modern Woman: The Lost Sex* by Lundberg and Farnham (1947), who urged women to find fulfillment in the traditional nurturing role and assured them that neurotic unhappiness was the fate preparing itself for those who did not.

Behind these attitudes, however, changes were already occurring. In 1960 women already composed one-third of the labor force, more than half of them were married, and a third were mothers. In 1963 a statement that became a rallying point for the rise of a new phase of feminism was published: *The Feminine Mystique* by Betty Friedan; and in 1964 Title VII of the Civil Rights Act banned discrimination by reason of sex along with race, religion and national origin. Friedan's book was of course not the first or the only declaration of a need for change in the position of women. Simone de Beauvoir's thoughtful, wide-ranging and, in the end, extremely influential *The Second Sex* first appeared in France in 1949 and in the United States in 1953. But Friedan's book came out at a time when an eager audience was ready to hear its message, and it spoke in a tone of passionate commitment that evoked a fervent response.

The Feminine Mystique was only the first of many serious works exploring women's situation, both past and present, and putting forward programs for the future. The written record is so voluminous and was so prompt in its appearance that it clearly points to the existence of an underground uneasiness among women related to dissatisfaction with the traditional family-centered "expressive" role.

In book after book the limitations and psychological distortions imposed by an image of femininity that seemed inappropriate to the actual demands of life were discussed, sometimes with considerable anger. (A representative sample can be found in Firestone, Greer, Janeway, Millett and Mitchell.) The general subordination of women as a group to men as a group was presented as a political act, enforced by the privatization of women and the devaluation of their skills. It was pointed out (to take one central example) that the "expressive" mother role asks women to evoke the emotions of their children and manipulate them as part of the process of socialization: Because children love their mothers, they feel guilt when scolded, and by this use of feelings, they incorporate sanctioned social responses into their behavior. The demand on mothers that they manipulate their own emotions in order to communicate the ideas and ideals of a patriarchal society in which they were confined to subsidiary roles was set forth. The valuation of women by taking the mother role as primary to their lives was questioned, particularly in terms of popular disapproval of women who were presented as misusing the role of mother by "holding onto their children" or otherwise exploiting the power they were permitted in the family and denied elsewhere. The effect on female self-esteem of a feminine image in which women occupied a secondary position vis-à-vis society as a whole was analyzed. The interest of the reading public in discussions of these and related topics suggests that a widespread alienation from traditional views existed.

The response was both private and public. Women began to meet in discussion groups to "raise consciousness" by comparing experience and sharing support for personal efforts at change. On the national scale, a conference of state Commissions on the Status of Women held in Washington in 1966 became the focus for the founding of a new feminist organization, NOW, the National Organization for Women. Friedan was a leader in its establishment, along with Representative Martha Griffiths and Kathryn Clarenbach, head of the Wisconsin Commission on the Status of Women. By September 1966, 300 educators, business women, editors and government officials, both male and female, had accepted membership on the board, and NOW began its program of political intervention, legal attack on discrimination, education on social issues, and efforts to achieve equality for women in economic life. Though NOW has been criticized by more radical groups for a reformist stance and a commitment to middle-class values, it has remained a highly effective arm of the movement and has concerned itself in many issues of interest to women of all classes.

Response to the renascent women's movement at the political level produced some quick advances: passage by Congress of the Equal Rights Amendment and early ratification by a number of states; executive orders designed to set up programs of "affirmative action" that would increase participation of women in the professions and in business management and skilled vocations traditionally reserved for men; greater opportunity for education in all areas; the banning of advertisements for jobs listed as suitable for one sex only; equal credit facilities; the official opening of government employment at all levels to women, including military service, except for combat duty; and many more. Some of these gains have been effectuated to a considerable degree: Enrollment of women in law and medical schools has jumped, and it has risen in architecture and engineering. Male universities have opened their doors to women students; and some penetration has been made into upper management and on boards of directors. Major social change, however, does not occur easily, and resistance to women's advance toward equality is evident. It is impossible to predict how effective this resistance will be over the long term. But it seems clear that political shifts cannot wipe out alterations in gender roles that are based on altered circumstances of economic and social life; and clear too that women are learning how to resist the resistance they face by political activity and by determined ambitious effort for individual achievement.

A public event that emphasized the solidarity of women coming from every state and territory, from all income levels and cultural backgrounds, and from a great diversity of occupations occurred in Houston, Texas, in November, 1977, as a climax to the government-proclaimed International Woman's Year. Thousands of delegates elected by state conventions, and many interested observers, gathered to pass an action agenda for the future. Provisions included a multiplicity of issues. Some headings: Battered Women; Business; Child Care; Disabled Women; Education; Employment; Health; Homemakers; International Affairs; Minority Women; Offenders; Older Women; Reproductive Freedom; Rural Women; Sexual Preference; Women, Welfare and Poverty. In spite of the variety of topics and the diverse backgrounds of those attending, the spirit of the meeting was one of community that allows and values diversity and finds common interests within it. Naturally all social movements aiming at change must expect periods in which their aims and activities are challenged and tested. If they survive, they can emerge with new strength and steadiness of purpose.

Characteristics of the Contemporary Movement

The diversity of the women's movement today is entirely real, as the goals put forward at the Houston Convention indicate. Some are political, some economic, some social and some, like the right to sexual preference, appear to be personal. Equally real, however, is the connection among these goals, and readers should be aware that few of them can be adequately understood if they are thought of as purely and simply "economic," "social" or "personal." A central point of Friedan's book was that many women during the decade of the 1950s interpreted the malaise they felt as being due to a psychologically caused maladjustment to the then-approved feminine role. When some of them became aware that their friends were experiencing the same difficulties, they began to search for a common, social origin of their distress. The very idea that the source of the problem was external and that their feelings were not individual neurotic symptoms brought relief.

Another example of linkage can be discerned by analyzing a goal that seems at first glance purely economic: the issue of equal wages for equal work. This is a major demand of the women's movement, and it is supported by many who do not think of themselves as feminists. In spite of the recent influx of women into the labor force, the great majority motivated at least in part by economic need, women's wages have actually declined over the last several years in ratio to men's and now stand at less than 60 percent of the male average (full-time workers in both cases). There are clearly some economic reasons: Lack of seniority on the job is an obvious one. But the social causes for this disparity are almost certainly greater, while behind these again lie opinions and assumptions arising from psychological attitudes, both male and female, including that which attributes female inequality to the much touted "fear of success" among women.

If we now undertake a brief view of this situation, we observe that a demand for equal wages cannot be satisfied without response to a less popular demand for equality of job opportunities. In point of fact women can never be paid on a par with men until they are accepted as plausible candidates for positions in any field, at any level, instead of being restricted to particular occupations or subsidiary levels of work. An example of the hindrance imposed by social factors can be observed when we isolate one that has recently received some attention: the mathematics skills acquired by women in their educations. "Math anxiety" and "math avoidance" severely limit the fields in which anyone can hope to find employment or success. Without calculus or statistics, preparation at postsecondary level for a number of lucrative occupations and professions is impossible. Even in general business the ability to evaluate cash flow and balance sheets or to follow the workings of systems analysis can be vital to advancement. Women as a group are not well prepared during their school years to take advantage of economic opportunities requiring math skills. This economic result is often the product of social assumptions that define mathematics as a masculine sphere and suggest, directly and indirectly, to teenage girls that it is "unfeminine" to do math well. Of course, the result is not only detrimental in restricting work opportunities. It reinforces the acceptance of a feminine image that incorporates sex-based intellectual limits. (See Tobias, 1978.)

Worked out in economic terms, the current effect is that opportunities in some fields that are traditionally masculine have been extended to qualified women but stop short at entry-level jobs. In other industries or businesses, a full two-tier system still exists: Women are confined to adjunct positions where the promotion ladder runs from file clerk or typist to executive secretary in contrast to the advancement open to men that extends to top executives served by these secretaries. An excellent firsthand study of the internal operations of a major American company, in which this system is only now being painfully supplemented (not superseded) can be found in Rosabeth Kanter's *Men and Women of the Corporation* (1977). Here we can follow the day-to-day interaction of social and psychological formulation on economic status and opportunities. Of special interest to students of psychiatry is Dr. Kanter's discussion of the effects on behavior, both male and female, of a changed status for women that is widely perceived (and reacted to) as deviant. The position of "token" is graphically analyzed, as is the result of moving from such severely "skewed" sex ratios to those that are merely "tilted." The surprising result is that an increased number of women present decreases the threat felt by men, presumably because gender stereotypes can finally be abandoned in favor of seeing individual women as individuals. The psychological analysis of role breaking, as felt by both the role breaker and role others, has seldom been better done.

The psychological stress attached to the position of "token" is clearly a component in the refusal of many women to try to break out of the area labeled women's work, a refusal that ensures the continuation of unequal wages. Paradoxically, the economic motivation that brings so many women into the work force may also decide them to stay in stress-free areas rather than take the risk of moving up: They need the jobs they have too much to take any chances with them. 1976 figures reveal that 98 percent of all secretaries are female, as are 94 percent of all typists, and 74 percent of all clerical workers. It is easy to assume that this kind of distribution is due to women's fear of success, but Kanter's work (along with that of many others) illustrates the real, often punitive, psychological price set on aspiration by women. The social costs cannot be ignored either, especially for women who are also wives and mothers, whose homemaking tasks continue to demand an average of two and a half hours of work a day. When gains and losses are weighed together, the decision to stay in a less demanding job may be completely realistic, which is not to say that it's satisfactory.

The mingling of social factors with economics can be found in many other issues of concern to women, especially to the growing number who are single parents: access to credit facilities, including mortgages; ability to rent living space; the cost of child care, at centers or in the home. The scarcity of child-care centers supported at least to some extent by local government, local industry, tax relief and volunteer contributions of time or money by members of the community points up a continuing, but now totally unrealistic, adherence to the image of a family as described by Talcott Parsons, which currently exists for only a fraction of the population. So does the limited availability of part-time work above the lowest level and of positions offering "flexitime" with adjustable hours. Industry welcomes women as labor; 60 percent of the three million incomers to the work force in 1977 were female. But, with few exceptions, it still envisages a family in which the sole breadwinner is male and social adjustments to accommodate working women are unnecessary.

By the same token, questions that appear to be mainly legal and political often turn out to have a social and economic component. The entitlement of women who have not worked outside the home to Social Security is through their husbands and begins only after ten years of marriage; till recently, it was twenty years. Physical abuse of women by their husbands is both a legal and a social problem, but an economic factor is present when women are forced to ask themselves, "What do I do now? If I leave, how can I earn a living?" Separated and divorced women may receive child custody and, supposedly, child-support payments. If and when these are not maintained (which happens more than half the time), the economic problem requires a legal answer. The definition of rape is also difficult: Is it a crime or the result of social maladjustment? Where does the psychological element come in? The right of a woman to a legal and medically safe abortion by her own choice is probably the issue whose social, political and psychological ramifications are debated in the most heightened and passionate tones. But now that Congress has refused to direct that Medicaid funds be made available for abortions chosen by women, economics establishes a subclass of the poor whose right to an abortion (stated by the Supreme Court) is economically unenforceable.

The experience and aspirations of women who are members of minority groups broaden the range of concern and of activity within the women's movement. Again economic problems, which affect all minority people, are primary for they bear hardest on black and Hispanic women. Their wages are lowest, they are more frequently single parents dependent on welfare, while education and training for work that pays adequately are harder to come by than for any other definable group. But these economic disabilities inevitably translate themselves into political and social questions, while even more urgent may be the psychological need to identify oneself and one's priorities. Should minority women support the efforts of minority men to step forward toward full equality in preference to insisting on their own rights? How do life choices vary from those open to other women? Do differing cultural backgrounds produce a family structure that differs from white patterns? Have oppression and deprivation set up a con- tinuing "culture of poverty" that tends to replicate itself? Not only do minority women confront these questions for themselves—they (like other women) are charged with raising and socializing the next gener- ation. What goals, what attitudes, can they lay out for their children to take as models? Faced with the violence of urban ghettoes, what sort of character structure can they try to develop in the young? It is also necessary to consider the effect of the experience of powerlessness on women in terms of the parenting they are charged with. Do victims tend to victimize their children? We note again here the kind of linkage between different aspects of central problems that is typical of women's situation today and typical therefore of the efforts to respond effectively to these products of social dislocation, which is the purpose of the women's movement.

If economic and political questions connect with other aspects of life and challenge social norms and psychological constructs, feminist views also diverge from orthodox interpretations when we turn to more personal matters. Indeed a division between public and private spheres is itself disputed by the movement. An image of women as private people whose principal concerns have to do with family and interpersonal relations is held to be politically meaningful, a definition arrived at by a patriarchal society committed to maintaining male dominance by distancing women from public activities. The paired terms "male/female" are held to imply comparable pairs of "active/passive" and "public/private." It is suggested that the spheres set off by these dichotomies are so separated in traditional thinking that they are not only valued as superior/inferior but are actually to be examined according to different approaches: cognitive and rational for the male, public, active sphere through the disciplines of economics, political science, or history; while the personal, private, emotional female area may be open to psychological interpretation but not in a scientifically rigorous fashion. This is the expressive realm of myth and poetry.

Characteristic of the women's movement is the positive rejection of this division of humanity and with it a purposeful effort to connect public and private areas of life. In the feminist view the limitations that the male role places on full emotional expressiveness are as harmful as the restrictions of the female role, and they follow from a devaluation and trivialization of private and personal activities. One well-used attack on the women's movement has been the declaration that its aims are trivial: They have to do with "who washes the dishes" or does the housework. (The contradictory approach, that feminist aims are revolutionary, has also seen much service.) In fact, the insistence by society that women are to be the sole agents of homemaking and child rearing is far from trivial and affects both sexes profoundly. Equally important is the parallel insistence that emotional satisfaction is of no importance in the active masculine sphere of paid labor. (Its effects are well studied in Studs Terkel's *Working.*) The effects of massive social change are now being felt in both areas.

Effects of Social Change on the Mother Role

The decline in the birth rate plus an extended life span decreases both the actual and the relative time that women now expect to spend as childbearers and rearers, a period that in the past was usually coincident with their total active lives. Another change is less obvious:

the tie between childbearing and child raising is less necessitous than
it was before nutritional knowledge permitted healthy children to be
raised without breast feeding. While there is a weight of argument to
the point that psychological health demands a close mother-child
symbiotic relationship in the first months of life, there is also an
opposite opinion. In *The Mermaid and the Minotaur* (1977) Dorothy
Dinnerstein argues that the omnipresent and overwhelmingly powerful "First Parent" who is now almost always female leaves in the
infant an ineradicable stain of fear of female power and of the need
to revolt against it in favor of patriarchal authority. She believes this
gender-related conflict has had incalculable effects on the nature of
society itself. Her views will be considered later as a part of a discussion of theory, but this (so to speak) reassessment of the psychic
turmoil that Freud named the Oedipus complex is reflected in many
other familiar and reinforcing statements on the psychological problems occasioned by overpowering and castrating mothers.

In any case, historical and anthropological data make it clear that
contemporary practices that expect American mothers to look after
small children by themselves without the more or less regular assistance of other adults is far from being the usual pattern. Less radical
arguments than those of Dinnerstein have advocated greater involvement in child raising by the father along with a greater use of beyond-
the-family institutions. Possibilities put forward range from almost
total care by professionals, as in some Israeli kubbutzim, to the familiar nursery school, the means by which relatively affluent parents
provide a stimulating social milieu for their children for part of the
day. The need of working mothers for trustworthy and reliable child
care is apparent, but in the demand of movement activists for extended
child-care facilities is also included a sense of the benefit to young
children of interaction with their peers and with a range of friendly
adults. Here again is an instance of the linkage between public and
private, economic and social needs.

So in fact the theoretical question that Dinnerstein raises is com-
panioned by practical questions: How possible is it for a mother to
fulfill adequately the role of principal child raiser in today's society?
When, in the past, the family was the locus of economic activity,
children were not left alone with one adult for a good part of the day
or isolated from the world of work. Often they were looked after by
other kin or by neighbors, and in a rural or village world the need for
supervision ended when they were younger. How extreme that family
isolation can be today is indicated by these instances listed in a study

undertaken for the Massachusetts Advisory Council on Education by the Massachusetts Early Education Project (Rowe). This group found:

1. Isolation of wage earners from spouses and children, caused by the wage earners' absorption into the world of work.

2. The complementary isolation of young children from the occupational world of parents and other adults.

3. The general isolation of young children from persons of different ages, both adults and older children.

4. The residential isolation of families from persons of different social, ethnic, religious and racial backgrounds.

5. The isolation of family members from kin and neighbors.

Such isolation means that the role of the family as the agent for socializing children is inadequately fulfilled at present *whether or not* mothers are at work outside the home. Children are now growing up without the benefit of a variety of adult role models of both sexes and in ignorance of the world of paid work. Returning women to a life centered in home and family would not solve the fundamental loss of connection between family and community. The effort by the women's movement to see that centers for child care are provided by society is not an attempt to hand over to others the duties of motherhood but to enlist community aid to supplement the proper obligations of parents, as was often the practice in the past. Other approaches to the same end are shared household and child care among several families, or actual communal living. They are less frequent and more marginal, but the impulse is toward enriching the immediate day-to-day existence of parents and children alike. It stems from a sense that the present isolation of family life is historically abnormal; and much data exists to justify this view. It also arises from a widespread fear of the invitation to competent women, who are not allowed a fair run of independent and autonomous activity, to overinvest emotion in their children. A good deal of literature, both popular and scholarly, testifies to the detrimental effect on children of demanding and manipulative mothers whose influence has been declared alienating and even schizophrenegenic. How can this be prevented? The women's movement replies, by making sure that other opportunities for activity are open to women and by bringing other adults in to direct responsibility for child rearing.

Effects of Social Change on the Role of
Woman as Sexual Partner

While different aspects of women's lives continue to be connected in many ways, a major disconnection has occurred with the development of reliable methods for controlling conception. Sexual activity can now be detached from childbirth, and in theory, at least, women are as free to take part in sex as men have been in the past. True, the contemporary world is still far from working out the repercussions of this fact, for old necessities linger on in the behavioral patterns that they established. The traditional double standard is fading, but as yet no accepted guidelines for the proper expression of female sexuality have taken its place. Once again we see the need to improvise ways of relating between men and women and of gratifying emotions.

In the past men were allowed more sexual freedom because they only begot children and did not bear them. The process of gestation both identified the mother and made her the responsible parent. The role of sexual partner then stood in some opposition to the role of mother, for female sexuality could only be satisfied when it was contained acceptably within a social structure called marriage; and marriage had many other functions. The long infancy of human children increases their dependence on the adults of the community, and the effect of this has been to emphasize the function of the mother role above that of sexual partner even in social systems that demonstrate a greater communal responsibility for children than does ours. Male sexuality has been expressed in ways that were not limited by social norms and familial obligations, but if conception follows, the physical fact of childbirth has to be integrated into the social structure. The child belongs somewhere, fitted into the system somehow even if its category is stigmatized as bastard. As a result, the satisfaction of sexuality for women has always taken second place to the social interpretation of the fact of motherhood.

Reliable birth control methods break the necessary connection between sex and motherhood, but they do not suggest an alternative way for women to value or to express their own sexual drives. The obvious model is for them to "behave like men"; which, rightly or wrongly, is held to mean the acceptance and gratification of sexual opportunities whenever offered. But the principle that male behavior in any area is the equivalent of universal human behavior is one that the women's movement questions heartily, whether we are talking about aggression or affection. And indeed the fact that women have very frequently been forced to restrain their own sexuality if only to curb the rate of population increase must have played a considerable part in the development of "normal" male sexual approaches and practices. Here again we are at sea in a world of change, in search of new kinds of valid sexual interaction.

Thus the relationship between the women's liberation movement and the great decrease of restrictions on sexual activity in recent years is not simple. Historically, the feminists of the nineteenth and early twentieth century tended to condemn the easy gratification of male sexuality. In part it was due to the simple physical drain of childbirth on women who did not have access to birth control or to modern medical science for themselves and for the children whose deaths were so much more frequent than today. In part it was due to fear of venereal disease, contracted by men on their sexual cruises and passed to their wives. In addition, orthodox cultural wisdom assumed that respectable women were usually frigid; and frigidity can become a self-fulfilling prophecy if both partners expect it and do nothing to overcome it. Eminent Victorian physicians like Dr. William Acton laid it down as truth, and mothers who had not known pleasure themselves taught their daughters that sex was something to endure in order to please their husbands.

A change in women's expectations of sexual pleasure began half a century ago, thanks to the impact and spread of the work of Freud, Jung and their disciples. The decrease in frigidity can be traced decade by decade through the figures given in the Kinsey report on women, while the data supplied by Masters and Johnson seem to indicate that women are capable of longer, more sustained and more quickly repeated orgasm than are men. But as yet social expectations have not adjusted to give female sexuality full expression.

Thus, if the perceived male pattern were proper for women, it should follow that women could as easily be initiators of casual sex encounters as men. Certainly some change has taken place here, but in most circumstances women who invite sex overtly are seen as behaving deviantly and are devalued. To be a stud is admirable in a male. To be a nymphomaniac is not a desirable female image. Other definitions for women who invite sex are prostitutes, or those who suffer from feelings of inferiority and buy male companionship in return for sex. In intimate relationships there is no doubt that women can more easily initiate sexual encounters than ever before; but the public stereotype still reserves the right to invite intimacy to men, unless the woman takes on the traditional position of inferior.

At the same time, the increase in sexual freedom has had a curiously prescriptive effect on male-female relationships. Men are expected to seek intimacy with women as part of a normal friendly relationship; and women are expected to comply. This may seem to increase the choices open to both sexes, but as long as invitation on the one hand and compliance on the other are felt to be required, choice is not free. In the past the male right to initiate a sexual encounter was balanced by a female right to refuse the man's request on general grounds of morality or propriety. Acceptance was then seen as a personal sign of affection and favor, but refusal carried no stigma of personal rejection. Today, since women are known to enjoy sex as much as men and need not fear social recrimination for their activities, it is expected that they will respond by agreeing. Consequently, refusal becomes as personally pejorative as acceptance was gratifying in the older situation. A woman who says "No" seems to be disparaging the man who asks. This is not only unpleasant at the time, it shadows the future of the relationship in a way that refusal never used to do. A woman who refuses a man's request is now no longer expected to be doing so on the basis of her commitment to moral or social standards that everyone accepts whether or not they practice them. She is taken to be saying, "I don't like *you.*" Paradoxically, she can perfectly well refuse an invitation to a concert because she doesn't care for the program or suggest that she'd prefer to do something more active than attend a movie; but refusing a sexual encounter is invidious. Some women who still feel themselves to be secondary people whose role calls for them to please men accept sex as a duty in the same way their great-grandmothers did. As long as the feminine role includes an injunction to please men, and a perusal of the popular press indicates that it does, a version of the double standard will still survive.

Women's Lives: A Field of Scholarly Research

One of the most fruitful developments of the women's movement has been the astonishing increase in our knowledge of the lives and potentialities of women. Unknown before the decade of the seventies (though of course explored by a few early researchers, such as Mary Ritter Beard, Margaret Mead and Simone de Beauvoir), the field of women's studies has been opened for investigation by historians, sociologists, anthropologists, psychologists, theologians and students of comparative religion, literary critics and philosophers. The rewards have been rich. Social historians had already been pursuing researches into past family patterns and ways of daily living; these obviously open doors to the study of female life-styles, obligations and expectations. As a result, a great deal of myth and legend has been replaced by factual information based on archival research, on surviving letters and journals and on neglected writing by women authors. Known historical work has also been made more accessible so that the related significance of all this material can now be seen.

In analogous fashion, anthropologists have increasingly focused on women's activities in other societies. Women anthropologists have naturally been accepted in areas where men had been barred, as in the case of secret women's rituals or traditional knowledge of legend and crafts. The question of women's contribution to early technology and food collection has been explored, and their experience reviewed for its weight within the social structure. (See Rosaldo and Lamphere, Friedl, Reiter.) Sociologists are reconsidering many structures and relationships within contemporary civilization. In a short essay contained in a 1975 collection *(Another Voice,* Millman and Kanter, eds.), Arlene Kaplan Daniels lays out over two dozen areas where women's impact on society needs scholarly study. Existing studies of psychological sex differences are brought together and analyzed in the work of Maccoby and Jacklin, while Jean Baker Miller offers a short but perceptive discussion of the impact of change and the need to create new and adjusted relationships in *Toward a New Psychology for Women.* In *Beyond God the Father,* Mary Daly supplies insight into the role assigned to women by the Catholic Church, while Reuther and McClaughlin discuss female leadership in Jewish and Christian traditions *(Women of Spirit).* Critics Elaine Showalter and Ellen Moers have illuminated past literature, bringing to women the sense of a strong, continuing literary tradition with deep roots in the past.

Such work can only be indicated in the briefest fashion. The scholarly journal of the field, *Signs,* is published quarterly, and those interested in the new learning on women will find it valuable, as is also *Feminist Studies.* The fact that this is a field to itself, not a conglomeration of pieces of others, has been foreshadowed by the earlier comments in this essay on the essential linkage between economic, social and psychological aspects of women's concerns. An example from women's studies will point this up: In what area should be discussed the effect of the division of labor by gender? It is clearly economic. It touches on biology; but the question of motherhood and child raising is also social. What are the psychological effects of directing one sex to one set of occupations? Historically, what do the records tell us about work assigned to women? Is it always the same? If not, what changes can be found, and with what other elements are they associated? What can we learn from the division of labor in other societies or as indicated by prehistoric data? How does it differ according to class and racial or ethnic background? No doubt there are more questions to be asked that would involve other fields, but perhaps this is sufficient to indicate the breadth of inquiry occasioned by the impact of the women's movement on research and education.

The importance of this new knowledge is not simply theoretical. It extends, as it alters, the perspectives by which women can view their lives, understand the attitudes they have accepted as normal and the behavior they see as proper, and plan (if they so desire) to alter life-styles and projections for the future. We are looking at a process of feedback and reinforcement. There is no reason to suppose that the process will stop in the foreseeable future. Clearly, too, these changes in women's perceptions of themselves and of their potentialities are going to affect their relationships with men. The new research on women should consequently be of great value to students of psychiatry, not only for treatment of women patients but for understanding resulting shifts in male perceptions, needs and aspirations. Moreover, where many early statements from feminists tended to be largely negative, reacting against masculine norms in the needed effort to disestablish such norms from their apparent universality, the passage of time has permitted the development of positive theoretical structures as well. Feminist statements of the late sixties and early seventies often had to stress the dissociation of women's actual experience from that described by orthodox social and psychological works. Even then, many went on to suggest alternatives; but the growing body of available data has been accompanied by a growing mass of alternative interpretation and constructive hypothesis.

Theoretical Considerations: From Negative to Positive

Although feminist theory is already developing its own evaluations of the effect of gender roles on individuals and society, some recapitulation of its reasons for rejecting standard social and psychological interpretations must still be given. Fundamental to this rejection is the orthodox assumption that male experience and behavior can be taken as the basis for general theory in almost any field. *He* is not only the generic pronoun subsuming *she*; the forms and norms of male-dominated society are taken to be sufficient for the study of humankind: The study of "psychology of women" thus becomes an addendum to the study of psychology.

In rejecting this assumption the women's movement both affirms a difference in women's experience and declares the equal importance of this experience. Equality, that is, does not imply sameness but rather the equal value of difference. Male patterns, or patterns that have developed under masculine dominance, are deficient. They not only ignore the patterns of behavior and interpretation of life taught to women by their variant experience, they also overlook the influence on the situation of humankind that arises both from male dominance and from inattention to women's lives. In addition, the causes for variation-by-gender tend to be taken for granted as following inevitably from physiological differences. Obviously, the fact that women, not men, bear children is important in determining the course of their lives. But how important is it? And is the importance overriding, or does it vary according to social circumstances?

The great majority of feminists would answer this question by saying that the child-bearing function of women is a rudimentary base for a vast structure of sex-differentiated behavior patterns that are, in fact, socially assigned. Moreover, the physical base changes through time with external conditions of life. Thus, in the past, human infants did not survive without intimate, long-term care by some female who could nurse them, mother or wet nurse: There was no adequate substitute for breast feeding. This *physical* need no longer exists, whatever may be the opinion on the psychological desirability of mother-child intimacy. Again, in the absence of a developed technology, pregnancy and the presence of young children assigned to female care affected the sort of labor that women could undertake. Technical and scientific advances have wiped out physical limitations on women's ability to do heavy manual work; indeed, they have practically eliminated such work. But its ancient necessity became incorporated in tradition and continues to mark some occupations as unsuitable for women, though the label is now merely metaphoric.

If the historical necessities that once dictated the status of women are no longer operative, the directions derived from them can now be modified—and should be modified where they have become counter-productive. If nurture rather than nature is mainly responsible for the way we order our lives, we can better hope to order them differently. Feminists point to the variety of occupations, of role definitions, and of social status among women in different societies and at different historical periods as an indication that the feminine role not only can change but has changed radically. As science, technology and medicine continue to extend human control over the physical world, the potential for variation increases.

Recent emphasis by sociobiologists on the impact of genetic determinants of gender behavior is of great interest. The eagerness with which it has been taken up and popularized tends to increase the suspicion felt by feminist scholars in the field that it is being used as a covert social control, no doubt unconsciously in many cases. Scientific evaluation of the effectiveness of biological directives and controls is clouded by an unfortunate tendency to advance it as a new form of Social Darwinism, so that it seems to represent an effort to maintain orthodox male-female patterns of dominance. It is thus reminiscent of many earlier declarations that whatever is is right because it is (obviously) the product of evolution.

However that may be, we need not deny that biology can influence human interaction in order to perceive the dangers of oversimplifying the mechanisms by which these influences may work. If genetic determinants do exist, they cannot operate simply even in physiological terms. "To equate biological with intrinsic, inflexible or preprogrammed is an unfortunate misuse of the term," writes H. H. Lambert (*Signs,* vol. 4, no. 1, p. 104); and points out how "innately determined structure and function normally develop in interaction with the environment," including the bodily environment in, for example, the maturation of the visual system. And beyond the complex and difficult question of how genetic directives may affect each other, there lies the even more complex questions of the intervention by social limitations, social opportunities and learned motivation.

The complexities of social and personal interaction are fundamental to the study of psychiatry. In many ways the feminist effort to discover and explore the "secret history" of women—that is, to investigate and revalue the events and interpretations that structure their lives—is analogous to the practice of psychiatry and the development of analytic theory, with its willingness to probe and question received ideas. Therapists treating women share the concern of feminists to improve and facilitate connections for women with the external world —though feminists perhaps believe more strongly that real improvement is not possible unless the external world is changed along with the individual's perceptions of it. Both groups also see repressed and denied experience as the cause of powerful disruptive results in the ability of women to use their energies well and would agree that because the apparatus of repression works unconsciously and is rationalized by social myth in the public situation and by neurotic structures in the individual personality, it is hard to deal with in a straightforward fashion.

In fact, the situation of women today is a place where public and private disfunction meet. Social directives that define the feminine gender roles in a limiting and even disabling way (as adjunct; as other; as private person; primarily as nurturing so that self-denial must precede self-fulfillment; as unfitted for creative and active intervention in society) invite a neurotic response. The approved self-image of women may be suitable for some, but even these women do not have an opportunity to choose it. It is laid on all women, whether suitable or not; and in any case, it is a definition *by others*. Moreover, it differs sharply from the aims and goals of the masters of our society as embodied in the culture that women, as well as men, are told to incorporate in their understanding of normal behavior. The idea that the individual self is innately deviant from the ideals of a culture affects others, not only women: Male members of minorities receive this message too. It is never a pleasant message, but the fact that minority men are in a position to pass some of the sting on to minority women (if they so choose) may somewhat mitigate it in their case. The bodily imprint of sex difference, interpreted as penis envy, is certainly taken by analytic theory to be of overwhelming significance and indeed as the root of female character formation. What theoreticians of the women's movement are disputing is not the physiological ground of difference between men and women—that would be ridiculous. What is being questioned is the significance of physiological difference and the universality and necessity of cultural interpretations of this difference.

True, men are also offered an incomplete self-image: They are limited not just in the expression of emotions that are regarded as feminine but in responding emotionally in an overt way to events and are thus inhibited in their ability to confront inner feelings and work them through. The women's movement is aware of the disabilities that the male gender role lays on men and is convinced that both sexes will profit from the overthrow of sexual stereotypes in favor of individual human diversity. But though the expression of machismo, of competition, confrontation and violence is not only socially unfortunate but personally painful to many men, the male role is less destructive to the psyche than is the female if only because it encourages action, not passivity. It also places men in the central position in society and declares them to be the important sex, since they properly originate activity, interpret and structure events, and administer the apparatus that deals with external reality. Obviously not all men welcome the burden of action and the responsibility of social administration, but the implication of the male role is worthiness for these tasks, while that of the female role is subordination by reason of unfitness for them.

Theoreticians of the women's movement are attempting to work out patterns of social interaction that can not only open doors to activity for women but also reduce the extremes of alienation, violence and drive to dominance that the control of society by one sex has produced. Jean Baker Miller (*Toward a New Psychology for Women*) speaks of the need to preserve women's ability to affiliate with others in bonds of affection while seeking greater self-direction. Is "autonomy" a desirable goal for women? she asks; and replies that they are seeking something more complete than is implied by the term in its current usage: "a fuller not a lesser ability to encompass relations to others, simultaneously with the fullest development of oneself." She is looking for *redefinitions* of goals that have been reserved for men, not simple-minded acceptance of them as they are now understood. For women to risk conflict requires that its definition be thought through and reinterpreted, so that conflict as paralyzing confrontation gives way to a process of sorting out reasons for disagreement, judging the need for change realistically, finding allies who share this need, and then embarking on the effort to arrive at an agreed-on goal by negotiation as well as by confrontation.

Dorothy Dinnerstein's analysis of the effect on infants of the family constellation as we know it has already been cited. The mother-child symbiosis, she declares, is primary to the structure of character and of society, and it is therefore the menacing cause of our contemporary problems, to which gender stereotypes are central. Infants who experience earliest socialization only through the mediation of one sex, and who must reject the relationship in order to form an individual identity, will see in the other sex a desirable, romantic and emotional goal for their own identification. These "mother-raised humans" cannot value the first parent in a way that separates her from the engulfing authority who was felt as monstrously powerful: If it creates the self, cannot it also destroy it? Such infantile memories form the background to human understanding of the world. "Male authority," she writes, "is bound to look like a refuge from female authority," and thus it presents itself as the source of individual autonomy. Our child-raising practices distance the father from the baby until the child is old enough to be less terrified of parental engulfment. Therefore the father is perceived as a means of escape from the symbiotic first relationship and a passage toward active maturity.

Dinnerstein contends that very early dual care of infants will prevent the perception of parental power as being located in only one sex. It will therefore work toward the disappearance of gender stereotypes that now support patriarchy as the alternative to a dreaded and menacing fantasy of matriarchy. She replies (as many feminists have) to Freud's famous question, "What do women want?" by declaring that it is "to stop serving as scapegoats (their own scapegoats as well as men's and children's scapegoats) for human resentment of the human condition." The subordination of women, she believes, is a function of the desperate need for children to escape from the female parent because this parent is seen as the all-powerful creator of the world, which she alone mediates in single-sex child raising. The introduction of a surrogate parent does little to change this as long as the surrogate is female. It is rebellion against this perceived power that produces the fear and resentment that creates and maintains the actual subjugation of women to rule by men.

A connection between the rejection of the mother by girl children and the devaluation of oneself as female is an area where feminist theory is now very active. In an interesting way this is a tribute to Freud's significant, indeed primary, insight that separation from the mother is an all-important first step in the growth of the individual to self-integrated maturity. For boy children, the reward for successful progress through the Oedipal situation is identification with the father in the role of legitimate authority figure and definition of the mother as female and other: not herself a legitimate object of sexual desire but one of a class in whom such an object will be found. Freud's studies of the female Oedipal development suffer, in feminist eyes, from being secondary to, if not adaptations of, male experience rather than independent analysis of an essentially different experience, whose difference is further accentuated by societal views and valuations of gender roles.

In Freud's view, and it realistically reflects the opinion of society both then and now, the truly essential bodily difference between the sexes is the possession or the absence of the penis. We are so accustomed to this view that we seldom stop to ask ourselves why it was made, and when we do the first answer that comes to mind is: The penis is a visible difference, the uterine cavity is invisible. Therefore the girl perceives that she lacks something that her brother possesses. However this perception is possible only for children below the age of puberty *looking at each other* and barred from the opportunity of observing the naked adult female body, which clearly displays visible breasts and, when pregnant, a protruding belly that differs from mere obesity. In short, Freud is asking us to posit a vision of bodily difference in a society that is not only clothed but prudish. The limitations of class and of period that affect the range of patients with whom Freud dealt have been remarked on often enough, but it's necessary to consider the actual perceived data that such a society presented to its members. In a community where naked adult figures were familiar to children, the male possession of a penis might well be offset by the female possession of breasts; and the nurturing value of the breast for the child would be demonstrated continually, while the bodily forms of pregnancy would be clearly known to all. In short, it would be much less easy to reduce all sexual difference to a male-penis-presence and a female-penis-absence. It follows that if the penis were still to be valued more highly than the equally visible breasts, there would have to be a societal reason for the valuation. It could not be merely physiological presence/absence of one organ, if the counterbalancing presence/absence of another were totally ignored.

Also present in Freud's discussion of the female Oedipal situation is a confusion between the absence of a penis and the "loss" of the penis. Now it would clear up this blurring if we could assume that Freud was speaking merely of the child's emotional perception of the situation, if he were positing only *her* confusion and her imaginative explanation: that she had once had a penis and had lost it. Unfortunately, Freud's usage is decidedly ambiguous. The child's "phantasy" of castration is regularly expressed as the discovery "that she is castrated" or even "the fact of castration." If this is shorthand, it is confusing shorthand; and particularly so because Freud consistently describes normal female physiology as a "deficiency" and its discovery as "unwelcome knowledge." At first the "misfortune" is thought to be peculiar to herself, but when the child learns that this is the general condition of women, "it follows that femaleness—and with it of course her mother—suffers a great depreciation in her eyes."

This is certainly true; to be female is to be assigned to an inferior position, and if the "unwelcome knowledge" is a little less shattering than it was in Freud's time, it is still no cause for rejoicing. The question does not have to do with Freud's perceptions of external reality and its effects on the psyche, which are profound and true, but with the reasoning that supports them. Freud himself occasionally warned ("Femininity") against the "superimposition" of unjustified significance on the facts of physical difference between the sexes. But these differences are just what he cites to account for the social roles of men and women, even though anyone reading him today can follow his arguments perfectly well (indeed better) by taking these differences as *symbolic* of assigned gender roles. Let the possession of a penis *stand for* the social right to male dominance, and Freud's three famous papers on female sexuality become even more illuminating, as if an intermediate step in his reasoning had been restored by returning to it a full sense of the socialization process of learning and accepting norms of behavior and expression. So much of the psychological insight that has stemmed from Freud's own work analyzes and illuminates exactly the systematic progress by which external events, including body structure, are related to the self via maturation-through-interpretive relationships that one almost feels within his writing a contradiction (repressed and denied as it is) of his conscious dedication to the invariant effect of biological determinants.

To a considerable extent the search of feminist theoreticians for a vision of the process by which girl children can move through separation from the mother in new ways is a tribute to Freud's insight. Is there a way, feminists ask, to avoid the necessity for hatred and hostility to this First Parent that Freud assumed? He wrote in "Female Sexuality" that the end of the pre-Oedipal attachment to the mother "is accompanied by hostility: the attachment to the mother ends in hate." The specific factor, he continues, lies in the castration complex: "Girls hold their mother responsible for their lack of a penis and do not forgive her for their being thus put at a disadvantage." It is clear that identification with the mother is made difficult not simply by the discovery that she too is female—that is, has been "castrated," but also by the idea that she is the agent for castrating her daughter.

Once we are able to see this "castration" as being social in nature —that is, the product of integrating into the (female) self the "unwelcome knowledge" of one's inferiority—it is possible to entertain the idea that mother-daughter hostility is not inevitable because it is not biologically determined but the result of significance assigned by a culture to physical differences between the sexes. Why should the penis be an object of envy unless it bestows on its possessors some advantage? Freud suggests that, in the experience of small children, this advantage is that of physical pleasure, that masturbation is more satisfying and longer continued among boys than girls. Again, one cannot help but feel that the contemporary assessment of females as finding *less* pleasure in sex than males somehow influences this assumption. As Kinsey, Masters and Johnson and others have now demonstrated however, this is incorrect. It would seem that we are again looking at an unconscious estimate of the meaning of physiological fact according to a societal assumption.

Current interest among feminists in the mother-daughter relationship does not so much reject Freud's interpretation of the way it appeared (and appears) to operate as it rejects the inevitability of such a sequence. Dinnerstein's suggestion of changing the nature of the relationship by avoiding its unique quality has been discussed: Break up the "inevitable" linkage between powerful first parent and femaleness by arranging for active male parenting from birth on. Another approach is rather to revalue the female linkage as carrier of profound affection and meaning within a female heritage so that knowledge of one's femininity need no longer be "unwelcome." Some explorations of mother-daughterhood explore the significance of the relationship in terms of female-to-female affection. These explorations lead toward a search for evidence of matriarchal traditions in the past, for a woman's culture that has its own essential values, and in the personal sense, toward a revaluation of lesbianism. Since the attitude of the women's movement toward the issue of lesbianism has been found distinctly puzzling by many men and women, a brief discussion of its importance to this aspect of theory may be helpful.

Efforts to reach across to the female principle are anything but easy, for this principle in fact represents the repressed and devalued part of human experience, which is identified and defined in any male-dominated culture not by its carriers but by those who see them as "others," and always (as far as we know) as inferior others. The attempts by women to explore inner reality appear, to those who naturally accept traditional cultural norms, as withdrawal and even rejection of accepted male-female relationships. In fact, they are regarded by those who make them as being—more significantly—efforts to discover what is essential to women's existence that is not derived from male definitions and male-related concepts. To withdraw from standard male-female connections is a necessary step for this (one might say) analytic plunge into hitherto unexplored areas of the unconscious.

To find and authenticate a new structure and a different definition of the essential identity of femaleness is obviously so demanding a task that few women will venture on it; and at the same time, so significant that many will understand (even if subliminally) why it is a vital part of the women's movement. The journey of women toward each other is a journey toward this goal. Psychologically, the sexual coming together of women is often seen as part of a search for a renewed identification with the mother and the lost affection between mother and daughter. Where Freud posited hatred and hostility, which had to accompany a break with the pre-Oedipal connection, theorists and lesbian actors-out of such explorations are testing possibilities for retaining a female affective contact that would not short-circuit maturation but would free it from occurring *only* in a hostile setting. As things stand now, "the loss of the daughter to the mother, the mother to the daughter, is the essential female tragedy." So writes Adrienne Rich in her probing chapter, Motherhood and Daughterhood, in *Of Women Born*. Rich's writing illuminates the psychic connection between a search for the lost mother and the sexual love for other women. She quotes the poet, Sue Silvermarie: "In loving another woman I discovered the deep urge to be both a mother to and find a mother in my lover." (Rich, 1971)

While it is certainly true that psychiatrists, and therapists generally, are increasingly tolerant of homosexuality in both sexes, it is still hard for most acculturated individuals, whatever their training, to perceive positive values in these relationships. To suggest that such values exist in the present and as part of a process of change is not to affirm that they are either supreme or eternal. The effort to create a new female identity, and the attempt to understand this effort theoretically, is at an early stage. Lesbianism is perceived by many feminists as a permissible sexual preference, in which the male-female dominance is absent and affection is therefore free to express itself in an atmosphere of equality. The more profound linkage with a rethinking of the mother-daughter connection is no doubt less often put forward, but the surfacing of this topic in much recent poetry and fiction by women indicates how central it is in current feeling. Both are perhaps best seen as manifestations of the process of redefinition of the female identity.

For most women interested in the goals of the women's movement, lesbianism is simply interesting as theory or is understood as an assertion of the individual right to live as desired in a pluralistic society. In public practice, support for lesbian rights is really a question of civil liberties; antilesbianism can be seen as an analog of antisemitism, with much the same motivation. Its inner meaning and function, as one strand in the female effort to explore and recover the unconscious life of women, has been dwelt on here for the benefit of students of psychiatry who can profit from some knowledge of the causative background and the analytic connections to Freudian theory.

Summation

The extremely diverse concerns and activities of the women's movement now link into many aspects of existence. Their complexity is so great that any simple description of the movement is necessarily false, while questions raised in one area turn out to resonate in others. Political, economic and social matters are joined. The impact on women's psychological aspirations and fears is multifarious. Images of the self and also images of the female role are fluid. Practically speaking, political or economic action responding to demands of the women's movement is perfectly possible, and the creation of new social structures and networks is badly needed by all. But these actions, while helpful, cannot be thought of as permanent solutions that will satisfy women, whose lives are now caught up in change. Their demands result from such change and will continue to be put forward in one form or another in an attempt to adjust human existence as experienced by women to the forces of change.

This sense of life as a process of becoming that can be modified just because it is a process is part of the ethos of the women's movement. Anger against limiting traditional social roles and oppressive institutions is certainly very much alive; but the attention of the movement is now increasingly turned to the future. Its present impact allows it to plan and to think ahead. As more and more women live various (often stressful) lives, resulting social pressures will not only be registered more strongly but will also affect new areas of existence. It will surely not escape the notice of psychiatrists that shifts in women's lives now impact powerfully on conscious and unconscious processes in men. This must be expected to continue, and an understanding of what it is that women want will prove useful in many circumstances.

Bibliography

Aries, Philippe. *Centuries of Childhood: A Social History of Family Life.* New York: Vintage Books, 1965.

Beard, Mary Ritter. *Women as Force in History.* New York: MacMillan & Co., 1946.

Daly, Mary. *Beyond God the Father, Toward a Philosophy of Women's Liberation.* Boston: Beacon Press, 1973.

de Beauvoir, Simone. *The Second Sex.* New York: Alfred A. Knopf, 1953.

Dinnerstein, Dorothy. *The Mermaid and the Minotaur, Sexual Arrangements and Human Malaise.* New York: Harper & Row, 1976.

Feminist Studies, c/o Women's Studies Program, University of Maryland.

Firestone, S. *The Dialectic of Sex.* New York: William Morrow, 1970.

Friedan, Betty. *The Feminine Mystique.* New York: W. W. Norton, 1963.

Friedl, Ernestine. *Women and Men.* New York: Holt, Rinehart & Winston, 1975.

Hole, Judith, and Ellen Levine. *The Rebirth of Feminism.* New York: Quadrangle Books, 1971.

Greer, Germaine. *The Female Eunuch.* New York: McGraw-Hill, 1971.

Janeway, Elizabeth. *Man's World, Woman's Place.* New York: William Morrow, 1971.

Kanter, Rosabeth Moss. *Men and Women of the Corporation.* New York: Basic Books, 1977.

Kinsey, A. C. et al. *Sexual Behavior in the Human Female.* Philadelphia, Pa.: W. B. Saunders, 1948.

Laslett, Peter, ed. *Household and Family in Past Time.* Cambridge: University Press, 1972.

Lerner, Gerda. *The Female Experience, An American Documentary.* Indianapolis: Bobbs-Merrill, 1972.

Lindberg, F., and M. Farnham. *Modern Woman: The Lost Sex.* New York: Harper & Row, 1947.

Maccoby, E. E., and C. N. Jacklin. *The Psychology of Sex Differences.* Stanford, Calif.: Stanford University Press, 1974.

Masters, W. H., and V. E. Johnson. *Human Sexual Response.* Boston: Little, Brown, 1966.

Mead, Margaret. *Male and Female.* New York: William Morrow, 1949.

Miller, Jean Baker. *Toward a New Psychology of Women.* Boston, Mass.: Beacon Press, 1976.

Millett, Kate. *Sexual Politics.* New York: Doubleday, 1970.

Millman, Marcia, and Rosabeth Moss Kanter, eds. *Another Voice: Feminist Perspectives on Social Life and Social Sciences.* New York: Anchor Books, 1975.

Mitchell, Juliet. *Woman's Estate.* New York: Pantheon, 1971.

Moers, Ellen. *Literary Women.* New York: Doubleday, 1976.

Parson, Talcott, and Robert Bales. *Family: Socialization and Interaction Process.* New York: The Free Press, 1955.

Reiter, Reyna. *Toward an Anthropology of Women.* New York: Monthly Review, 1975.

Reuther, Rosemary, and Eleanor McClaughlin. *Women of Spirit.* New York: Simon & Schuster, 1979.

Rich, Adrienne. *Of Women Born.* New York: W. W. Norton, 1976.

Rosaldo, Michele, and Louise Lamphere. *Women, Culture and Society.* Stanford, Calif.: Stanford University Press, 1974.

Signs: Journal of Women in Culture and Society. Chicago: The University of Chicago Press.

Shorter, Edward. *The Making of the Modern Family.* New York: Basic Books, 1975.

Showalter, Elaine. *A Literature of Their Own.* Princeton, N.J.: Princeton University Press, 1977.

Stone, Lawrence. *The Family, Sex and Marriage in England, 1500–1800.* New York: Harper & Row, 1977.

Terkel, Studs. *Working.* New York: Pantheon, 1974.

Tobias, Sheila. *Overcoming Math Anxiety.* New York: W. W. Norton, 1978.

Strouse, Jean, ed. *Women and Analysis: Dialogues on Psychoanalytic Views of Femininity.* New York: Grossman Publishers, 1974.

Wertheimer, Barbara. *We Were There: The Story of Working Women in America.* New York: Pantheon Books, 1977.

WORK

Work is action, and consequently it is both a break in the walls between public and private space and a path that connects them. But work as mere doing is meaningless. Without purpose and goals, without endurance and persistence, work becomes drudgery, or its direction wavers. Without the structure provided by theory, activist work for common goals can go astray, or it can founder in frustration, all meaning lost. Individuals and groups of human beings need all these things for satisfaction: personal ambition, which draws strength from a belief that action can be effective; theory, which both explains the way the world works and connects the personal and the political—and action, which is the instrument for intervention in events.

The limitations on acceptable action, which hedged women in for so long, always tended to break down under social or economic pressure, in time of famine or war or cultural shifts. What has freed women recently has been exactly the social and economic changes in the circumstances of existence that have moved society from small-scale, family-based, pre-industrial production with its great emphasis on agriculture to the world we live in today. We have lost a great deal—ties of kinship, ties of region, sense of community—but we have gained a great deal too in the loosening of social imperatives and the opening of opportunities to those denied them previously. Any climactic shift, such as humanity has experienced in the last two hundred years, obviously brings both loss and new chances for undreamed of advance. We have them both today.

Do the losses outweigh the gains? No. But they may well be felt more quickly and they are easier to articulate. Losses are present, and though hope and aspiration may be present too the full value of gains lies in the future. In addition, the outward sign of women's opportunities and independence is pretty unromantic—the chance to work for money that comes to our own pockets as a result of our own known efforts. There's nothing glamorous about that and a good deal that's grubby, but it's the bottom-line alternative to being looked after for those of us who aren't heiresses. It has its costs, but at least they are explicit, clear, and open to attack, to change by action. What are the costs of being looked after?

This section deals with the work place as it is, with its impact on women moving in there and with the interweaving between women and work now taking place and sure to continue. Some things need to be said: Celebrating the opportunity to gain independence by one's own activities does not mean celebrating drudgery. Getting paid doesn't make a job better in itself: A lot of necessary and valuable work is done for other reasons, and more ought to be. Voluntary work that is chosen by the worker and that evidences its value by its public results and its personal rewards is vital to social life and always has been. But in our cash-related system, unpaid work that is not under-taken by choice, that is assigned as part of a permanent condition and that defines one's place in life, seems to me to approach the meaning usually understood by the word *slavery*. If you have been a member of a group that normally existed in such a condition, money in your pocket, put there by your own exertions and usable by your own decision, is not just grubby cash—it's the key to a lock on your life.

In our time more and more women carry that key with them. That's important. Also important is the undeniable fact that women don't earn as much as men, are not easily given the training and access to the tracks that lead to success in the mainstream world of business, politics and the professions, and are instead shunted toward jobs that pay less, that may be unpleasant and routine, and that are definitely undervalued. In large part that is due to the lack of linkage that society sees between public and private, work and home. The costly splits in our society will come up over and over in these discussions. A very painful one is that which is held to lie between work and home. A woman's value in the work place is kept down by the general opinion that she is and ought to be the main, the almost sole, source of domestic labor. There are reasons: in the first place, a still-pervasive image of woman as nurturer and homemaker. Psychologically that doesn't accord with success in the rat race. But in addition, and leaving psychology aside, a person who has to spend two and a half hours a day doing another job is not taken to be good material for the higher reaches of employment. We all know the old "joke" about keeping women subservient by keeping them barefoot and pregnant. In a pinch, housework can also serve.

Psychology enters the situation again by associating the traditional feminine role with the kinds of work-for-pay that are seen as appropriate for women, jobs that can be related to household chores. Cleaning and cooking are female concerns, so who cleans offices at night? Who packs fruit in canneries? Who waits table in less-than-elite eateries? Clerical work is equivalent to dusting and tidying. Personal service— retail sales that cater to personal needs, cosmeticians, nursing—parallel in the public area the care for family members assigned to women at home. Another factor that limits jobs open to women swings round once more to the housework still expected. Routine jobs are not exciting or well paid, but they tend to have regular hours, and if you must be sure that you will be able to pick up the children from the baby-sitter by five o'clock, you can't afford the time that higher-level positions require.

In addition, keeping women's work-for-pay unattractive inflates the value of being taken care of. If work is so unpleasant, why do women want to take it on? Why not stay home, mutters The Thing, where they really belong? The answer that's most acceptable in public discussion is money, and it's a true answer, as far as it goes. But no matter how family-spirited the impulse to earn may be, the *capacity* to earn implies something more: freedom, independence, the power to disagree about serious matters and be listened to. Some of the very first victories for the women's movement in the nineteenth century gave them the right to own, as individuals, the property they might inherit and the wages they earned, property and wages that had passed with marriage to husband and head of the household, and that's a bit of history worth remembering. Over the past decade the idea that equal wages ought to be paid to women has gained wide support, even though equal wages have not followed. The general respectability of equal pay in the abstract, however, means that other methods of preventing it in reality have to be found. Restricting the kinds of jobs usually open to women by the social pressures of housework to be done and the psychological pressures of what is held to be appropriate are good ways of maintaining the familiar link between female workers and low-paid work.

But none of this is going to stop women from going outside the home to work for pay or from pushing past the barriers around the permitted kinds of work that can be undertaken in the female ghetto. Women in the work force are now too normal, too common, for the crippling of affirmative action plans to hold back our entrance. Although resistance to women's progress toward higher levels of positions is certainly with us, we have already gone too far to be stopped, though there may be a slowdown. Any slowdown, however, is going to be met by feminine action, by a coming together of women and an increase in support networks and service organizations, by self-help and useful alliances. By this time women know a lot about the business world and how it operates, and though you can fool a good many of the people most of the time, you can fool them least easily on matters of money, for the value of money is open and countable. Food prices, rents, mortgages, car payments—these are no longer mysterious matters that are properly left to the man of the family to deal with. Housewives have long been charged with a great deal of consumer spending. Now many women are well informed on both sides of the earning and spending equation. If salaries are still unequal, it's hard indeed to hide inequity and its consequences from those who earn as well as spend.

An inescapable part of the story of women and work-for-pay is the context, the nature of work itself in our time. Discussions of the drudgery and boredom inherent in many jobs surfaced toward the end of the sixties. Inflation's pinch and the threat of unemployment have lessened the attention now being given the question, but the existential circumstances have not changed, and the results of job dissatisfaction continue to surface individually as "midlife crisis" or "burn out." Inattention doesn't cure problems, even though hopes that were not made effective in action may end for a while in apparent resignation.

Or have these hopes sought another kind of outlet? Is it possible that the various kinds of religious revivalism, and interest in novel cults, that are familiar today express distaste for the drab triviality of existence, for its recurrent flaws and its lack of reward? Are we witnessing the reappearance of a context of life that makes the consolations of religion the only plausible offset of daily frustration? If so, one wonders how long a civilization as material-minded as ours, as addicted to status-symbol possessions, and as dependent on commercial turnover for its economic life, can invest its emotions in spiritual values. If this society were really to reassess its principles and its behavior by such standards, we would be in for revolutionary change; but that does not seem to be what most of those who have (they say) been born again have in mind. The Moral Majority appears to project a return to the past; a nonexistent past, as a matter of fact, that Clio, Muse of History, would not recognize. The desperate joiners of extremist cults seem to be in search of discipline and strictness as a defense against disorder, not in order to create a positive new structure. These are both negative views. They do, however, present a judgment that finds the present state of things unsatisfactory. Turning away from the world as it is does nothing to change it and attempts to bring back an imagined Golden Age of traditional order have never worked yet, but both responses speak of an inarticulate need for change.

Healing the splits in our lives can start anywhere, as long as the process is rooted in the here and now. The paid work done by most people in the industrialized West is far from Utopian, but it's what, here and now, we live with, and its details and operations are where change has to begin. The change over the last generation that has brought more and more women into the labor force hasn't made us equal to men there, or anywhere else; but it does increase the similarity in our lives and decrease the forces that make each gender a mystery to the other. We have to expect that old patterns of thought, which have a life of their own in the minds of those who can see no pressing reasons for change, will try to maintain themselves by emphasizing gender differences. Thus women will be invited to go on taking women's jobs that pay little and lead nowhere. Women who want more will be offered techniques for advance that copy confrontational machismo and isolate them from each other. Heirarchical ranking will continue to ignore the inventive capacity of working people and to place their ideas, coming out of their experience, below the theories of management teams. Nonetheless, human beings can and do recognize each other as individuals who share aims and interests and dislikes and memories. All of us dream of some kind of world where community can really include the lonely and sharing can sometimes replace competition. I do not think that the growing numbers of women in the world of work can make those dreams less likely, nor the overlap of humanity between individuals, of different sexes and ranks and backgrounds, less evident.

In my life, "work" seems to be more talked about than written about. Three of the papers collected here were given at conferences, and the sound of a human voice rings through them. I've left them as they are in the hope that their rather conversational style makes them more, rather than less, accessible. Two of them date from the late seventies, one from 1981, as does the fourth selection, written for *Prime Time,* a magazine directed to those who have passed their fortieth birthday. All of them deal with the labor that engages human beings from different starting points, all of them are sensitive to the phenomenon of women entering the paid labor force in large numbers, and they occasionally touch on the same points. I hope that these connections will not seem to be repetitions of the same old dull facts but rather recognition of strong currents in our society that affect numerous fields of action and to which many sorts of inquiry must avert. I have not been able to write about the world we live in, in these years, without referring to the great need we have of understanding process and change; without reflecting on the effects of painful schisms in our accepted social mythology and—concurrently—the underlying linkages between many problems, often taken to be separate. To say that we can solve our problems by healing the splits in our world view and that the process of doing this will move us toward a more satisfactory future is of course just a form of words that should reveal, not hide, the need for earthshaking, active struggle if humankind is to survive. Well, the words are laughably insufficient, but I don't think they're untrue.

So. Reflections on work.

Rehumanizing Work

I'D BETTER BEGIN by defining terms. All of us, I think, have a strong awareness that a great deal of the work people do today is profoundly unsatisfactory, simply drudgery to be got through, which provides no return to the worker other than the money it earns. Recently there's been a good deal published about this state of affairs and a bit published about possible remedies. Most of the latter seem to be still in the realm of hope for the future, while the reality of work today is experienced as something to be endured and distanced from oneself.

To quote Studs Terkel's opening paragraph in his book *Working* is to read a description of disaster: "This book, being about work, is, by its very nature, about violence—to the spirit as well as to the body. It is about ulcers as well as accidents, about shouting matches as well as fistfights, about nervous breakdowns as well as kicking the dog around. It is above all, or beneath all, about daily humiliations. To survive the day is triumph enough for the walking wounded among the great many of us." And then Terkel quotes a few of the people he interviewed. "I'm a machine," says the spot-welder. "I'm caged," says the bank teller. "I'm a mule," says the steelworker. "A monkey can do what I do," says the receptionist. "I'm less than a farm machine," says the migrant worker. "I'm an object," says the high-fashion model. Blue collar and white collar call upon the identical phrase: "I'm a robot."

Most of the people that Terkel talked to are in fact blue or white collar workers. But we would be wrong to think that the pervasive dissatisfaction with one's occupation is confined to the lower echelons of our society. When Prof. Seymour Sarason of Yale recently completed a study of the relation of professional people, doctors, lawyers and university faculty to their employment, he turned up a picture that doesn't differ too much from Terkel's. Sarason reports on a doctor in his forties, so highly respected in the profession that many of his colleagues come to him. Asked about his overall impression of attitudes among the physicians he treats, he replied, "In the last five years ninety percent of what I deal with is depression"; depression, he adds, that is directly work related. Lawyers confront the same feelings of entrapment; and when Sarason and a colleague asked permission to gather data from the faculty members of some three state universities, they were unanimously turned down. The reason? Administrators suspected that so many faculty members were disaffected that they would find even an anonymous questionnaire too threatening and disturbing if it asked about their desire to change careers. And now, Sarason reports, he finds among his students the sense that making the choice of a life-long career, even an elite, professional career, means walking into a trap.

Work, in short, is defined and experienced as a rat race; but in spite of this bitter judgment, there is very little will to try to change its circumstances. It's as if people at all levels have given up on finding rewarding work. Sarason tells us that even professionals who say they are relatively satisfied with what they do still feel distanced from it, alienated. It appears that they *expect* so little from their daily labors that they're willing to *settle* for that little. This is, so to speak, the opposite of the famous revolution of rising expectations we used to hear about. It seems as if we are going through a revolution of falling expectations.

Clearly this somber prospect is of enormous importance to women today, women who want and need to enter the labor force and find positions of equality there. If this situation is both real and inescapable, unalterable, then we must resign ourselves to lives that deny the basic requirements of human connection and community. One high-powered executive to whom Studs Terkel talked described the corporate world as "a jungle" in which "you're thrown on your own and you're constantly battling to survive." He himself found that exciting. But the penalties he describes are pretty grim. Thus, he says, "I don't know of any situation . . . where an executive is completely free and sure of his job from moment to moment . . . You're caught in a squeeze . . . Fear is always prevalent . . . Gossip and rumor are always prevalent . . . The executive is a lonely animal in the jungle who doesn't have a friend . . . The most stupid phrase anybody can use in business is loyalty. . . ." And so he goes on. It's hardly surprising that the speaker left the corporate business world "because suddenly the power and the status were empty." Reflecting on his experience, he told Terkel that he'd really always wanted to be a teacher, but when he looked at Academia, he found another jungle there. How much of this bitter judgment is personal? Some, no doubt, but not all. Too much has a familiar ring.

Should we, however, accept this vision as conclusive? We certainly have enough evidence to show that dissatisfaction and alienation are rife at many levels of employment; but I'm not so sure we ought to agree that these conditions are inevitable. If we go deeper into the causes that people give for their unhappiness, we discover some clues. Those may point to remedies. I've been a long time getting around to defining terms, but perhaps we can make a stab at it by saying that "rehumanizing work" means getting the rats out of the race. Let it remain a race, but let it be one that's suited to men and women rather than rats.

Looking for remedies to the ills reported from the world of work is not a task for women only; but because we are still largely new entrants, our view of the situation may be fresher, we may take less for granted. In addition, the kind of mind-set expressed in books like Terkel's often gives a woman the sense that the world of work is structured so grimly because it takes account only of masculine experience and the shibboleths that the macho mystique exalts. Women don't live by those rules. While we may think that they are more valuable, or pertinent, than our own methods of getting on in the world, and a lot of us do, we nonetheless know that they are not absolutely required, because our own lived experience differs. In saying that, I by no means want to suggest that men and women are innately different in their psychology, their potential for achievement, or their ability to relate to their fellows. But for centuries, for millennia, our daily lives have led each gender to interact with other human beings according to a different style. Our social system is based on male needs, and the public section of it, where women have seldom ventured, is attuned to masculine modes of communicating, relating, and getting things done, and these in turn derive from a primary, if unconscious, drive to keep the second sex secondary. The women now entering positions of authority in government and business have had very little time or chance to factor female perceptions and female ways of behavior into the system.

At a time when changes are needed, our variant experience can be a real resource. Our vision is not confined within blinders that point our gaze to the "One Right Path," a path that appears to be overgrown with weeds and poison ivy if the testimony of dissatisfied workers is to be believed. A wider view may find some alternatives. Needless to say, they won't all be advantageous or even workable. We will have to approach the task of analysis humbly, aware that our own experience is limited and must be sorted out for its good and bad qualities and that in any case the institutions of the world possess a dynamic of their own and will not change their ways because of good intentions, even if they are embodied in good ideas. But we shouldn't write off the chance that new ideas are good ideas. We do have a wealth of unused knowledge, much of it dealing with an area that is evidently a source of trouble: human management and communication. One thing that women have been doing forever and a day is listening to complaints and judging the depth and the causes of the dissatisfaction revealed. The next step has often been ours too: introducing and implementing the changes that will lessen difficulties if it can't remove them.

Take, for example, the jungle-dwelling executive who thinks that loyalty is a stupid phrase. He is mistaken. Anyone who wants to work successfully with other people has to know that teamwork, involving connection, consultation and trust, is needed. Any analysis of successful corporate or governmental operations shows up the necessity to delegate the implementation of decisions to others, who are relied on to carry them out loyally, though not blindly. Ongoing enterprises posit a common goal. Now, it may well be that the notion of "rat race" elevates the value of individual success until the common need to arrive at a shared goal all but disappears. Women, who have had little opportunity to set independent goals outside of the traditional ones dictated by an assigned or expected social role, are obviously going to be more aware of what we're doing when we become part of an organization in which our actions are not traditional. We will be less likely to lose sight of the purpose of the exercise because we have to pay attention to the whole process of action. When we work for our own ends, in alliance with other women, we have to invent a structure of reciprocity that's taken for granted in the male world. And if we are working for change, the need for cohesiveness increases in importance. No one changes the world alone. Only loyal comrades and trustworthy allies can do that. People new to a setting can't take the implementation of orders for granted. Male or female, newcomers are more aware that loyalty from others is something that has to be worked at by those who desire it, that alliance is a two-way street.

Think again of those depressed doctors and academics mentioned by Professor Sarason. Their depression, he says, comes from a sense of losing control over their activities. That can indeed be frustrating. But it occurs to me to ask whether the control they have expected is valid. Should professional people be able, because they command expertise, to define exactly how they interact with the rest of us? Are patients people who can ask questions, or are they properly components of an assembly line, waiting in clinics for prescriptions and directives? Women have been chided for the volume of tranquillizers, weight-loss pills and sleeping tablets they take. Well, it isn't the patient who decides. Perhaps it's time that medical men lost a little control and even began paying house calls again. And when academics, even the most dedicated, come to believe that institutions of higher learning exist primarily to support them and their research and only secondarily to educate their students, I feel it will do them no harm to rethink their attitudes.

I do not want to belittle the frustrating, psychologically destructive effect of losing control over one's work. It is central to the question of giving back a human dimension to the hours spent in making the money we live on. But I think we should do more to analyze it, not simply take for granted that it is there, part of life today as the world of business, industry, the professions and government are set up, and that it can't be altered. That's more or less where we've got to, hung up and resigned, for almost everything being done to address the problem accepts the idea that work has to be terrible—this terrible.

And it is terrible. Professional people grumble about dealing with bureaucracy, but workers on an assembly line have lost even the control over the way they apply their own muscular strength to the tiny, broken-down bits of production that they contribute to a finished object. Clerical work is just as bad. Much of it requires no skill at all. If it weren't still too costly to build robots to file or to fill in forms, robots would be doing it. In fact, computers are doing as much as can be systematized. In the long run that will be all to the good. But meanwhile the mechanization of work continues to treat the human beings who handle the grubby unsystematized details as if they were machines. And the great mass of people stuck in these routine clerical jobs are, of course, female.

So women have a special interest in seeing work upgraded and stretched to ask something from the capacities of the people who have to earn to live. Our major move into the labor force comes at the very time when the world of work is beginning to acknowledge, however grudgingly, that something is wrong. At the same time, women are penalized in getting work and in having access to promotion because we are said not to know how to do things right, the company way. Which means that we have not been trained and indoctrinated to do things the painful, wrong, crippling, frustrating inhuman way. So stick us at the bottom of the heap, don't listen to us—and make sure we know that our independent ideas have to be trivial nonsense; that we don't know how to behave like "one of the boys" and consequently our ignorant suggestions are only funny. If we want to succeed, we must learn the bad old techniques that are even now being identified as contributing to the rat race. There's a double bind if ever I saw one. But if you read some of the silly books that are supposed to tell you how to get to the top in management, you will find that what is advocated is always inhuman, manipulative behavior that is designed to intimidate others and establish you as the little sister of a man-eating tiger. Or they tell you to do your best to create the nasty jungle where abrasive executives stalk and confront each other.

So if we take seriously our analysis of what women are up against as they increasingly move into the wide world of activity outside the home, where paid work is done today, we will want to ask why it is that human control over the work human beings do is being lost. To whom is it being lost? The professionals declare that they are losing control to the bureaucrats. Bureaucrats mutter that they must comply with all these regulations that the idiot public insists on having for protection. Executives say that the unions have taken over; and union members declare that production schedules are still set by management. And of course you can be sure of finding someone, at every level, to tell you that these crazy rules about affirmative action have made trouble everywhere.

This isn't analysis—it's reflex action.

Since everyone else has an opinion, let me try my hand at analysis. The dehumanization of work began long ago, with the introduction of machinery. Of course there had been terrible drudgery before that, where men and women were used more or less like machines; but unless you were a slave driver on a plantation where you had no trouble replenishing the supply of human machines you overworked to death, you did not lightly ignore the demands that human capacity laid on you. And few plantations, or latifundia, really could ignore these demands. Human creatures carried physical work loads in the past much, much greater than anyone does today in any developed country; but by the same token, there was a premium for them in discovering and developing better ways to do the work they had to get through. In order to do that, they became involved with the work they did in something of a creative way.

Let's not be sentimental about this, which is easy to do. We all like to imagine that somewhere, sometime, there was a stretch of Good Old Days. Well, I guess some days, short of bloody invasion, A-bombs or the Black Plague, have always been fairly good for some people. But I am not talking about good old days but about a specific question: the reward that it has been possible to get from doing one's work with a skill that raises one's self-esteem and offers a kind of pleasure in sheer accomplishment. It's what we look for today almost only in sport. But the satisfaction of doing a good job used to be present in work—even work that was conducted under very unpleasant conditions.

Let me give you an example, a quotation from a book called *Akenfield*. It's a study of an English village made a few years ago by author Ronald Blythe, drawn from interviews with people of all ages. Some of them remembered far back toward the beginning of the century, when times were very hard indeed. This passage comes from the memory of Jubal Merton, a wheelwright and blacksmith, who was sixty when Blythe talked to him. He left school at thirteen to learn his trade. One of the things he remembered was going hungry during the First World War, when the rich farmers kept their food for themselves, and rationing was not strict. Let him speak now about men at work, poor, but proud of their skill:

"Things got worse after the war, yet the land didn't suffer. It went on looking pretty good. The houses came to pieces and the people were hungry and keeping themselves warm with bits of old army clobber, but the fields stayed absolutely perfect. The men forgot that they were the farmer's fields—(the rich farmers, that is, for whom these men worked as laborers)—and decked and tended them most perfectly. They were art itself. The farmers like to think that the men did this fine work for them, but they did it for themselves. The farmers had got the upper hand now and wherever he could he made his worker a slave . . . Have no doubt about it! No man dare open his mouth, or out he went."

It wasn't compliance or submission that made these men work the farmers' fields so well, Jubal Merton is saying, it was *defiance*—a dedication to the work. They were not compliant, and when times became good enough, many left the land behind, and the farmers had to learn to get on with men who knew they had an alternative. Which was, as Merton knows and says, absolutely necessary. I cite his story not to suggest that we want to go back to those terrible old days, when men could not speak their minds, but instead to illustrate that even in such times there was a human connection with work that could be drawn on to strengthen the workers in their knowledge of their skills and abilities; and they worked well not to please the farm owners but to assure themselves that they did possess the skills. They showed them off—as a losing pitcher today might show off his own skill even though he knows the game is going to be won by his opponent. Now, that kind of pride in one's work can't be conjured up to order. It comes out of a sense of the value of what is being made and of the value, therefore, of the maker's skill, time and energy put into the product. There used to be a more general relationship between worker, product and the public it was made for. This is a very human vision. A recent study of working conditions in a hospital kitchen reports that the women doing what appears to be mechanical work—setting up trays and serving meals for patients—have a perfectly sensible appreciation that their work is important: Sick people need to get the right meals, or they will get sicker. Salt-free meals should go to the patients on salt-free diets. Mechanical kitchen chores are a part of their treatment, and the chores must be done right.

So the prevalence of machines makes it hard for us to see the human capacities and skills required to tend machines or do routine work. Have we given machines too much space in our thinking? In asking that, I do not for one moment want to suggest that it is the machines that have made work inhuman. When we do that (and again, it's tempting), we are anthropomorphizing the machines and giving them power they do not possess. We do that, we humans, rather often. We pass the buck because we don't like to think that we ourselves are responsible for our plight. But it is not the machines that took the human dimension out of work—it is the way that they have been used. By us. By nobody else but us. And the more we avoid that thought and cover it over in our minds, the less able are we to do anything about changing the evils that make so many jobs today simply examples of the rat race.

If you look at the cures that we've tried, you can see that we know this is an accurate description of work as it is. We shorten hours, we raise wages, we come up with a dazzling galaxy of fringe benefits; the only thing we don't do is try to set the machines working to our time instead of people working to machine time. Thank God for high wages and shortened hours—thank God for flex time and part time that let people have some say about how long they want to spend tending a machine; but why do we stop there? We created machines to do the awful physical labor that broke and killed people in the past; and then we handed over to the machines, which were saving our bodies, the control of our psychic energies, of the pattern of our lives, of the greater part of our waking hours. For the first time in history, the idea that someone might enjoy what they do so much that they choose to go on doing it longer than is required has become something rather shameful. These people get called workaholics—indiscriminately. I'm one, unashamed. It's assumed quite generally that we work this way because we're scared to do something else, that we are neurotically defensive. Maybe some of us are. I'm sure that there's not one reason for it any more than there's one right way to do anything. But some of us work because we enjoy it.

It's this element of personal, human involvement that gets left out of our present definition of work. The inhuman machines set the standards and the hours in the factories, back in the early nineteenth century; and later on, at the end of the century, you began to get an extension of these standards to all work, under the names of "efficiency" and "rationalization." The whole business enterprise came to be seen as a machine. Its parts were of course made up of human creatures with human emotions, but these emotions were declared to be counterproductive, inefficient. Where flair and intuition had once been quite valuable assets, they were now abandoned in favor of the "rational" following of orders from a central headquarters, which, in turn, distrusted flair and intuition and substituted cold, tough-minded decisions, based on the analysis of data. Just as mass production allowed any part of a machine to be substituted for by another like it, so human beings were supposed to be replaceable, one by another.

It's worth noting, by the way, that during this century the expression and the handling of emotions were assigned especially to women. Earlier, men had been allowed to weep as well as to rage; we can read about it from Shakespeare to the Romantic novelists and poets. The stiff upper lip, the insistence on a masculine ethic that made cold analysis a virtue among men, this is a product of the nineteenth century, and it paralleled the development of a business ethic that puts efficient operation in the central place, whether such efficiency is achieved over the depression, the nervous breakdowns, and the emotional deadening of its managers and workers or not.

Dehumanizing work, then, is not just something that happened. Certainly the advent of machines invited the subjection of workers to their schedules; but a deliberate effort was made to get rid of, or prevent, the emotional involvement of individuals in what they did.

Workers were best used, this theory of efficiency maintained, when they were reduced to cogs in the overall machine, replaceable parts, whose human characteristics were totally irrelevant to their work. And so these human characteristics were increasingly downgraded.

But human beings aren't interchangeable parts, whose feelings can be checked outside the office or the factory door. Eventually a new generation of efficiency experts discovered that if some account were taken of people as people, production levels actually improved. One famous study found that just having a team of experts looking at the work people did improved morale and productivity, whether the experts actually redesigned work programs or not: The control group did just as well as the group that was the subject of the altered programs, because for the first time someone seemed to be interested in them. So, bit by bit, some efforts were made to permit or even encourage human interaction among the workers.

This effort was limited. Up top, executives continued to function by abstract, rational analysis; and a manager who operated by flair and intuition had to be terribly good to be let alone, because he made everyone else nervous. Equally, women continued to be thought of as the presenters of emotion; and consequently, as being unfit for management work. They might—horrible thought—actually take personal considerations into account when they made decisions. Well, myself I don't know how anyone making decisions manages to leave personal, human considerations out. If you try to do that you just fool yourself, instead of confronting the facts of the situation, which have got to involve feelings—your own and other people's—if the facts have anything to do with human beings. But this is still heresy, in the world of industry and even in commerce and the professions. Even where it is recognized that emotions exist, they are suspect. And the areas of management and operations that deal with them are less prestigious than those handling production or even sales—where it's assumed that the customers' likes and dislikes have to be taken into account.

Consequently, when we try to think today about rehumanizing work, we almost inevitably think too small. Three or four years ago, there was an upsurge of interest in questions about the nature of work. It stemmed from the increasing economic costs that businesses were feeling because of absenteeism, job turnover, and sloppy work. The usual remedies—greater management control, simplification of jobs—totally failed to deal with the problem. So new ideas were heard: such as "job enrichment," industrial democracy, and the use of work teams that could control the entire production of some manufactured product. In Scandinavia especially, these ideas were tried out, first as pilot projects but later at some new factories built to replace the ubiquitous pressure of the assembly line with layouts that made possible more flexible work patterns. There were other experiments, both here and in Europe, but these were the most ambitious.

Reporting on one Swedish experiment in the *Scientific American* for March 1975, Lars E. Bjork described, with cautious optimism, the effect of allowing one department of twelve men and a foreman to work out new methods for producing drills that didn't tie one man to one machine and repetitive operation. This was a well-watched pilot project, and it appeared to work. Most of the men involved found the job more pleasant and less stressful. One said that laying out jobs in an individual way "makes you feel like your own boss." But Bjork also noted the constant puzzlement that beset upper supervisory levels as they were asked to relinquish control, and their resistance (it was finally overcome) to something as simple as guaranteeing the workers in the experiment that their wages would not drop during the transition period. In fact, productivity did not decline, and even when some absenteeism occurred, it could no longer shut down the whole line. Still, one swallow does not make a summer; if change is to continue, Bjork remarks, there will have to be changes elsewhere in the company. And clearly management does not welcome change that reduces its responsibility for planning and hands it over to individual departments.

In short, efforts to rehumanize work run into very much the same kind of difficulties that efforts to upgrade women and minorities through affirmative action have encountered. Not a great deal is done without outside pressure. The cost of absenteeism, badly done work that necessitated recalls of goods, and actual difficulty in hiring people for certain jobs have provided the economic pressure to think about changes in the pattern and content of work. Political pressure for equal opportunities for women and minorities has forced a change in hiring and promotion practices. But neither motive has really been internalized within current management. On the one hand we get tokenism, on the other we get the assumption that higher wages will solve all problems. But basically neither answer addresses the reality of unequal opportunity, limited responsibility, mickey-mouse control from above and, perhaps most destructive of all, the accepted idea that life divides itself in half, with work, a burden, here; and leisure, an irresponsible rootless passing of time, there. All of us are living divided lives today; even the housewives outside the world of work are restricted to the half-life of the private, personal sector and denied engagement with much of the active world.

Real remedies are going to require that we find ways to put our fragmented lives together. And that in searching for a better "quality of life" we no longer overlook the need for a better "quality of work." Those of us who believe that feminism points in the long run to an enlarged humanism understand the importance of lifting limits from narrow, circumscribed roles for men as well as for women. The masculine ethic and the macho mystique have deprived the area of work of badly needed human characteristics and elevated the idea of a ruthless efficiency as the overriding standard. Many men resist the movement of women into the work place because they fear that emotional qualities will be imported along with the female sex. I can only hope that they are right.

Naturally our mere presence as employed women isn't going to do a great deal, particularly if we allow ourselves to be sold on the idea that the only way to get ahead in business—or wherever we're heading—is by means of learning to be one of the boys and employing standard tactics of domination and intimidation. But it's obvious that women who are appearing on the work scene in such numbers at a time of change are also a harbinger of change. There is dissatisfaction with old methods. And so there is opportunity for the input of new ideas. The number of men who have changed their careers midway through, and the larger number who want to, point to an increased flexibility in male minds. Some men have been able to make that switch because their wives had decent jobs. But beyond that, dissatisfaction with work, even at this personal level, and the determination to change one's own life may indicate a greater willingness to accept change in a wider context.

Rehumanizing the rat race will not be a quick process. It is much too big a task for any single remedy to take hold. But the reinvolvement of women with outside-the-home economic work is being paralleled—as yet to a lesser extent, but still to some extent—by the reinvolvement of men in family concerns, especially in child care; that is, in areas of life where emotions count. And the ability to imagine and practice a variety of life-styles instead of just one proper, middle-class "normal" progress from the end of education to retirement—this too raises male tolerance for flexibility. As we widen our ideas about how it's possible to live, I think we are bound to widen our ideas about how it is possible to work and particularly to reunite time spent at work with other interests. Women who demand child care point to the intimate connection of ability to work for the money they need and the responsibility of the rest of society in raising children. Experiments in part-time and flex-time work may well lead to shifts in established work patterns. The movement of factories out of urban centers has an immediate unhealthy effect on the inner city; but in time—I said that this will not be a quick process—it may have the effect of reuniting work and community. Certainly recent isolation of middle-class families in residential suburbs and other restricted areas contributes to the image of work as a rat race, because it ensures that work is a mystery, fenced off from leisure and pleasure; something so bad it has to be hidden away. If we could re-create some kind of apprentice system, where young people *included* work skills in their education, we would be moving toward rehumanizing work in still a different fashion.

Heaven knows, the return of some sort of control of work patterns to the individual worker is vital; but in thinking up ways to enrich jobs, we must not imagine there is any easy panacea. When the only suggestions come down from experts and management; when they are based on the "let us do you some good, we are the ones who know how" conception, they will operate as Band-Aids on a major wound. To end job dissatisfaction, one must invite—and welcome—worker involvement, ideas and techniques. And even, perhaps, the stunning thought that the folks at the bottom might have some useful suggestions for running things higher up. No doubt we must begin this enormous effort to reunite work and the rest of life by means of small experiments, but let us see them in the widest context; a human context, where women's experience as part of the category of the rest-of-life is given full weight.

Coming into
Your Own
in a Man's World

IF THERE'S ONE thing women would agree on about the facts of female life, it's surely that our roles and activities are subject to change, often without notice or much input from us. Traditionally, we've moved house as our husbands' jobs demanded, sometimes enthusiastically, sometimes with considerable anguish over the loss of our friends and our children's roots. We've been expected to implement or organize the volunteer work that communities have depended on for generations. We have fund-raised, car-pooled, undertaken Den Motherhood, steered the wheels with the meals that go to the elderly, helped to plan parenthood or else not, manned (or womanned) phones for myriad causes ranging from good to moderate, and we know well who's going to be asked to lick stamps and address envelopes, ferry voters or baby-sit on election day—you may add your own specialties to this list. We've grown used to becoming experts in model plane building, batting averages and horsepersonship as children's hobbies require. And now, of course, more and more frequently we go to work at that job outside the house for which we get paid, while still holding down the one we do at home for love.

Flexibility has been our middle name, and an honorable one too, as long as its purpose has been to support the activities of other people. But with the growing participation of women in the job market, appreciation of our capacity to do six things at once has become more problematic. As well it might. Working wives and working mothers know they are juggling an awful lot of breakables. But it isn't exactly our skill at juggling that seems to be in question. What causes concern is not our ability to adjust but the uneasy feeling that our loyalties may shift. Will a woman with a paid job be as ready to move from Boston to Denver if her husband's company schedules a transfer? Who's going to ferry the young from one stimulating activity to another if the ex-head of ferry command is now newly fledged as the holder of a law degree? Will a devoted Frau Professor enjoy typing her husband's research notes if she's pushing to finish her own dissertation?

The return of married women to a labor market they left as brides has been going on for a long time, but for a couple of decades it was seen as pretty much an individual matter. Yes, so-and-so's wife was selling real estate or mutual funds. Mrs. this-and-that was after an M.A. in social work at the state university campus, while many a mother of schoolagers had refreshed her typing skills or dusted off a teaching certificate and headed back to work long before the phenomenon went public. In fact, more women were in the labor force in the mid-fifties than when Rosie the Riveter was a cover girl during World War II; and their number has grown steadily ever since. New entrants to the job market, the statistics tell us, are overwhelmingly female. Back in 1950, six married men were breadwinners for every married woman; now it's less than two. And these aren't short-term jobs to tide a family over difficult times. Women currently stay in the labor force for an average of more than twenty-five years.

Sooner or later, working women are going to be taken as normal, but that hasn't quite happened yet. On the one hand, the economic value of a two-income marriage rises along with the rate of inflation. On the other hand, there's still a felt need for married women to justify working for pay. Either money pressures require it (and plenty of husbands find that a painful admission to make), or the working wife should have more than just a job. Only a professional career is considered acceptable as a reason for moving out of the domestic sphere. If the best you can do is another routine job, you might as well carry on with the PTA.

This attitude says something about the ambiguity our society harbors about a woman's proper role. It also displays a good deal of ambiguity about our view of work. The double doubts feed each other. How positive do most people feel about their jobs? There's been a fair amount of negative testimony on this point, going back at least as far as Thoreau's famous observation, "Most men lead lives of quiet desperation." The conversations Studs Terkel reports in his book *Working* indicate respect for work honestly done, resentment toward the pressures that often surround it and toward the hype that can falsify its purpose. A number of studies have been made of "job satisfaction." But satisfaction obviously depends on what one expects from a job. Is it "meaning, purpose, intrinsic enjoyment and self-development" that professional people expect from their work? If so, they can be more easily disappointed than blue-collar workers assigned to routine, mechanical tasks. Most of us assume that professional work is indeed more satisfying, but a number of recent studies cast doubt on the rewards it brings, pointing to the incidence of "midlife crisis" and depression. Job alienation, it appears, can show up where it's least expected.

If man-the-breadwinner is dubious about the rewards for his activity in the work place, why should woman-the-homemaker be fleeing the haven of family and feeling in so determined a fashion?

Primary is the inarguable need to earn. Widows, women responsible for themselves and, even more necessitous, women who are also responsible for children are primary breadwinners in exactly the same sense as any male head-of-household. They are not, however, the only women aware of money pressure. And why should they be? The idea that one pair of busy hands, one working adult, can support a family may contribute to masculine pride (or shall we call it the macho mystique?), but it's a very recent artifact. Women have worked throughout history—worked hard and long, using remarkable skills and great creative talent.

Still, though history may make the idea of women at work legitimate, it doesn't necessarily make it desirable. The fact that our ancestors did things one way while we do them another doesn't imply that we should, for example, trade in our automobiles and get a horse. The record of women as competent workers should have something more to say if it's going to persuade us that work's good in itself. Does it? I think it does—something important. Women's ability to do well the same things that men take pride in doing well points to the wide overlap of human feeling, capability and experience that both sexes share. It underlines our common interests. Too many stereotyped images picture men and women as different kinds of creatures with different missions in life, so different that we are taken to be unable to share work and purpose. The sturdy, laborious lives of our ancestors, forefathers and foremothers too, reveal an enduring capacity for both to learn new ways of living and managing.

This doesn't mean that men are going to turn into women or women into men! Human beings provide a rich diversity of potential for change. If women begin to do some of the things that men alone have undertaken in the recent past, and we can see them doing so; if young fathers take a hand in the daily care of their children, and we can see that as well; then both sexes are evidencing a profoundly significant capacity for growth.

But, though the psychology of men and women may be adaptable to different life-styles, aren't there real physiological differences that direct women away from some kinds of work? We certainly hear more about sex differences than about similarities. Yet when the U.S. Employment Service tested sex differences in the seven areas important to success in the skilled trades, where women are regarded as most disadvantaged, they turned up only one area—spatial reasoning—in which women tested lower than men. In two—numerical reasoning and manual dexterity—no difference was apparent; and in four, women were superior—form perception, clerical perception, motor coordination and finger dexterity.

Most jobs today don't call for appreciable physical strength or more dexterity than is needed to use a typewriter or word processor. If we can accept the idea that it's psychology rather than physiology that dictates our notions of sex differences in the work place, we'll be better able to deal with the problems those notions present.

Our biggest problem is adjustment to change in the world around us and in intimate relationships. It's a problem that's complicated by our tendency to carry images of each other that are appropriate to one place but not to another. Men may assume that they can adjust their behavior from public arena to private sphere but doubt that women (so emotional) can do the same. When changing roles force us to improvise new ways of dealing with each other, we can do it best if we hold to a sense of the similarities between the sexes, instead of scaring ourselves with the notion that men and women, like east and west, are a twain fated never to meet. We do meet, often, and our feelings frequently run the same course. If women feel shy about moving into new settings, men are still worried about being turned down when they ask a woman for a first date. It seems that we're all sensitive to making a wrong move and being rejected.

Or take that well-known study on women's fear of success. Before we jump to the conclusion that women are nonachievers, we ought to ask about the kind of achievement that did not attract the young women who took this test some fifteen years ago. It was "leading her class at medical school," that female students at a Midwestern college shied away from, while men did not. At the time, however, going to medical school was a daring venture for a young woman. They expected, and got, fairly tough handling from their male comrades and their male professors too. Anyone who aspired to lead her class in medical school would need quite exceptional motivation plus a thick skin. Today, of course, women in medical school are much more

numerous and a good deal more welcome; and today several attempts
to duplicate the earlier study have failed. We have to ask whether it
really indicated fear of success or a prudent realization that pioneering
in a field where you're unwelcome is a tough job, better not taken on
without great self-confidence and dedication. Heckling and ostracism
act as real social and psychological deterrents for those who would
otherwise want to enter new fields. Once the pioneers have broken the
barriers (as they also have in law school and are doing in engineering
school), others follow promptly.

Of course deterrents remain. Today they operate most strongly
with mature women, even those whose daughters have eagerly em-
braced nontypical careers. Some are home-grown. The reactions of
husbands and family are seldom totally positive when a woman in
middle-life first speaks up about career ambitions. She herself may be
doubtful of her own drive and potential. Women returning to college
to finish undergraduate work or to get a higher degree typically express "fear of success." And then they go on to place in the top tenth
of their classes and often lead them. A little counseling helps at the
start, and it's most useful when it comes from returning women
who've been there a little longer and have found that courage can be
learned just as well as fear. We see here the factor of normality, the
strengthening sense that plenty of others are doing the same thing.

This isn't always easy to communicate back home. Helen Yglesias,
who herself embarked on a new career as author at the age of fifty-
four, followed a couple of successful novels with a book, *Starting:
Early, Anew, Over and Late,* investigating just this subject of people
of nontypical ages taking up new activities or trying to—for, of course,
it doesn't always work. One comfortably-off husband responded to his
wife's desire to take a job quite simply. "I said no, I need you at
home." She gave in and, he reported, "has been perfectly happy with
volunteer work." But don't her obligations there, Yglesias asked, keep
her as busy as if she had a full-time job? "Yes," was the reply, "but
she's not committed to that work. She can refuse to take on a particular task when I need her at home." Interestingly, this gentleman went
on to praise the women in his company for "native brilliance, dash,
intuitive business sense" and support of each other. His wife's comments, however, are not included.

Here again is ambiguity surrounding the proper role of women—
paid work is all right for others but not for "my wife." Perhaps less
evident is the valuation of work that comes through. Volunteer work
is all right because it can be put aside when family obligations arise.

Work for pay cannot. What does that say about the work that women do at home? It isn't paid for. Is it, therefore, worth less than the labors of the breadwinner? Breadwinners often say no, that it's simply "different." If that's all, why isn't it as suitable for men? Why is working for money specifically male, working for love specifically female?

We are back to the old doctrine of innate male/female differences that outweigh our similarities in importance. And one of the differences is cash value. Women can work, yes; but they must put family first. Of course, if what a wife earns is essential for the family, then it's okay for her to take a job. Even so, it should be an undemanding job so that she can still fulfill her family duties. In such a job, of course, she'll never earn what a man does. Which goes to prove that breadwinning is really man's work. Excuse me—that's *proof*? It looks rather more like a deck that's been stacked to give a woman a primary mission that has to be done before, or while, she works for pay. The lower pay that she naturally receives from routine and undemanding work is then taken to show her inability to manage jobs that pay well (and are demanding of time and energy). Those jobs may bring more satisfaction, meaning, challenge, opportunities for self-development, but they ask too much of homemakers, says the stereotypical image of women. And they do. Which seems to mean that the greatest deterrent to success in the world of work isn't a woman's fear of achievement but the fear felt by others in her life that ambition, normal to men, has to be turned off in her case. She can take a job, *if* she refrains from acting in a way that will get her anywhere. The proper attitude of women toward work is summed up in the description of volunteer work: You can opt out when you want to.

I don't think that view has much to do with the psychology of women, but it has a lot to do with the psychology of men. It turns up in the work place as well as at home; not everywhere but in many settings still. Male bosses, too, expect that working wives and mothers respond to family demands and that this is a "proper" way for a woman to behave. As a result, though entry-level jobs have certainly been made more available to women (with pressure from affirmative action directives a factor), promotion beyond them is harder to come by. Higher-level jobs require long hours; frequent travel; independent, swift decisions. And (the stereotype repeats) women are family oriented, putting others first. Male executives can be sent off to San Francisco on short notice or transferred from Omaha to Daytona Beach, but the boss who considers doing that to a woman is very likely to ask himself first, "How will her family react? Will her husband put up with it?" If the answer carries the overtone, "I wouldn't like it if she were my wife," another element may enter the picture: the image of an ambitious, hard-driving boss lady whose femininity is very questionable indeed. It is difficult, one must conclude, to be both a normal woman and a normal human being.

According to masculine psychology, that is; but women are very sensitive indeed to male thinking. We needn't attribute that to a special kind of female intuition. It's due to the fact that men are the holders and wielders of power. A woman whose work is confined to the home is dependent on the male breadwinner both for her status in society and for plain old cash. A woman in the work place knows that top bosses are male and expects the commonplaces of male feeling and thinking to be guidelines to behavior—theirs and hers. Women moving into new activities carry with them an old image of woman-as-man-expects-her-to-be, "normal" woman geared to her "proper" role of nurturing, caring, responding to demands and guiding personal relationships. That role doesn't fit the work place. Consequently, women at work feel themselves under the shadow of contradictory expectations that don't originate with them but that have to be taken into account in public and in private too. Female flexibility is put to a particularly grueling test when it's asked to satisfy such ambiguous assumptions.

Certainly many men are getting over that double vision as more perfectly normal females turn out to be admirably competent at their professional vocations. But the confusion is still widespread enough for women to be wary about it. And, if it's there, dealing with it is usually up to women themselves, for even companies that proclaim themselves "Equal Opportunity Employers" seldom feel it their duty to try to change the inside of executive heads. Reducing male sexism is taken to be a female task; which is like saying that racism is solely the problem of blacks or other minority members.

In *Men and Women of the Corporation,* her study of how a major American company operates at the human level, Rosabeth Moss Kanter discusses the management problems that result from this sense of *difference* from women and from minorities. Uncertainty, she observes, plagues all bureaucracies. It is "the fundamental problem for complex organizations, and coping with uncertainty [is] the essence of the administrative process." Uncertainty is countered, she goes on, only when those charged with making decisions know and trust each other. But how is this trust established? By forming "homogeneous groups" whose "mutual understanding [is] based on the sharing of values." There is no room here for difference.

Input from strangers is unwelcome, whoever the strangers may be: It's taken well over a year of a disastrous economic squeeze for American auto companies to begin investigating the remarkable success of their Japanese rivals. Women are seen as at least as different; Simone de Beauvoir put it succinctly when she used the word *other* for the male description of women. One wonders whether the free-floating dissatisfaction with work, noted earlier, may not be connected to this "uncertainty" at large in major companies. People who aren't sure about the effects of their policies are bound to be uncomfortable about making plans for the future; but that, of course, is what male executives are supposed to be so good at. These doubts, I believe, should be seen as the result of pressure from the limitations of the *masculine* role. By devaluing the experience of others, it serves to keep what used to be called "the white man's burden" weighing heavily on the same male shoulders.

So we come round again to the question of women's ambitions. If decision making is uncertain, if job satisfaction means settling for little, if those who have traditionally sought meaningful work are experiencing depression and opting for shifts in their careers, why do women want to get out of the house and into the office?

One unpleasant answer rears its head promptly: work at home is so isolating, so unrewarding, that anything is preferable. I'm reminded of George Bernard Shaw's reply to the reporter who asked whether he was happy to have attained the age of ninety. "Only when I consider the alternative," said Shaw. But the truth, as well as the prevalence, of such a reply simply can't be estimated. For one thing, it's extremely personal, depending (like job satisfaction) on expectations. For another, its implications are very upsetting, not easy to face even if true. "And so they were married and lived happily ever after," say the fairy tales, and we hate to give them up. Instead, women tend to assume that unhappiness is a sign of personal failure: Dissatisfaction with the job done for love at home brings on a case of the guilts more readily than does dissatisfaction with work for pay. Homemaking is still very deeply felt as our primary job. Expecting little reward from marriage is much harder than expecting little satisfaction from a paid job, where we all tend to be reasonably skeptical rather than romantic.

One problem is that we fail to see that many elements that operated in the past to keep marriages together have diminished or vanished entirely—the profitable work done at home, the active companionship between husband and wife who were managing a farm or a business in tandem, the longer time spent raising larger families in which fathers at home took a greater part, closer ties with kin and the neighborliness of small-town life that provided affectionate friendships. All these contributed support to the central male/female relationship and supplemented it if difficulties arose within it.

Let us remember, too, that we all live longer nowadays. The *New York Times* recently quoted Dr. Holger Stub of Temple University, a specialist in the study of aging. "Longevity," said Dr. Stub, ". . . exposes marriage to a phenomenal increase in disruptive influences and culminates in high divorce and separation rates." In response to this increased life span, the good news is that "almost all women can plan for a second career of twenty to thirty years." But the good news of active golden years is mixed with the bad. "Increased longevity allows men and women virtually to bargain for two marriages, one for the young family years and another for the postparental period." Dr. Stub makes no judgment of this new sort of ambiguity, he simply states that it's "not merely a possibility but is actually taking place." If Dr. Stub is right and the fairy tales wrong, it seems that older wives have two choices: either to stay home and pray that their husbands will too, or go after that second career that can provide a suddenly necessary paycheck.

Dr. Stub declares his data to be realistic, however amoral or cynical they may sound "to romantics or the religiously oriented." I must confess that they sound a bit exaggerated to me, even though I'm neither of the above. But if they are increasingly a fact of life, even if not a major one, they add other reasons for women to think seriously about that second career. In any case, modern science and medicine have given us many more years of healthy life. If, with children grown and gone, we find ourselves severely unemployed at the old job of homemaker, those years will be more rewarding if they are filled with self-directed activities that build competence and self-esteem. Volunteer work can serve this purpose—but only if it's taken seriously; when it's perceived as something that can be put aside at will, it is being trivialized. I am sorry for that. Volunteer work is at least as valuable and as needed as it ever has been, but in a society that reckons the worth of labor by how much it brings in, we can't be surprised by finding work done for free dropping lower on the scale of values. At present, women who have been involved for years as volunteers know that top posts often go to professionals—that is, to workers who are paid and who will therefore not take off when demands from private life pull women away from their responsibilities in this area of public service.

We humans are social creatures. We all need some part in the web of community, some involvement in the networks that bind us together and serve common purposes, whether the work we do is paid for or not. Each of us aspires to be more than a helpmeet to someone else. We have a psychological need, as well as a right, to aspire to success without fear, success that is more than vicarious, even though it will often be shared with others. A true community is made up of individuals with ideas and resources that are both personal and accessible for use by society. I believe that such authentic individuality grows out of continuity in action, engagement in ongoing processes of effective work. One way to think of it is by the rather clumsy name of a "career identity"—the sense of a repeatedly competent, activating self, trustworthy not simply by living-to-rule but as an individual capable of judging, acting, learning, persisting, gaining in knowledge and skills; a person willing and able to engage directly with events and analyze them on the basis of her own experience, female experience that is part of human experience; a person moved by unsuppressed ambition toward achievement that can be enjoyed *realistically*—neither doubted, nor overvalued.

The development of such an identity brings a confidence that enlarges the familiar image of female flexibility. It assures us that we can learn new skills even if they lead us into unfamiliar territory. It points to the common humanity of men and women. Married couples who have shared their lives long past the period expected by Dr. Stub often arrive at this sense of mutual understanding by another road that embodies the real meaning of living happily ever after. But that private road doesn't diminish the value of public evidence testifying to human mutuality, visible along with the differences that male or female experience engenders. An awareness of human similarity speaks to the growth of trust, the decrease of uncertainty and anxiety, and an increasing conviction that neither sex should function as "other" in private or public.

The entrance of women into the work place is not going to cure the ills that have accumulated through the proliferation of repetitious, routine jobs, timed to machines and hard to call "meaningful" by any standard except that they provide the wherewithal to live by one's own efforts. The knowledge that you can do that is not to be sneezed at, but if we're ever going to make work more satisfying, we need to see "earning a living" as a part of living, not necessarily a burdensome process to groan our way through. I believe we got ourselves into that fix because we have split the human race in two by gender and have assigned the task of earning a living to one half and maintaining important personal relationships to the other. Both segments lose value and significance as they diverge. The rising concern with "quality of life" may well be a consequence of our unfortunate estimate that work for pay has to be a "rat race." When we assume that competition and confrontation are needed for success on the job and that these are strictly male qualities, and add the corollary idea that women don't and can't employ these useful qualities but are uniquely fitted to express the warmth and affection all humans require to thrive, then we are dividing not only society but our own feeling, reasoning, active and responsive selves. We are denying the essential mutuality of male and female members of the species *Homo sapiens.*

If we downplay the simple gender difference set up by the stereotypes of masculinity and femininity, we open the door to a richness of individual differences instead of scaring ourselves with a polarized view of the world. When each sex is ignorant of the life experience of the other, attraction is shadowed by fear of the inner mysteries of your closest companion. I don't think the fear is necessary to the attraction! Indeed, people who understand the pressures and pleasures of each other's lives are surely able to establish better and more permanent relationships than those who haven't a clue about what's going on with their nearest and dearest.

The work roles of women are here to stay. The psychological problems they raise don't have to be. They can best be solved if we trust ourselves—and each other—enough to share them.

Women and Technology

THE TOPIC I'VE BEEN ASKED to address, "women and technology," is as interesting as it's wide-ranging. I've always found that my lecturing provides me with invaluable research material and unique opportunities for insight into the ideas and concerns of students and professionals in different disciplines all over our country. But this time you have forced me to plunge into an exploration of an area with which I was familiar only in principle and not in detail. I certainly can't pretend that I'm an instant expert, but I have had my mind stretched and my level of knowledge raised dramatically in the last few weeks by talking with deans of engineering schools, affirmative action officers, executives of professional societies, women evaluators and executives in major industrial companies and by reading papers and reports that they have kindly supplied to me. As a result, I have a much clearer picture of this growing trend—the entry of women into the technological fields that we associate closely with the phrase "man's world." Clearly you're aware of this phenomenon, or I wouldn't be here. It's my hope that you also approve and support it.

The entry of women into the world of technology, I said; and I want now to rephrase that and, rather, say the *re-entry* of women into these fields. Before we come to the pointers and the data that I've picked up recently, let's take a look at history; yes, and at prehistory too. That's not because I have a passionate regard for the Good Old Days—some of them were terrible. But too many of us, at this point in time, are stuck in exactly that—in this point of time. We imagine that the way things are now is the way they've always been; and that tends to persuade us that it's the only way they *can* be. We suffer from what philosophers call the Solipsism of the Present, and we badly need to widen our view.

It's true that the future is more attractive for most people today than is the past, that futurology, not history, is the trendy subject. But let me remind you that history is, after all, a little more accessible and amenable to testing. Even the great Niels Bohr was once heard to muse, "It's very difficult to predict—especially the future." Fortunately for us, it is not quite so difficult to predict the past, not so difficult, even, to look at it objectively. And what we find there is quite as different from the present as the future is likely to be. Historians who tell us the way things were done before we were born and, by extension, anthropologists who tell us how things are done in societies other than our own can help us to get rid of the Solipsism of the Present and thus to imagine that things can be different, without the world actually falling to pieces around us.

Very well, then. Once upon a time every human creature lived as part of a small group of foragers and hunters. Often these groups gathered together for part of the year in larger aggregations, but it's improbable that even these companies amounted to more than a few hundred men, women and children; while the smaller, roving bands numbered no more than thirty or forty. Studious anthropologists and archeologists have woven together many shreds of knowledge to create an image of how these folk lived, checking their ideas against direct observations of peoples discovered in the age of exploration and investigated since then with increasing profundity by students from our own culture. We know that these people were fully human, for they were capable of high art—the paintings they left on the cave walls in southwestern Europe tell us so, and they are echoed by rock paintings here in America and in desert Africa as well. Meticulously carved figurines have been found across Siberia, and northern Indian hunting peoples and Eskimos have created their wonderful carved wood, bone and stone sculpture under our very eyes.

Hunting peoples, I said, and no doubt the fact that so many of their images have to do with the hunt and the animals hunted contributes to our seeing them as hunters only. But they were foragers too, gatherers of nuts and fruits, of insects and small animals. And everywhere that we have evidence of such activity we know that it is carried on by women. Sometimes it is carried on exclusively by women, but even where it is not, they always play a large and significant part. It seems to exist everywhere south of the circumpolar Eskimo culture, where the occupation of women is the preparation of the meat and skins provided by male hunters—preparation that is undertaken, incidentally, with great technical skill.

Where foraging exists, it usually produces a large proportion of the food supply. I've no time to lay out the different social patterns of foraging, which depend on region, climate and available food supply, of course; but anyone interested can find a brief, cogent summary of the subject in a little book called *Women and Men, An Anthropologist's View,* by the chairperson of the Department of Anthropology at Duke University, who is a past-president of the American Association of Anthropology. Her name—yes, *her* name—did that surprise you?—is Ernestine Friedl; and in some forty pages she gives us a clear picture of how these cultures managed to subsist.

Most writing about the progression toward advanced culture of more primitive peoples has laid emphasis on Man the Hunter and how his invention of weapons led to the creation of artifacts and thus to the beginnings of technology. OK, no doubt the invention of weapons played a large part in this process. But I would like you to turn your attention also to the tasks of Woman the Forager and ask you to imagine her, accompanied by her children, at work. She left the camp, or the temporary sleeping base, more regularly than did Man the Hunter, for foraging, if not an everyday affair, must go on three or four times a week at least, while a successful kill of big game will supply food for a longer period. Often she would be carrying a small child. Perhaps she would be pregnant with another, though the custom of lengthy breast feeding was certainly used to space births. Bushmen women, whose material culture is very simple, ridicule those who have children less than four years apart. She and the little ones might very well have to walk some distance. Among desert Bushmen, it may be anywhere from two to twelve miles; and she will carry back a load of food that can weigh up to thirty pounds.

Well, now, how does she do that? Not in her hands, especially if she is also carrying a child. No, she invented the container. I don't know what it would have been made of at first—woven twigs that were green and supple; big tough leaves pinned together with thorns; nets or baskets of fiber from vine stems—all these are possible and all will have vanished into dust, of course, while stone arrowpoints and adzes survive. But invent it she did, because it was absolutely necessary for the female tasks of carrying food and carrying children. She surely slung the new baby on her back in some kind of sack or net even before she learned to lace a papoose into a carrying board that could be hung from a tree branch while she worked.

And imagine what a contribution those fibrous braids turned out to be for other purposes: They could lasso some animals and snare others. They could net fish. Woven into baskets and daubed with clay, they stored gathered seeds. Baked hard by the sun, such containers led the way to pottery. Nor should we overlook the evolution of the digging stick, picked up to make it easier to get roots out of the ground, which led to the hoe that worked the land and became the first agricultural implement. I won't deny the contribution to technology made by the weapons of Man the Hunter, but please do *you* allow also for the contribution made by the peaceful inventions of Woman the Forager. She was no stranger to work or to the efficient techniques whose development, in her hands, were a major part of the long process toward civilization.

Let us now leap forward a few eons. We find our foremothers quite as skilled at their work as were our forefathers. Let me read you a short description of the work undertaken by colonial American women along the Atlantic seaboard, as our nation was being founded. It's from a recent study by Barbara Mayer Wertheimer of Cornell on working women in America, and its title is *We Were There* (Pantheon, 1977).

"A woman's work began at sunup and continued by firelight as long as she could hold her eyes open. For two centuries almost everything that her family used or ate was produced at home under her direction. She spun and dyed the yarn that she wove into cloth and cut and hand-stitched into garments. She grew much of the food her family ate and preserved enough to last the winter months. She made butter, cheese, bread, candles and soap, and knitted her family's stockings." Ms. Wertheimer doesn't mention it, there's so much to record, but she also made the bedding—those wonderful quilts that we now see as works of art.

"Her day began as she coaxed the coals to a flame to cook the first of the three meals she prepared for her large family. Bending over the open fire, summer and winter—(the cooking range was a nineteenth-century invention)—she hoisted the heavy Dutch oven or water kettle into place on the swinging iron fireplace crane. If she had a well in her own yard she was among the fortunate: many women fetched water from a town well some distance from their cottage.

"She had other skills . . . (as well). The small businesses that supplied the growing needs of the rapidly increasing population were usually conducted by husbands and sons within their houses or on their property. For additional labor they depended on their wives and daughters. Thus women learned to shoe horses, cut and trim tin plates, sew uppers onto leather (shoe) soles, tend the store and keep the books, or operate a saw or grist-mill. They could also handle a musket when need be, and often did." A few pages later, Wertheimer lists some of the occupations undertaken by women in the southern colonies in the seventeenth century. Here we find upholsterers; glaziers and painters; Jane Inch, silversmith; Mary Willet, pewterer; a gunsmith; a blacksmith; tanners; shoemakers; tinkers; Elizabeth Russell, shipwright; Mary Butler, blockmaker and pumpmaker; and Cassandra Drucker who owned and ran a fulling mill. In short, women did their own skilled jobs, and sometimes they did those of men as well.

What happened between then and now to remove women from the world of technology? It was not, I assure you, a refusal on their part to get their hands dirty. Indeed throughout the last few centuries, both here and abroad, wherever industrial society exists, women have done dirty jobs in mill and factory or just as office cleaners and charwomen. Juliet Mitchell, in *Woman's Estate,* recalls a foreman who explained that one particularly grubby and repetitious job, carried on in an atmosphere so noisy that everyone who did it learned to lip-read, couldn't be given to anyone but women. "If we give it to men," he said, "they fall over in an hour or two." So please, gentlemen, don't tell us that you have been protecting us up here on our pedestals. We're more likely to think that you've been excluding us from competition for the jobs that offer better pay and some advancement.

What happened, I believe, is that much work withdrew from the home and vanished into factory and mill, into office and commercial establishment. Women who needed to work for money had to follow it, and when they arrived where it was done, they came as supplicants. Moreover, there was—there *is*—still laid on their shoulders the social injunction that primary to any woman's endeavors is that of keeping a home and raising children. A woman at work in the labor force is a woman with two jobs. If she has young children, she's a woman with three jobs. And they can no longer be carried on in the same place, to her own time, with the easy natural assistance of others in the family or of neighbors. It is not women who fell out of skilled work. Rather, it was a mindless, idiot restructuring of work that failed to include and to profit from the aptitudes and the expertise of women. Mindless and idiot, I said; and I mean it. Already the first directives and limitations of factory work have been remade because no human being could survive with them—hours had to be shortened, machines had to be made safer, inhuman heavy work had to be eliminated or taken over by iron and steel and steam or electricity, not muscle power. Men and their unions forced these changes. But very, very little has been done as yet to adjust work to make it fully human—human enough to welcome the child raisers into it. At present, there is a very large component of economic need in the motivation of women in the labor force. Oh, I know lots of women work because they want to, and more are coming into technical work all the time; I told you I'd got some figures. But believe me, they are still climbing over obstacles to get there, and most of them are still carrying that double job, one at work, one at home, as men do not. I think men suffer from that, by the way; I hope we'll have time to talk a bit about what the exclusion from family and child raising means to men. But my topic is women and technology, and I must stick to it before I wander. What I'm telling you therefore is that women have been removed and excluded from technology in the recent past *not* by the lack of intrinsic ability or aptitude for math or the manipulation of machinery—they have used these aptitudes in the past and they still do in other societies. They have been excluded because we have organized the structure of most work today in a humanly destructive fashion that hurts everyone and, in addition, makes it infinitely more difficult for those who are charged with the survival of the human race in this society to contribute their gifts and capacities to the production of material goods or to recognized professional fields. This has got to stop.

I think it will stop. I'm an optimist. And I think the re-entry of women into the labor force, especially into technical work and into executive levels in industry as a whole, will help to stop the blight. Now, don't get me wrong. I do not think this will happen because women are better than men; I do not think they are innately more moral and loving and nurturing and clever at personal relations than men are. I just think that women have had to preserve these abilities in our society in recent times if we were going to survive—because the world of action as structured by men abandoned these qualities. And these are necessary human qualities. We have got to care about each other, we have got to live together in communities that offer rewards that are emotional and aesthetic as well as material. *All* of these values must be present, because they are all needed. Well, some of them got laid on women to keep alive, while male values moved toward competition and confrontation. I don't belittle the value of competition or of willingness to confront those who attack your person or property or ideals or aspirations—I just say that they are not all of life. We cannot live locked in a power struggle, perpetually at war with each other—not if we expect to stay sane. You know that as well as I do.

But men have tended to make my sex *the* one that had to pay attention to it.

And because my sex, which has had to keep alive and think toward the future of our children and to use these particular human assets of caring and connection instead of issues of confrontation and competition, is now moving back into the main stream, I think it is inevitable that along with us will come a sense of the great value that these qualities confer on all us humans.

I notice with interest, therefore, some bits and pieces that seem to surface in my conversations with men and women who are deeply concerned with the re-entry of women into technological fields. The dean of the Cornell School of Engineering remarks that he is a bit worried about the effect of the fact that so far women at Cornell appear to be heading toward a range of fields that overlaps but differs from that of the men students there. There is a tug toward environmental and general social concerns among the women. Now, obviously, this is in part due to completely realistic factors: Women who are heading toward new areas are not going to run into as much frozen bullshit as women who are heading into traditional fields, where they will succeed or fail to the extent that they can persuade their superiors to look at them as "one of the boys." Of course some of them are going to opt for analytical jobs, research jobs, where they don't get flack and hassle from men whose minds have been baked into chauvinism. Women don't expect to be welcomed in masculine citadels. They are quite capable of being objective about the treatment they receive and to report on it with humor. "Oh no, it isn't exactly hostility that I get from my colleagues," said one of the women full professors in a science at Princeton last spring. "It's more as if they thought I was a dancing bear." But to expect a cold shoulder is not the same thing as being indifferent to it. Some women are going to decide that they will not go into the coldest part of the deep freeze or the hottest part of the oven.

The difference Dean Cranch notes in feminine goals also has something to do with a preference for working *toward* goals by means other than competition and confrontation—by working with conversation, compromise, a sense of the value of sharing. In addition it has to do with the injunction to women to do most of the work of family support—emotional support, I mean, though plenty of women support families economically too—and of child rearing. We do value these personal, human ties as good things. We will always think twice about entering a career that tells us we can't succeed both places;

which, let me point out, is not a thing that any career outside the Catholic priesthood tells a man in our day and age. So a good deal of what worries Dean Cranch about women's career choices is the result of utterly realistic and hard-headed decisions on their part. I am sure Dean Cranch is aware of that; when I say he's worried, I think that what concerns him most is finding that his faculty is skewed toward predominantly male interests and doesn't take sufficient account of the push toward analytic and human environmental work that women are importing. And frankly—I hope that his worries are realized. Because I believe that his male students are going to profit from an opening toward a greater concern with the demands of ecology and with factors in engineering that relate to human values, not mechanical principles. To my mind, mechanical principles must be learned, and must be well used, because they serve human values, and if they don't do that they are not being well used.

I find it extremely interesting, in the same vein, that Dean Jahn of Princeton reports that his freshman engineering class, which consists of 22 percent women, is not all planning to go on to engineering but is treating this knowledge as a possible basis for other careers. This seems to me a good and practical way to begin marrying two cultures, of science and the humanities. I am not surprised to be told that the faculty women there are clustered in the Center for Environmental Studies. This fits expectations—and it fits roles and life-styles as they are at this stage of transition. I do not, of course, want to see us stay where we are. I hope that a generation from now women will be heading into mechanical, electrical and civil engineering as readily as they now move into the more obviously humanistic fields, because it seems clear that these fields need humanizing. But the fact that women are starting other places suggests to me that they are both sensible and here to stay—they are going where they can be accepted now most easily. This is a sign, I think, of a reality-oriented process. But let us be sure not to cut the process off and decide that women *must* head for human-related areas, because they are naturally suited to them. The process I note is valuable just because it is a process of *change,* and change is needed most where it has not yet reached.

Another point of great interest to me is the value of counseling for women going into technical fields. Some of you will remember, I imagine, a book that came out five or six years ago that made much of male bonding, Lionel Tiger's *Men in Groups,* and assured us blithely that women didn't bond—he could tell because they were not volunteer firemen, nor did female baboons appear to care for each other's

company. Well, women are not baboons, even if they are not often
volunteer firemen. And they bond. They connect. David Johnson of
Cornell very kindly sent me a report on a conference held there in June
of 1975 on Women in Engineering. Included is a report from Lynne
Harrington Brown of Purdue on the effect of intensive counseling for
women in the science majors there, and I'd like to give you a quick
rundown on it, not only for the points it makes but because it widens
our view of present students.

Unlike Cornell and Princeton, Purdue is a middle-western institution in the public sector drawing local students and open, in the
sciences, to any high school graduate from the upper half of his or her
class. The institution thus expects to take in a broad spectrum of
students, including high-risk students. As might be expected, the attrition rate in the School of Science was horrible; 60 percent for men,
75 percent for women. However, when they analyzed the women who
were leaving, they discovered that it wasn't marks that were making
the difference—that is, the women who left had grades as high as the
women who stayed. It wasn't academic performance that pushed them
out of the field; it was the strain of going it alone in an unfamiliar area.
These students didn't drop out; they simply transferred to fields more
traditionally open to women—home economics, nursing, the humanities. In 1973, with a grant from FIPSE for two years, the School of
Science targeted a program at women in the first two years; for it
appeared that if they survived to become juniors, they pretty much
stayed to graduate. The first item on the agenda was to provide intensive counseling, with no restrictions on what could be brought up, and
easy access to six counselors, half men, half women. "What actually
happened," writes Brown, "was that most of the students went way
beyond the three forty-five-minute periods that had been planned.
They began to develop very close relationships with their counselors."
Not only did this support work well, it was perceived, by both students
and counselors, to point to the same areas of confusion, so that problems could be predicted and defined.

In addition, role models were imported, since there were not
enough on campus: women from industry, or women who were present but not easily visible because they were in research work, and
female faculty from other institutions. These people provided career
counseling, they came and talked about their jobs for several class
periods, and these were followed by informal sessions where concerns
about personal lives for women in science could be raised. And, third,
each student did a research paper on some topic relating to women,

from child care to ERA. That was it. And in one year the attrition rate was cut in half. It appeared, at the time this paper was given, that this drop would be replicated as the program continued.

Some of this success comes from learning that other people have done what you want to do, part comes from finding friendship and support from each other and from the slightly older students who came into the classes and talked about their experiences. Peer counseling for women has everywhere proved its worth. But what we also see here is the formation of networks and of bonds that will continue to support these women and give them the attachments to colleagues that men have taken for granted but that have, in the same taken-for-granted ways, been refused not always but often to women.

For these bright spots that I've noted are still only spots. Horror stories can be told about even the best institutions; and though good engineering schools have managed to help their entering women connect with each other into that exciting state that is known as "critical mass," women at work in industry are often still very much alone, still under enormous, silent pressure to act like one of the boys and to repudiate either their normality as—let's say—an engineer or a physicist *or* their normality as a woman. The idea that one can be a normal scientist and a normal woman at the same time is astonishingly hard for the male mind to cope with. Here are a few quotes from a paper by Mary Rowe, Affirmative Action Officer at MIT, called "The Saturn Rings Phenomenon," in honor of the particles of dust and ice that, like Saturn's rings, produce a marked change in the environment but are hard to identify individually. These are instances from 1973 to 1976, not the remote past.

How about the vice president of a large firm who when asked about appointing an able woman to an operations manager replied, "I couldn't do that; she's black and a woman. She's not even pretty." Or the scientist at a university who wrote, "Despite the fact that women may be even more qualified, I believe we should curtail the admissions of women; they will deter men from doing their best creative work." Or the reference given a woman scientist (not to Rowe but to a masculine colleague), "You can hire this woman for your lab if you want to, but I'd rather have her body than her mind." Then there was the ad hoc committee at a New England university that solicited letters in support of tenure for a famous archeologist, Jane Doe, and got back replies that "Dr. Jane Doe is probably the outstanding woman archeologist in the world." Dr. Doe was deeply offended—and discovered when she called the referee that her department *itself* had

asked that she be ranked among "women archeologists," not simply
as an archeologist. And then there is the continual minor harassment
of jokes, the ignoring of women or perception of them as being of
lower rank than that which they actually hold, the salesmen that don't
call on them, the invitations that aren't extended, the assumption that
a married woman will go where her husband goes if his job changes—
and the shock and horror that a man may find responding to a decision
on his part to move with his wife instead of vice versa. I was told of
one young scientist at a major eastern university who was offered a
prestigious appointment in his field and asked whether it could be
deferred for the months that it would take his wife to finish law school
work and receive her degree. He was told that he would never again
be recommended by his department if he did not accept at once,
because he would clearly mark himself as not serious.

I feel, as I stand here, that I've hardly begun to raise questions of
the utmost importance to all of us; and yet, I can't go on forever. Let
me come back, then, to what I said at the beginning—that I hope you
approve and support the movement of women into man's world of
technology. You see, lip service is not enough. Unless you do truly
want to reach the unexploited talents of women and direct them into
this area, you will not begin to remove the obstacles that keep them
out, and you will involve yourselves in a self-fulfilling prophecy of
failure. Since the end of the last war, women have moved steadily into
the labor force until they are now over 40 percent of those working
or looking for work; and yet their salaries have not risen in proportion
to those of men. There are some side effects that keep them down, it
is true—seniority, length of continuous work, and so on; but there are
much bigger discriminatory forces at work too. And the result is the
misuse and under-use of women's abilities.

In the technical field, your best workers are those whose dedication and whose creative talents are enlisted. What are you doing to
reach women? Believe me, you need us. You desperately need our
experience and our knowledge of life. In the last ten or fifteen years,
urban planners and architects have managed to construct a whole
series of unlivable buildings and badly malfunctioning work spaces.
Why in hell, in the face of an energy crisis, can't I open the window
in a Holiday Inn? Why do the beautiful all-glass buildings climbing
toward the sky in New York overheat every summer on one side and
freeze everyone on the other? Who in the name of God designed
high-rise, low-cost housing for families and imagined that putting
playgrounds around the base of the building would do anyone any

good? Why not put some communal space inside, arranged by floors—little kids here, and let their parents live on that floor; adolescents in another place; older people somewhere else. Use an apartment on each floor for public space. What you lost on rent, you'd make up in the prevention of vandalism, because you'd be building a community spirit at the same time as you provided unpaid observers and guardians, like those whose passing in the destroyed neighborhoods around the high rises Jane Jacobs lamented so eloquently.

As I was writing this speech, my husband happened to remark on the sad situation of St. Louis's hockey team—a big, beautiful one-use building for their home and a fuel bill that's quintupled; and no one seems to know what to do, except contemplate bankruptcy. Well, I can't tell you what to do without seeing the place and knowing St. Louis, but I bet that a group of women, engineers, residents, architects, urbanists, planners, businesswomen, all of them with minds that have to be flexible, have to adjust to the everydayness of life, its nitty-gritty details—I bet such a group could come up with a whole slew of ideas. Women are still immersed in process and interaction. All of us are used to doing two and three things at once—we just pray for a little quiet time to concentrate on our main job. Every time I pray aloud that when I'm born next time I want to be born triplets, another woman says, "Oh God, so do I! What I could accomplish then!" And we could. But that sometimes maddening, distracting flexibility keeps us in touch with the way things work in this world; material things; ice-box doors; clocks that one presumably ought to be able to wind without breaking fingernails; knives for steak that cut steak; washing machines that can be repaired; need I go on? The world of work and the world of ordinary living has been separated and, believe me, that's bad for everyone. We need to get put together again.

What women are going to bring to this joint enterprise is not, I repeat, something special and quintessentially feminine; it doesn't spring from intuition that grows out of the genes or nurturing care that comes with mother's milk. Men are entirely capable of providing every bit of that, except for the milk. Female virtues are human virtues, and they need to be more widely distributed because without them our society, dominated by men, is depriving itself of extremely valuable qualities. But they are qualities that can be called forth, and trained, in both sexes. Of course there are individual variations, which is what makes life interesting and amusing; but the weight of social training is sufficient in itself to offset any sexual differences that might surround the overlapping central section of likeness and similarity that both sexes share. The great movement toward equality for women is beginning to erase the stereotypes that have blinded us in the past to the ease with which we can talk and work together, to the qualities that we share and can enjoy together. At the same time, it will increase the diversity of our world, because we will be able to think of each other as individuals, each with his or her own strengths and quirks and anomalies and weaknesses.

I travel a lot and usually, on planes, I find that I'm sitting next to a man who's going somewhere on business. Sometimes one or both of us wants to work, or read, or take a nap; but quite often we fall into conversation. It always interests me to note how many barriers my companion has to climb over in order to talk to me as one individual to another. Sometimes we don't make it; but when we do, we usually find each other stimulating and informative. That doesn't surprise me—but it does most often surprise the man I'm talking to. Why should it be so hard for us to get the insides of our heads together? It's because of those stereotypes we have of the other sex as being different, and frightening, or boring, or incompetent, or unable to see another point of view. The women who're putting their minds and their skills to work again in the eternal business of getting things done in public, of making a living and keeping the world on its ordinary usual course are not frightening, not extraordinary creatures from some queer inner space whose synapses and reflexes work differently from those of men. Some of them are bright, some are strong and creative, all of them are motivated, and if they have got themselves into this field, they have stamina. You can use them here; and the overall changes in society that this move of theirs will bring about are overdue.

Career Identity

"CAREER IDENTITY" is rather a clumsy phrase and not one that I'm very happy with. But when people confront changes in the context of life, new circumstances and emergent entities have to be given some label if they're to be talked about at all. We can hope that a poor or insufficient first label will be changed if the phenomenon persists and in time superseded by a better one. What I mean by "career identity" is not just the simple record of work done, as listed in a curriculum vitae, but rather the assimilation into the self of continued and consecutive active experience, moving with some purpose toward a goal. The variety and multiplicity of roles in women's lives is now more apparent than it has ever been—and more demanding too. Yet even in more settled times our lives always contained shifts in relationships and in status over time just because the context of life made us adjuncts and assistants to others rather than prime movers. Countering, but also complementing, such flexibility is the identification of oneself as an active agent, increasingly knowledgeable within a field and increasingly able to imagine meeting new challenges with invention and competence when they have to be faced. With such an identification goes increasing autonomy and initiative.

Perhaps I can illustrate what I mean by a personal anecdote. When the Minnesota Multiphasic Personality Test was enjoying a peak of interest some thirty years ago, I remember going over it carefully and with the sort of curious personal interest about myself that must be frequent in any such situation. What could the test reveal to me about hidden ranges of subconscious motivations? Might it not serve to show not just what one thought oneself to be but what one really was? One of the questions involved self-description: "Who are you?" to be answered in a fairly complicated way, as I recall. This, I should remind you, was at the height of the period of "happy-wife-and-motherdom," and in fact I was a fair example of just that at the time, a suburban housewife with a couple of school-age children. But there was no way that I could accept that definition of myself as sufficient or even as primary. Try as I might, the words "I am a writer," kept forcing themselves to the fore, center stage. Before I was ready to fit myself into a relationship, even a satisfying one, I had to name myself as a worker, a writer, who regularly practiced her professional activity, who wrote books and articles and reviews. Here was where I recognized myself as an active, autonomous person, and the presence of that person had to be listed first.

Now, I had the advantage of being able to lay claim to a familiar and rather prestigious work role. People know what writers do, though they overestimate what we are usually paid for doing it. Recognition of the role certainly made it easier for me to assert my claim to a career identity. But I don't believe that such recognition is the essence of the situation. What I had to emphasize was not so much being known as being active. It was the process of doing, of continuing and developing, that created and sustained an identity because it led—and leads—to an overall capacity to look at life and form an independent judgment about the significance of some set of circumstances. To any active person, there comes a confidence that you, that person, are capable of sound decisions because you've made them before, because you've had to form opinions on which you can proceed to your own ends. You can put your observations together into a reasonably trustworthy explanation of what's going on, which will allow you to interpret the present and predict coming events and suggest helpful ways of dealing with them. You have access to a realistic system of cause and effect, inside your own head, which has worked often enough in the past to be relied on, at least as a start. Even if you are facing new conditions and know that flexibility is called for, you assume that you're competent enough, in your relations with the world of action, to give coping a try. You do not panic and retreat in a fit of "imagination-anxiety," which is sister to "math anxiety."

What you are doing is recognizing and trusting yourself as a primary agent, not as "other." In her famous description of the "otherness" of women, Simone de Beauvoir wrote, of the occupant of the female role, "To be a true woman she must accept herself as other." Now, the continuous, autonomous, originating subject can't do that. She doesn't fit into a life that is judged merely by connections formed with other people, valued by their reactions. Pride in activity has got to be there. Without it, one's identity is filtered through someone else's experience. True, human beings are social creatures; we do count on the opinions and responses of others. Indeed, we grow to maturity and reach the stage where we have a chance for independent life choices only through the mediation of many "someone elses" who are kin, were teachers and mentors, continue as companions—or opponents. We live in a world with a vivid and influential human context. In important ways we do know ourselves through recognized relationships.

In women's lives, however, there is a special and limiting element in this situation. The human context is there in force, but the frame of reference it employs to name and define and assign significance to events and relationships is not derived from the experience of women. Our social mythology, our accepted system of cause and effect, come out of the lives of men. The image of woman that little girls learn from their mothers is one whose form and structure are designed to fit the perceptions and desires of males. If inner knowledge conflicts with the expected image, inner knowledge must be discounted or even denied. Within the growing, learning self of the girl child, her own intuitive responses to the physical or social world can't be trusted. They must be referred to the codified system of thought based on other people's thinking. The immediate impetus of autonomous action then is often caught and checked.

The essence of otherness is that any direct link between an individual and her own sensory perceptions, her own judgments and evaluations, can't be taken for granted. These links must always be dipped into the body of wisdom drawn from someone else's experience, while one's own is devalued, and responsive action to deal with events has to fit a pattern of acceptable behavior based on expectations that aren't your own. Feminine initiative is thus held back for a devastating moment of groping, of denying the first response. This delay surely reinforces the picture of men, not women, as being shapers of events, decision makers, daring interveners in action and risk takers. If women act at all, they are expected not to be leaders but to serve as helpers and handmaidens. What we might decide and do will not be credited—even by us.

Note how this validates the socialization of girls, who are taught to put relationships ahead of independent action, ahead of their own direct connection with the ongoing events of life. Growing up, we have all been taught to wait and see what is happening, which is sensible enough, God knows; but we have been told that our own assessment isn't enough to act on, no matter how long we wait or what we see.

Our activities should follow directions from one of those someone elses to whose commanding role we should not aspire.

If women hesitate to take prompt and decisive action, the reason is rooted in this disallowance of our cognitive initiative. It isn't a fear of success, it isn't a Cinderella Complex, it's sheer learned self-doubt. There is nothing that ties a group down to powerlessness and isolation more effectively. In Hitler's camps and Stalin's Gulags, it was conscious policy to disrupt the capacity of prisoners to foresee the future. The administrators of both holocausts built unpredictability into the daily lives of the inmates. Not only does this uncertainty promote anxiety in itself, it increases the load of anxiety to such a degree that one retreats from the burden into sheer indifference as the only possible defense. Feeling, hoping, imagining—they hurt too much. One ends by simply not daring to care or to think ahead of what may be.

And this kind of indifference brings us to the well-known finding that women and members of powerless, inferior groups and classes have trouble delaying the satisfaction of their desires. We want things now; we can't restrain ourselves in order to achieve later and greater rewards in the future. Those who can sublimate their immediate wants grow toward power in an incorruptible bourgeois heaven on earth, piling up savings, investing in future security, looking well beyond the fleeting moment at hand. The feckless poor and frivolous women, on the other hand, will run up bills until we fall on welfare or have to be bailed out of our debts and allowed only minimal sums for daily spending. Well, there's a chain of cause and effect here that the powerful don't see but that our experience makes quite clear. If you can't tell what's going to happen to you, if your judgment of events has been rendered suspect even in your own mind, how can you possibly waste time trying to imagine a future? Your vision of one has been labeled worthless. How silly, then, to try to form one. Seize the moment, *carpe diem,* becomes the only wisdom.

Another powerful element is at work in the image offered women as mirroring the self: It is a divided, a polarized image, and that too is the result of seeing ourselves first and foremost in terms of relationships with others. I have written elsewhere of the effect of the sexual images offered women by our culture: images of "Eve" and "Mary," of sacred and profane, which contradict each other. The effect is a profound confusion in one's own sense of identity, and that is merged with a rejection of much that is natural in oneself—and with a split among the ranks of women over a morality that takes its form from male needs and desires. Neither Eve nor Mary can provide any model for self-chosen, self-directed activity in the real world. For that we need the sense of a repeatedly competent, activating, doing creature, this thing I've tentatively called a career, or work, identity, who is trustworthy not merely by living to someone else's rules but as an individual capable of judging, acting, learning, persisting, gaining in competence—and so on and so forth. I mean a person willing and able to engage herself directly with events, as well as in relationships, and drawing on her knowledge of both kinds of living in order to shape her own existence.

The discussion planned for this meeting today addresses ambition and achievement. A certain amount of hostility is still mounted against ambitious, achieving women, on the dubious grounds that society needs selfless followers of paramount chiefs more than independent critics and innovative implementers; and that females have been marked out to specialize in this role, whether by God or our genes, or our history and prehistory. Before George Gilder became an expert on the workings of capitalism and free markets, he was telling women, in *Sexual Suicide,* that our abdication would be terribly tough on men who, without devoted, dependent, homekeeping women, could never be socialized away from natural masculine brutality. A more serious thinker, Carl Degler, has recently assured us that the moral authority granted us in the domestic sphere a couple of centuries ago opened a new era for women by increasing our stature and enlarging our role—still within relationships, of course. He goes on to acknowledge regretfully that our needed presence in this role of domestic moral authority will always conflict with our active selves, a judgment that has social force but does not grant much in the way of creativity and active invention to the women who find themselves in this dilemma. In fact, it is we ourselves who will have to think—and act—our way out of this situation. What keeps us still in this place, I think, is less the current animadversions of masculine thinkers than it is our own general commitment to the need we perceive to keep things running, even if it means self-sacrifice. We have always lived in the nitty-gritty of daily life, cooking, cleaning, minding the baby and the store, because someone has to do it. And yes indeed, someone does.

But why is it only women who are expected to smooth out the bumps of daily existence? Men might not be pleased to hear us say that we accept the duty because we don't trust them to do it. That's true. But one reason is bound in with our acceptance and their withdrawal, and that is the trivialization of the chores of the daily round. The combination of everydayness with femininity has, in fact, worked to trivialize both. Our commitment to keep things running, without protest as a group, without offering and insisting on new ideas and new ways, without structured rebellion, has operated as a very strong social control on ambition and achievement in other fields. We accept the fact that before we turn to our outside jobs or professions we must responsibly see that all runs well at home; if there are conflicts, we take solving them to be our responsibility because our duties—not our moral authority!—in "the domestic sphere" still bind us. How long will it take us to begin to see that any problem that affects millions of human beings (and holding down two jobs, one for pay and one for love, does just that) is a problem that requires a social solution? Which will only be achieved by political and economic action?

I don't know the answer to that question, but I know that if we are going to operate as agents of change and thus adjust social structures to real changes in underlying ways of living, we need the strength that comes from possessing vital and trustworthy selves, the ability to form and to abide by our own judgments and to go forward in the face of disbelief and hostility. Activity in the mainstream world of politics, business, the professions, is a necessary factor in gaining this ability. Yes, motivation is vital too. The same thought that has led us to say "We will do it because someone has to," about the obligations that now shape women's lives, can lead us to apply that statement more widely than we have done before. Both at home in the household and outside it, the skill to do well what has to be done and the persistence to keep at it till it has been done effectively are reinforced by the doing.

In addition, action that is continually mindful of the need for change is a powerful antidote to the co-option of women by the existing system. As we work toward change, wherever we begin, we will find ourselves working together and discovering again and again how self-trust leads to trusting the capability, creativity and endurance of other women. One of the greatest rewards of the women's movement has been the growth of strong ties among us, both emotional and cognitive. My own writing and speaking have led me to understand and value the talents of many other women. Their insights flow into mine, our books and thoughts reflect each other, we march together. Ambition and achievement, that is, do not isolate women from each other. On the contrary, they bring us together in a way that we have not been able to enjoy for—who knows how long?

The self that is actualized by steady and persistent interaction with events, that is powered by ambition and attracted to achievement, is a self that can invent and create, that is self-confident enough to take risks, to try putting its perceptions of the world together in a new fashion—or in more than one new fashion. It is also a self that is strong enough, centered enough, to accept setbacks and delay in reaching a desired goal. It can wait for gratification and learn from mistakes. It can disagree with orthodox descriptions of the world and assign its own values to those things adjudged great or insignificant by tradition. It can distrust dogma as well as trust its own intuitive knowledge. It can even agree with orthodoxy and tradition, when it has had a chance to think and to test these doctrines.

To achieve that kind of identity is a human triumph. It is now open to both sexes. Some of our foremothers certainly lived such lives, but we have to suppose that their gender kept their achievement unknown to a public wider than kin and friends and lost its memory for them when those who had known them died. We have a few records of remarkable women, but they have mostly come down to us by way of male memories and consequently are colored by traditional myths of how virtuous women behave. Where we have women's letters and journals they are generally concerned with the human relations that had to be their primary business. I suppose that the truest and most revealing records we have of women's ambitions and achievements of the past are to be found in the anonymous works of art created as handicrafts: quilts, embroideries, baskets and weaving, knitting patterns, anonymous tales and songs, regional and seasonal recipes; and these are still undervalued because they were so much a part of dailyness. They are evidence, however, of a continuing woman's culture embodied in creative work, which is both functional and beautiful, its everyday purpose enriched by and enriching aesthetic intent. They are the roots of what I've called career identity. I hope our work, with its greater breadth of opportunity, will be worthy of them.

SEXUALITY

I'VE BEEN ARGUING that this generation suffers from a good deal of misunderstanding about the world as it is because the data on which we human creatures base our overall views are deficient, although our ideas are changing. The ability of women to undertake energetic, goal-directed public activities has not been given full weight. Throughout history the economic and political arena has been allotted to the male sex; although women are to be found there now in steadily increasing numbers, male patterns of behavior and interaction have traditionally shaped the structure and the rules we think of as appropriate to this part of life. These rules are attuned to the image our culture has framed of the hero, the effective, daring male doer, the responsible father figure. We've all been brought up to admire that figure, but he hardly incorporates the whole range of human existence.

One might assume that reciprocity would arrange for the female image and women's patterns of action and modes of being to prevail in private life. That doesn't seem to be the case. Female sexuality does not set the tone of intimate relations any more than it directs foreign policy or political campaigns. Our visions of female sexuality, in fact, are not stable or centered but differ widely across time and space. They are also capable of contradicting themselves within a society. In part that's because women's lives have not been much examined by the makers of our cultural concepts who prefer their own vision of life, which is projected onto the social existence of others. In part it's because women have seemed to accept the standards in public and often in private, too, if it seemed wise or necessary to do so.

When unexamined lives change, as women's have in recent years, what the culture makers see first is the impact on themselves. (Sometimes they never get to see anything else.) So it's understandable that women's liberation has got mixed up, in the public mind, with sexual liberation. A decrease in restrictions on sexual intimacy is a pleasanter way to look at women's drive for equality than is the coincidental push for equal pay and equal opportunities at work, which tends to register itself, originally, as a threat of increased competition and undesired social change. Eased morality is a much more welcome change, by the guidelines of macho mystique, with its investment in "scoring." But the result is a confusion of mind.

In the articles that follow I have tried to untangle sexual liberation from women's liberation. The assumption that they are the same thing, or at least very closely related, creates troublesome ambiguities in contemporary thinking. Add the historical shifts in sexual morality that have taken place over the last century, and that are not yet fully assessed, and confusion deepens. Victorian morality, which we tend to take as "traditional" to an unwarranted extent, has vanished almost as completely as have horse-drawn traffic and hoop skirts. The fact of this disappearance is generally taken as a good thing, and I'd hasten to agree. But I don't see how we can drop the subject there and rush on to assume that the garden of earthly delights lies about us. What kind of a good thing is the decline in sexual restrictions? How does it affect other phases of private existence and public existence too? Are there social costs, and if so, what are they? Until we confront such questions they will continue to trip us up.

Let's start with history and a glance at the very different sexual morality of the 1880s. Among the respectable classes, public behavior was straitlaced and prudish, and private behavior was certainly affected by Mrs. Grundy's rules, though it can never have obeyed them all. Prostitution and pornography were rife, while being officially condemned. A double standard of conduct allowed men considerable license even though they were supposed to conceal their illicit doings, and many must have suffered pangs of guilt. Women were expected to be virgins at marriage and chastely faithful thereafter. If they disobeyed and were caught, guilt in private and shaming in public followed.

Consequently when women began to gain more freedom in public and to enjoy more choices in their private lives, sexual liberation and liberation for women took the same road, though change came more quickly in some places and for some classes than it did for others. When I was growing up, Victorian morality was still close enough behind to have shaped the lives of some of my nearest and dearest, and the struggle against it wasn't entirely over. Those of us who were young in the twenties and thirties were close enough to the pioneers of change to share their detestation of the hypocrisy and dishonesty of stuffy middle-class morality and their heady joy over its downfall. Lytton Strachey, Freud, Marie Stopes, James Branch Cabell and Havelock Ellis were all bundled together as prophets of freedom. Nineteenth-century feminists had tended to demand that men adopt the strict moral standards required of women; but after the First World War, it was the right of women to move toward wider sexual choices that promised an end to the double standard. It wasn't pleasure alone that was being honored, not that pleasure should be sneezed at. It was the right to pursue it, to feel and express feelings openly. In those days, then, fifty or sixty years ago, there was a real tie between women's liberation and sexual liberation.

Come now to the present. Today any connection between the two sorts of liberation is much more tenuous. The most overtly oppressive limitations on female sexuality have disappeared, and to a large extent male patterns of free choice have become acceptable as guidelines to feminine behavior, owing (it hardly needs to be said) to the availability of efficient techniques of birth control. Because sexual activity is no longer necessarily connected to pregnancy, it has moved into a very different area of experience.

But that doesn't mean that the overall significance of sexual activity is the same for women as it is for men: The pattern of our lives is dissimilar. The ancient directives that grow out of male dominance are still actively involved with the way each sex lives and values existence. Yes, both sexes are now allowed to find pleasure in sex—but whose pleasure is held to be most important? Who defines the terms of the relationship within which sex takes place or even shapes it as a relationship instead of a casual encounter? A woman who makes the running, and some do, is still operating within a system geared to male superiority. A shift in sexual attitudes has certainly occurred, but that doesn't mean that encounters can be neutral. They still take place against a background of social conditions that have not been transformed so greatly, and this context of life flavors the relationship at its center. Approaches or invitations to sex are not made in the same way by women and men, nor do they carry the same meaning to each partner. Male and female experience is not interchangeable, and the links between sex and existence in general aren't identical. Even though women have benefited from new opportunities to enjoy sex, the way we take it into our lives, judge it, build on it, is not yet our own creation. Until it becomes so, society is not offering us liberation but simply another set of directives. Now, if society, in time, really grows into the pluralistic equality that gender liberation would bring, female sexuality would find its own kinds of expression within intimacy that reflected equality. Because they would be expressions of human emotions, they could ease anxiety and widen the possible range of human connections and human pleasure for men as well as women. But it's premature to think we have reached such a stage as yet. Real sexual liberation has to grant women the opportunity to choose a partner and define a relationship, not simply to say yes when asked.

In a way the recipes offered women today on how to feel and act in dealing with sex recall the situation my generation faced in a larger context, when all our goals and almost all our mentors were masculine. We thought we had to reject all the values of femininity if we hoped to avoid being trapped in the narrow traditional role that our mothers (or so we thought) occupied. We plunged into playing the male role. Sometimes we failed; sometimes we overdid it. Today's publicized vision of sexual liberation appears to offer women the chance to play a male role—which is defined as having a lot of sex whose meaning is summed up in physical pleasure and which is often followed by a readiness to move on. The exercise is only loosely connected with the rest of life and need hardly be connected at all.

In fact, playing the male role in either public or private life seldom satisfies either the woman involved or the men in the picture. There is a subtle underlay in the current image of an attractive, "sexy" woman in which her pleasure is valued not for her sake but for the assurance it brings to the man that he is a good stud. She is still a purveyor of pleasure to the important participant, the man, not a full and equal sharer in the encounter. At the moment of pleasure, then, she has to fall out of the status of equality that the masculine ways of behaving and feeling are supposed to bestow and go back to the old feminine role in which her attractiveness, her compliance, her service to him identifies her function. Her pleasure is not only allowed it's expected; but its significance is not the same as that granted male pleasure. As long as this kind of secondariness exists, we haven't arrived at sexual liberation; we have not got rid of male dominance, and we can't say that we have removed from sexual relationships the masculine element of aggression that has been a part of such relationships, in many guises, for as long as tongue can tell.

Needless to say, these public attitudes are not universal. But they are part of the general atmosphere, and so they are apt to be the "givens" people turn to in defining, or valuing, a sexual encounter, they are the circumstances that have to be taken into account as likely to prevail until warmth between individuals and shared experience build a different sort of relationship. The power of masculine displeasure is still given much weight in our social mythology. Growing girls are brought up to be attractive and to value their attractiveness for its useful public effect. Boys are taught to shape the world their way by aggressive action. Make these qualities essential to the image of each sex, and girls are being invited to offer their attractions and compliance to the male sex in return for undertaking action in their behalf. The old social contract made female sex a bargaining counter for male intervention in the public world, and the contract's not dead yet. Did either sex ever feel it had the best of the bargain? If it felt cheated, and each often did, resentment and hostility became part of the expected relationship. Not always, of course, but often enough to label the shadowed relationship as average and name the one in which trust prevailed as fortunate, a matter of happy chance.

The continuing presence of male dominance and the expectation of female passivity in sex encounters supplies one obvious reason for experiments with woman-to-woman sex, just as emphasis on women's otherness has had a hand in persuading some men to prefer their own familiar sex to the mysterious, unexplored, and frightening other. As long as gender inequality is a taken-for-granted part of the rest of life, sexual encounters will include an element of confrontation between strangers, of danger, of suspicion and holding back. The exaggeration of gender difference toward polarization is an ancient habit of patriarchal thought, which often becomes, by habit and analogy, a handy tool for defining other people, things, events and relationships by differentiation, by dichotomy. But if men are this way and women are that way, then how do you deal with anomalies among men or women? The assignment of gender roles is reinforced by the fear of anomalies and ambiguities. There must be a "right way" for each sex to act, feel, and deal with the world, and those who don't behave that way consequently tend to get read out of court, stigmatized as abnormal.

My generation's rejection of femininity is one example of dichotomy. Such a rejection is often assumed still. Women in this time of change are often seen, and sometimes see themselves, as carrying a label that reads: "I'm feminine," or else being thought to forswear the female role hook, line and sinker. Individual personality is denied in both cases; though more and more often we do find our way to saying, instead of either of the above, "I reject your definition of my femininity." Even so we don't as yet have a simple and comprehensible label to offer in place of the choice: male, female, or odd. In truth, we need not one overriding label, one role that goes everywhere with us, but a chance to develop into a lot of different, many-sided people. One advantage of our complicated and changing world is that such a pluralistic personhood may be easier to achieve and to present to others than in the narrower communities of the past. If the difference between the sexes could be seen as an important and interesting difference but nevertheless one among many other enriching differences, we'd all be spared a lot of grief, frustration, neurotic anxiety and general misunderstanding.

How utopian that sounds! We have lived with danger, suspicion and the expectation of confrontation for so long that we take them for granted as an essential element in real, true, adult sexuality. Is that true? Having written a book that looks at power from below, from the point of view of the governed, I wonder whether the universal idea of sex difference, and the value we attach to it, does not serve as a division among the governed mass of humanity that profits our rulers. To seize on natural differences and assign enormous importance to them, whether they have to do with gender, skin color, religious faith, language, place of origin—it's so obvious a way to maintain a central place of control that it hardly requires planning. In the case of gender difference, the explosive, emotive power of sex and the intimate involvement with it bound up in all our lives insulates this area from the easy reach of rational thought. The very irrationality and intensity of our sexual feelings mean that social ways of dealing with them are desperately necessary to all of us and desperately hard, too. How do we control, direct, satisfy this demonic urge? The laws of society, the judgments of our culture and the interpretations of our arts are the areas to which we turn for guidance. Of course the power elite doesn't create the direction or the varying parameters of such guidance, but may it not monitor, approve and strengthen different tendencies? At any rate, the rulers of a society represent the ethos of that society and incorporate within the process of rule the accepted values of the mythic cosmology of that society.

In our society the possibility of violence gives an edge to sexual pleasure. Sadism and masochism are often treated by psychologists, and certainly by sexologists, as being matters of individual preference. Are they? Or are they a result of social conditioning toward hostility between men and women through emphasis on unlikeness, not toward common humanity?

Provoking violence by one group of the governed against another has a long history, the foreseen result of using "Divide and rule" as an instrument of dominance. Violence by nondominant men against even less dominant women provides a satisfying outlet for frustration; it can also channel resentment away from the powerful. An example from the past with overtones of meaning for the present describes exactly the use of sex to turn hostility that might threaten the powerful toward the weak by means of gender difference. A study on prostitution in late medieval France, by historian Jacques Rossiaud, which appeared in the magazine *Annales,* illustrates a technique by which The Thing managed to control threats of rebellion in urban centers 500 years ago. As population in the towns grew with migration from the countryside, so did the threat of riots and violence, especially from the young men who had not yet been absorbed into economic and political life. A simple solution was to provide community brothels. A bow to official morality suggested that these be advertised publicly as only for bachelors and travelers. A more discreet alternative, however, was available for the respectable family men of the town, in public bathhouses, with private rooms reserved by female "attendants," the massage parlors of the time. Some of these establishments were owned by great nobles and some, indeed, by members of the upper clergy, bishops and abbots. Thus was male sexual pleasure supplied with outlets in a way that many people today would take as being eminently sensible.

But not so fast. These outlets for pleasure did not prove sufficient to keep order in the streets, and so an alternative was offered that addressed the question of violence directly; violence channeled by gender difference. Young men, adolescents and up, were encouraged to join the medieval equivalent of youth-group gangs; they were known as "abbeys." Their meetings were occasions for jollification and rowdyism, after the manner of *Animal House.* Says Rossiaud, "The *juvenes* of closed cities, from sheer boredom, spontaneously set out in search of nightly adventure and fighting, defying the patrols, chasing girls, and engaging in rape." Spontaneously? Or was the action tacitly sanctioned? On the next page Rossiaud remarks, "In all the towns of south-eastern France, the abbeys . . . were recognized institutions that constituted an integral part of municipal life. Very often the abbot, his treasurer and his priors were elected in the presence of the town's magistrates." So it looks as if these activities, while overtly disapproved, were felt to serve a useful function. Specifically sanctioned was violence against members of the community whose behavior gave rise to scandal. It was almost always women who were attacked: the servant girl who was said to be kept by her master or the priest's concubine. But the victims also included those who were guilty of nothing at all: wives whose husbands were traveling on business, respectable young girls whose lives rape would ruin—and who were raped as a form of vandalism. All this in spite of the "sensible" provision of prostitutes for the wild young men.

Rossiaud does indeed suggest that what the authorities were doing when they shut their eyes to wildness and sexual damage was opening a channel that would drain off the hostility of the young and direct it against the weak instead of the old, the rich and the powerful: the men of property and status, the widowers whose fortunes gave them the pick of the young girls to marry as second wives—which may be a reason for those exercises in rape as vandalism. If the young men could not have the girls for their own use, they could spoil them for their elders. The women became a weapon for clandestine social struggle. What happened to them didn't matter much. Some kept mum about their disaster in the hope that they could still find a husband—a comrade, perhaps, of one of the rapists. At least public knowledge would not shame the family. Where the spoilage of female property could not be concealed, the brothel offered a depository for the damaged.

Sexual exploitation has changed some but not all that much. Young women are not ruined for life by rape, but the impulse to rape is still with us and so is the image of women as mere matter to be used and hurt when an outlet for violence is needed. Why is violence so easily channeled into attack on women? What deep hostility between the sexes expresses itself in this way?

Incest:
A Rational Look
at the Oldest Taboo

ARE THERE LIMITS to liberation?
The women's movement has all too often been confused with the
so-called sexual revolution for that to be an easy answer. Glad as we
are to free ourselves from confining stereotypes, we still face some
uncertainties. Can we assume that freedom to choose a sexual partner,
any sexual partner, is always liberating? Are sexual tastes always,
properly, a personal matter? Should no social constraints apply?

The affirmative response seems to promise healthy freedom, but
such views run into a challenge when they touch on the question of
incest—sexual encounters between close kin.

Recently, discussion of this "last taboo" has become much more
open than it could ever have been in the past. But it must still rely,
largely, on personal testimony. Few objective studies have been made;
moral horror is matched by psychological (particularly Freudian)
disapproval, and any disagreement is going to have to be very vehe-
ment indeed to survive. Moreover, if we rely entirely on the emotional
experiences of the participants, one set of feelings can be contradicted
by another. The result is emotional confrontation between tales of
exploitation and defiant reports of personal pleasure.

Finding trustworthy data from an extensive and diverse group is
hard. Judith Herman and Lisa Hirschman produced an excellent
study of father/daughter relationships in *Signs,* which went beyond
the personal to consider causative family constellations and therapeutic approaches. But the subjects of all fifteen cases studied were
women, and all were in therapy. Aside from being a small sample, the
subjects were per se sufficiently disturbed to have looked for help. Can
we assume that every incestuous relationship produces an equivalent
trauma? Not without investigation.

Warren Farrell, author of *The Liberated Man* (Bantam), has been interviewing male and female participants in incest who are not in therapy, and though some certainly speak of the experience with distress, others report positive pleasure. We must have personal testimony, then, but we also need a wide range of data—and qualified judgment, too; judgment that looks at the social context.

One bit of social context is the fact that incest includes several sorts of relationships and that we value them differently. Sex between brother and sister of similar age approaches the currently acceptable idea of sexual expression being governed by mutual consent, and sex between first cousins (defined as incest in some states and by the doctrines of some religions) is generally seen as even less deviant and more forgivable. Much more disturbing are parent/child encounters, but we look at those between mother/son differently, again, from those between father/daughter. Relations involving stepparents and children carry some of the overtones of parent/child connections, but they can be more easily faced because the distressing blood tie is absent and also perhaps because so many fairy tales alert us to the possibility of distortion in step-relationships. Intrasexual incest is disturbing in another way. Its existence is sometimes denied and sometimes placed in a category of "grotesque," which is another sort of denial, for it removes the matter so far from normal behavior that we can simply condemn without really thinking about it. In short, the difficulties we run into in thinking about incest derive in part from the variety of incests, which we don't judge in the same way.

Philosophically, incest asks a fundamental question of our shifting mores: not simply what is normal and what is deviant, but whether such a thing as deviance exists at all in human relationships if they seem satisfactory to those who share them. Psychologically, we confront the strange phenomenon of taboo, strengthened by horror and loathing of deviance and shadowed by the unsettling suspicion that such horror is required as a restraint on behavior that is secretly very tempting.

Some supposedly practical questions about the consequences of incest are not really that practical. It's true that inbreeding can produce birth defects when both sexual partners carry defective genes. It is also true that two members of an afflicted family will be more likely to be carriers than are strangers. But the idea that incest automatically produces damaged children is not true. Studies of abnormal births begin with the result, not the cause, and they consequently ignore the children who are normal. Since incestuous illegitimacy still carries a stigma that, in the past, rested on all illegitimate children, their existence is suppressed as thoroughly at least as was the bastardy of out-of-wedlock offspring during the reign of Mrs. Grundy. We simply don't know how many children of incestuous matings exist, and until we do, we cannot estimate the results. The big, mixed populations of today enjoy built-in safeguards that tiny, isolated communities lacked in the past. The tragic gene defects that produce sickle-cell anemia and Tay-Sachs disease are not the result of incest, but of long continued intermarriage among a group of connected families who have been subjected to the same environmental pressures. Mutations can wreak havoc quite apart from incest: Sturdy old Queen Victoria apparently suffered one, and bestowed hemophilia, through her daughters, on both the Hapsburg and the Romanov families, without benefit of any history of incestuous relationships.

We can rule out, statistically, that is, anxiety about inevitable, or even probable, biological damage to a child conceived in an act of incest. The problems raised by these illicit encounters are psychological, with psychological effects intensified by social judgments. It's too early for recent social changes to have arrived at any consensus on acceptable sexual practices; but though a feminist approach may not yet offer solid answers, it can certainly help to formulate useful questions. Those questions center on power relations. A great deal of our current thinking (and feeling) about incest comes out of Freudian theory—where power is at least as important as sex. The two mingle in Freud's description of how individual selves are integrated and labeled with gender-roles by the workings of parent-child relations, enshrined as the "Oedipus complex." Freud assumed that the sex drive innate in every human led each child to desire the parent of the other sex, as Oedipus unknowingly courted and won his mother. Growing up to normal maturity demanded that these desires must be put by, and the strength of character thus learned shaped the adult for the conflicts and connections of life. In Freud's view, our horror of incest arises from the fact that we have all experienced illicit longings for a beloved parent. We have given them up, but not forgotten the primal temptation.

How did we come to give them up? We were disciplined by those for whom we longed into renouncing our forbidden desires. The power of parents is as much a fact of family life as is affection, and children experience both, being born dependent and powerless into a world inhabited by giants, who may love them but add scoldings and punishments to rewards. That period in our life goes on for a long time, too, for human children live in a state of dependence for much longer than do the young of other species. Growing up human is uniquely a matter of social relations rather than biology. What we learn from connections within the family takes the place of instincts that program the behavior of animals; which raises the question, how good are these connections? Are parent-child bonds trustworthy and healthy—or exploitative? Overall, do they benefit the child or the powerful parent? Are they evenhanded, or do the Big People play favorites?

Obviously, the very fact that healthy growth is dependent on powerful others means that something can go wrong. And if relationships go wrong, the process of growth will go wrong, too. Incest has been seen in the past as something going terribly wrong, but wrong as a violation of morality or a religious code rather than as a psychological illness or a product of social breakdown. It was ordained by angry gods or grew out of personal, willful sin. To look at it as a "disease of the family" defines it as "wrong" in a different way. Contemporary commitment to personal freedom invites us to challenge old taboos as being obsolete: Feelings about adultery and homosexuality have changed dramatically. Is the incest taboo another such? Or are there real grounds for holding that *this* relationship is indeed something to be feared and shunned?

The old argument against incest is both simple and practical. If girls are not virgins, they are much less valuable as barterable merchandise between families or clans. Past marriage patterns were controlled by ongoing political and economic needs of families, male-headed families. Marry a virgin off well and you could gain powerful allies, or a chance at inheriting valuable property, or a friend at court.

Once this kind of value was placed on chastity, it extended to the sexual activity of older women: Mothers had to be controlled so that no questions could be raised about the legitimacy of their offspring, and thus about property or rights or titles within or between families. The incest ban guaranteed that daughters would be delivered to their husbands in a condition of virginity that would prevent occasions for disturbing the peace and that mothers would not be exposed to intrafamily encounters that could raise doubts about the legitimacy of heirs.

Unsurprisingly, these considerations were overlaid with patriarchal myth. In *Totem and Taboo,* Freud attributed the origin of the incest ban to a "primal horde" of young males who attacked the dominant father in order to gain possession of desired sex objects, of whom the mother was primary. The taboo was set up, he argued, to prevent a repetition of patricide and son/mother incest. In a recent book, *The Red Lamp of Incest* (Dutton), Robin Fox has worked out a variation of this vision that dips back into prehuman prehistory (incidentally telling more about the sexuality of baboons than this reader cared to know) and claims that control of the food supply gave dominant males control over access to females. (The contribution to feeding these groups made by food-gathering females is largely overlooked.) The power of the patriarchs forced young males into competitive struggle to survive and, Fox believes, set off the development of the human brain. So the incest taboo, according to Fox, is the Darwinian creator of humanity itself, via masculine competition. Women apparently sat at home breeding, waiting to be fed and sexually assaulted. It seems to me I've heard that myth before!

Unlike Fox's fantasies, Warren Farrell's investigations have to do with lived experience today. Farrell has asked ordinary people who have taken part in incestuous relationships to speak about the personal consequences freely, anonymously, and perhaps honestly. As with those interviewed by Kinsey and his associates, Farrell's self-selected respondents can be suspected of exhibitionism and exaggeration. Mostly they preferred to tell their tales over the telephone, under false names, which provides no guarantee of their truthfulness or opportunity for pursuit of uncomfortable topics. While it would be foolish to take this testimony at face value, it would be equally foolish to reject it out of hand. These are almost all the reports we have (outside of fiction) that are not based on interviews with people who were preselected in another way—who were in prison or in therapy. If nothing else, Farrell's talkers function as a control group.

About 200 of them responded to advertisements in a range of publications. Some had had more than one experience of incest. The largest number had taken part in brother/sister encounters (85), and the next largest in father/daughter relations (57). Brother/brother, cousin/cousin, and uncle/niece incest showed roughly the same frequency, in the twenties, and so, astonishingly, did mother/son incest —astonishing because other studies have reported it very rarely. In most cases (20 out of 24), the sons' reports were positive.

Which of course brings us to the important question of *who* was reporting. Men tallied a total of 82 percent positive reactions. Women, on the contrary, told of only 29 percent positive experiences with 52 percent negative and 19 percent mixed. Only in the case of cousin/cousin incest did women show a strongly positive response, and many people do not consider this type of relationship incestuous. In broth-

er/sister incest, 47 men found it positive, 1 was negative, and 3 had
a mixed reaction. Among women, 9 reported enjoyment, 15 were
negative, and 10 were mixed. The greatest difference occurred in the
reports on father/daughter incest: for men, 18 positive, 5 negative. For
women, 4 positive, 28 negative, and 2 mixed.

Farrell has some interesting speculations on these overall figures.
How many participants, he wonders, declared the experience negative
because of social expectations of guilt? Were women more easily
influenced than men in this way? How many illicit relationships came
out of difficult family situations that would, in themselves, do psychological damage to children? How much did age difference affect the
outcome? Farrell is aware of the power factor here: He found that
young girls involved with older men, whatever the specific blood tie,
suffered the most traumatic consequences. The lesson that they were
not valued as individuals but as sex objects directed them toward
taking on traditional sex roles and acting out the manipulative, secre-
tive, and isolated stereotype our society assigns to women.

Farrell's findings seem to me to be as honestly ambiguous as are
many feminists' attitudes toward incest: The possibility of pleasure in
permissive personal encounters is offset by the reinforcement of gender roles. These data, I believe, support the interpretation of incest
that I am using here: a disease of families today existing in a patriarchal system. Modern families may differ from those of the past in their
social connections and functions, but most still embody the ingrained
role prescriptions and gender behavior conveyed and enforced by
patriarchy. Like all institutions, families reflect and perpetuate current
social norms. Males dominate the existing power structure. In spite
of the self-serving notion that women wield power at home to match
that of men outside, male dominance also extends to family relations.
When in the past all intrafamily sex was seen by the power structure
as damaging to its interests, the incest taboo prevailed. Now the need
for family control of women has diminished in tandem with the decline in the importance of inherited property: Individuals now mostly
earn their own way, women as well as men. Virginity has lost a great
deal of its commercial value—to dominant males.

Of course, sexual pleasure has not lost its value, and what's wrong
with that? One thing: This pleasure is still defined by dominant males
in the terms satisfactory to them. It is still interpreted by old gender
myths, still something done by the powerful to the weak, still an
encounter between agents and others. Now, that's certainly not true
in the case of *all* encounters; increasingly, relationships can and do

approach equality, so that mutual, reciprocal pleasure enjoyed by both partners is a fact within them. But for the most part, gender stereotypes are alive and well—and dangerous. Women have been released from the sexual bondage of enforced chastity but not into our own, freely chosen pleasures. Social demands to please men have not relaxed. Rather, these demands have extended to include pleasing sexually, inside the family and out. Calling this a "permissive" society is inaccurate. All societies are permissive about certain activities and relationships, *because they do not see them as important.* In the past hundred years, chastity has ceased to be important, and our values have shifted in consequence.

But the shift has not been toward real liberation. The shift, based on the demands of dominant males, is toward woman as sex object, woman as more accessible than ever because she is less needed in an individualistic society as a social link in a family-related power structure. As fewer limits are placed by social controls on male desires, we can see from movies, television, advertising, how the acceptable age limit of the female sex object is declining toward the Lolita stage. We are also aware of an increase in broken marriages, and that too is an ambiguous finding, positive in the case of women finding better ways to survive than as long-suffering wives, but also evidence of a decline in family bonding and family loyalty on the part of men. Patriarchy, of course, sees this decline as the fault of women, and where it has power it proceeds to enforce traditional, archaic norms, which incorporate male demands. Removing the ban on sex arising from the usefulness of chastity (to men) "permits" women to be unchaste. It does not permit us to be free.

The persistent influence of patriarchy is evident in the attention paid to father/daughter incest, which is indeed typical of male dominance reinforced by parental authority. But other forms of incest are also shaped by gender hierarchy. As long as the world is divided into male and female spheres, the freedom of women to seek gratification outside the home, on their own terms, is limited. Sibling incest, one suspects, is often a matter both of convenience and of fear of the outside world. A girl who undervalues herself as a person is likely to accept affection with thanks and sex along with it. A boy who puts male desire ahead of personal understanding and interaction will look for sex where it's handiest. A woman tied to the home may fall into the habit of exerting power there in the only situation open to her— over her children, who are the only creatures she can dominate. Mother/son incest fits such a pattern. Father/daughter sex, then, is not the only form of the incest disease that stems from patriarchy, but it is the classic form, as it has been, and is the most widely discussed.

One obvious effect of patriarchal domination is the continuing isolation of mothers from daughters, which is indeed intensified in families suffering from the disease of incest. Father/daughter sexual relations are commonly justified by the father's need for affection that is denied by the mother. Farrell reports a frequent description of mothers as *aloof.* Indeed, this lack of expressed affection appears to motivate sibling incest, as well as making daughters ready to accept advances from fathers. The Herman-Hirschman study noted "shared . . . common features in the pattern of family relationships. The most striking was the almost uniform estrangement of the mother and daughter [that] preceded the occurrence of overt incest." In many cases the reason for estrangement was an incapacity on the part of the older woman: Mothers were alcoholic, tubercular, mentally ill. Household duties were taken over, not by the other parent, for patriarchal norms define these obligations as feminine and unmanly. They fell, instead, on a daughter, usually the eldest, who became in fact a surrogate wife. Among other distortions of relationships, such a young woman found herself the protector of the woman who should have protected her. Some pitied their mothers, some felt abandoned, others "saw their mothers as cruel, unjust, and depriving."

In this situation, feelings about the male parent were "ambivalent." Even when a girl felt "overwhelmed by her father's superior power," felt "disgust, loathing, and shame," she often thought that "this is the only kind of love she can get, and prefers it to no love at all." To a powerless girl child who could turn to no female champion, "the incestuous relationship did give . . . some semblance of power," by her accession to the mother role with its control over other family members. In addition—and here we see the deeper, less obvious damages of the incest disease—it gave these girls a special sort of malign authority: "They also knew that, as keepers of the incest secret, they had an extraordinary power which could be used to destroy the family." Secret power is even more isolating than the standard female stereotype: One dare not speak its name, one achieves it by action felt to be guilty, its enforcement proceeds by blackmail.

Is this family disease a strange infection? Or is it rather the intensification and spread of an ailment endemic in our society? It is not only incest, it is male dominance that devalues women's selves and women's bonds and reduces the family virtues of nurturance, of affectionate, long-standing loyal relations to duties and characteristics of one sex alone. The male right to function irresponsibly in personal relations is demonstrated in exploitative illicit connections, but it is present in all male-dominated ties. What happens in incest is that supposedly valuable family roles are subordinated to another force, potent and prevalent enough to overwhelm them. That force is male sexual dominance and the primacy of male definitions of female roles. There is no way that women will enjoy sex that is in fact "permissive" to both partners equally while male dominance exists.

As contributions to a continuing discussion, let me try to sum up these reflections on the present meaning of incest. Under patriarchy, diseased families of one sort or another are fairly common. Lack of community support and the difficulty of building female bonds isolate women and make mothering precarious and bereft of assured help in times of strain. The exploitation of sexuality in our culture is long-standing, but in the past it was offset by other important relationships. Many of these have vanished as social conditions and connections shift and break. As this happens, the sexual component within almost any relationship tends to increase, for it is taken to be one sure factor connecting human beings. Loyalty, friendship, family ties, the duty owed to an ideal—in our time, these obligations seem to have lost their force as motivators and connectors. When "sex" is used to sell clothes, cars, cigarettes, and *Cosmopolitan,* our expectation that it plays a part in every human relationship isn't surprising.

Capable adults can choose to accept the sex element when it pleases them or ignore it when it's unwelcome, though not always easily: Sexual harassment has only recently come under attack. For those who are still growing up and uncertain about the value of values and the meaning of meaning, it's hard to know what to accept or how to reject what is troubling. Power of any kind has its attraction: It appears to offer independence and autonomy, freedom of choice. The female image still projected to young girls tells them that the best way *they* can enjoy power is by manipulating a male person who claims it, some older male of whom the father is of course the prototype. In families where the older woman present seems to wield no influence or autonomy, that image is reinforced. Possible costs to the self, possible consequences for other relationships are far from clear. But when a bond of affection is based on the sexual exploitation of the young by an older, powerful "big person," the damage can be great.

Such distortions of family role are intrusions on the selfhood of the child. They violate the conditions of growth toward true independence and real autonomy. They betray trust. These reasons for condemning incest as the exploitation of power are not the same as those of "once upon a time," when patriarchal parents assigned a high value to virgin daughters; and not an entirely selfish value either, for protected girls could marry more luckily into better circumstances. Today, there are other more substantial and significant reasons for counting the costs of incest.

The first cost is the experience of exploitation, of seduction by a powerful person to whom affection is owed. Will affection always be tainted, afterward, by the expectation of exploitation? Will this experience teach the clever use of counterexploitations, of manipulation, of blackmail?

The second cost is incorporating into sexual pleasure the titillation of secrecy and mystery and, perhaps, shame and the search for domination. These are circumstances conducive to the birth of old, expected female masochism.

The third cost is the sacrifice of female connections to one another to patriarchal loyalties to the male. Incest often culminates in cultivating competition between female generations or between sisters, one of whom may see herself as the loved and favored one because the father, brother, or uncle has chosen her over the rest.

The fourth cost is the establishment of the girl child's perception of herself as a sexual being instead of a complete person who can enjoy and control sex as she wishes and can also enter into other sorts of relationships as she chooses: nonsexual relationships of friendship with either sex, of shared work, of continuing, cross-generation respect.

The current discussion of incest is healthy, to the extent that it is undertaken not in search of shock value, nor for easy moral condemnation on outworn grounds, but as an exploration of what this kind of deviance—particularly damaging and prototypical father-daughter incest—means in our society today. Efforts like Fox's, to ground incest in sociobiological history and prehistory, seem to me intellectually ridiculous and dangerous in their implications, for they attempt to give more than social weight to a social problem. Those of us who understand the need for change in our society had better watch carefully the efforts of supporters of the status quo to justify that status quo by presenting it as anything more than a social convenience for our power system. The dominant are always pleased to be told that the system as it stands is right for some eternal, inevitable reason—God or Nature or Genetic Imperatives Built into Our DNA, or what have you.

We should also judge incest as a deviance *in this society,* not because we hate deviance but first as revealing of the nature and forces operating in this society and, second, for the damage done not only by deviance but by these social forces themselves. For example, can we even condemn incest as "deviant" when it is compatible with the patriarchal vision of women as objects, servants, and isolates?

Where we can and should condemn this disease of the family is for the misguidance it brings into child rearing, the damage it does to relations between generations as well as to relations between sexes, which are already conditioned by male dominance. The function of families today has been cut down from much larger operations in the past. No longer centers of production or part of kin networks in necessary, everyday ways, no longer charged with vocational or apprentice training or with revenging injustice (all once part of family obligations), the family today is a place for relaxation, for the expression of emotions—and for the raising of children to emotional maturity, to the capacity to live freely in a world larger than the family. Incest turns the family into a fist, clutching at those it should be preparing for autonomy. It misinstructs by acting out the most disabling of patriarchal restrictions.

Let us not imagine that this disease is a counterforce to the directives of society. If the taboo endures, it is because the tabooed acts still have an attraction, they are tempting: tempting to the powerful male because any and all sexual gratification is held to be desirable. Tempting, again, to men and also a bit to women because it is a violation of rules, and just as in our grandparents' day, violating rules can be a sexual turn-on. Which is a comment on "sexual liberation" as it's understood today. We live in a world that tells us that it is enjoyable to break its own regulations; we assume that civilization, in Freud's words, must have its discontents. Which means that we're condemned to live in something worse than ambiguity—in muddle and confusion.

But let's not assume, on the other hand, that the way to get rid of muddle and confusion is by simplistic denial of their existence. The cure for this incest disease isn't to get rid of personal guilt and judge it by one's own positive or negative reactions. True, guilt can easily be laid on people, can be made to work as an effective social control, but there are some actions that are really worth feeling guilt over. I am not sure how many "sins" I would recognize in the world. Some would surely be defused by changed circumstances. But I can imagine none that is more irredeemably sinful than the betrayal, the exploitation, of the young by those who should care for them.

We do that every day, in public. We have elected an Administration committed to betraying the weak in the interests of the dominant. The disease of the family we call incest is not self-engendered within the family; it is a contagion caught from the surrounding social environment. The exploiters, the betrayers, are themselves sick, victims too. But you don't cure ills by forgiveness of others any more than you cure your own ills by denying guilt for their consequences and justifying relationships on the basis of personal pleasure alone. Circumstances themselves have to be changed. This women's revolution knows that, has undertaken this task in many ways. Rethinking family roles is infinitely more difficult than changing the rules of the work place, but if we really want to strengthen families and preserve them as secure places for growth and emotional learning, we are going to have to think our way toward equality, toward respect, and toward the ability to refuse to act out the exploitation of the weak that society makes all too easy for the powerful.

Who Is Sylvia?
On the Loss of
Sexual Paradigms

WHEN THOMAS KUHN, whose work on *The Structure of Scientific Revolutions* gave the word *paradigm* a new currency, was taken to task for employing the term ambiguously, he undertook to rethink its usage. In a postscript to a new edition of his book, he sorted out four major connotations of the term. They can serve equally well as guidelines to the present inquiry. To wit:

As an overall descriptive equivalent of *paradigm* Kuhn chose the phrase "a disciplinary matrix." One component he labeled "symbolic generalizations." These offer a basis for communication and shared judgment. To analogize, a society expects that in normal times sexual relations will follow some pattern or patterns that may differ individually but will fit comprehensibly into the accepted structure of behavior.

Kuhn's second component is a shared commitment to known beliefs that provide a source of "preferred or permissible analogies and metaphors. By doing so, they help to determine what will be accepted as an explanation" of the puzzles that the physical world sets the scientist. Emotional relationships are puzzling too. Privately, sexual paradigms allow an individual to explain to her- or himself the attitudes and conduct of the beloved. Publicly, they lay down the gender attributes that define masculinity and femininity.

Third on Kuhn's list are shared values. These assign weight and priority to the agreed-on beliefs that underlie scientific speculation and communication. We can extend this process of discrimination to ask how well sexual paradigms fit other standards of social behavior or agree with the sort of identity structure that is reckoned to be normal in any particular context of life. Are they part of a relatively seamless web of cultural connections and directives, or do they force contradictions upon one's sense of self? Do they encourage active engagement with the world around, or are they binding and limiting?

Kuhn's fourth element in the disciplinary matrix brings us back to the adjective, for it is the paradigm as "exemplar." These he describes as "the concrete problem-solutions that students encounter from the start of their scientific education," practical illustrations of theory, such as "the inclined plane, the conical pendulum, and Keplerian orbits." Sexual paradigms are learned in part from the anonymous pressure of prescriptive social mythology, but of course they are also taught intentionally. Exemplars of good, proper behavior and the rewards that it brings, plus horrible examples of disastrous impropriety, have been rehearsed to more or less patient listeners from the time that time began. The very fact that so few exemplars of female sexuality are now dinned into the ears of young girls is clear proof that old paradigms are losing their vitality.[1] One more text from the gospel according to Kuhn. Paradigms fade when their usefulness diminishes. An obsolescent disciplinary matrix not only stops answering questions adequately, it also ceases to generate good new ones. Meanwhile, accumulated data that do not fit easily into old theoretical patterns pile up. These amorphous observations can be assimilated only with difficulty, forcing makeshift, patchwork additions to and emendations of orthodox theory, as if the scientific mind had fallen back to the primitive level of "bricolage," à la Lévi-Strauss.[2] Things fall apart, and if the center holds, it is only because of outside pressure. No longer does this disciplinary matrix find its purpose to be coping efficiently with everyday events in the world of reality. Paradigms cease to be recipes for managing processes and getting on comfortably with one's life. Instead they are preached as ideals to which a life should be dedicated.

Female sexuality, I think, has always been used by society as a sort of glue to hold structures together; we shall come to this. Attempts are still made to enlist its aid in preserving order within family and social relationships, but more and more they take on the air of desperate bricolage. The power of sexuality is being invoked in semimagical fashion, to support outworn paradigms that no longer explain and predict events in the world. The salt has lost its savor, the glue its glueyness.

So much for the word. It is time now to consider its use in the

---

1. Thomas Kuhn, *The Structure of Scientific Revolutions*, 2d ed. (Chicago: University of Chicago Press, 1970), pp. 181–87, passim.
2. Ibid., pp. 82–83.

context of sexuality. What is it exactly that we are losing as our images of femaleness shift? What are the exemplars that our culture's definitions of women's sexuality have presented to the young? Western society has long offered two pictures of woman as sexual being. They are not simply contradictory; they have existed in a balanced polarity of good and bad, sacred and profane. In one the female symbolizes chastity; in the other she embodies insatiate, nymphomaniac greed: Pasiphaë, Lilith, woman as whore. In Christian legend, she is Eve the temptress, eternally confronting Mary, virgin and mother.

This bipolar split is in itself evidence of the external origin of our paradigms of female sexuality. There is no central core here, no kernel of feeling from which puzzled emotions could have diverged to become opponents in confrontation with each other. Eve and Mary are products of divided minds, but they are minds divided by masculine emotions at work in a male-dominated society. So, in Kuhn's terms, the shared beliefs and values expressed in our paradigms of female sexuality are not, in fact, shared fully by the women who have had to take them as models. They do not grow out of the interior emotional reality of the female self. Because they are learned as a means of surviving from the surrounding context of life (or have thus been learned in the past) and are also taught as exemplars, they are of course incorporated into the personality in varying degrees. But coming out of alien understanding as they do, they are never really satisfactory even when they seem to be accepted and absorbed quite thoroughly. This lack of "fit" is surely one source of the sense of "otherness" that Simone de Beauvoir elucidated a generation ago.

All this is well known. The new disciplinary matrix of feminist studies has begun to generate a shared critique of patriarchal thinking. "Otherness," in its social aspect, sets women apart from mainstream ideals and norms of behavior. Feminine goals are deviant even when they are prescribed by the social structure, for they always differ from the true peaks of aspiration, which are reserved for males. Males who forswear such ambitions are unmanly, that is, they act like women. Women who try to attain these normally desirable ends, however, exhibit unfitness for their proper role. It is thus impossible to be both a normal woman and a normal human being, surely a catch much older than "catch-22"—catch number one, perhaps.

Beyond its direct social stigmata, the impact of otherness is psychologically disorienting. Intuitive perceptions of the world cannot be trusted if they are made by an interior self that has learned that it is not considered primary. Its judgments always have to be adapted to those based on male experience. Female a priori knowledge, then, cannot be taken as valid by the female self who is required by the laws of otherness to live as a displaced person not only in man's world but also within herself. As a result, her primary impulses to action are always caught and held on a frustrating brink. Even if the delay is only momentary, the need to overcome it by an act of conscious will changes the quality of female activity by robbing it of the full, playful freedom of spontaneity.

We cannot evaluate the effect this hesitation has had on female sexuality until we have gotten rid of it. We must assume that the impact of otherness on women varies with the weight and extent of the patriarchal belief system in any society. No doubt where a fair area of free action falls within woman's place, the effect is less inhibiting. In Western society, however, we also have to consider the result of a polar split in our vision of female sexuality. Eve and Mary have presided over our existence, offering that meanest of options, an either/or choice. This adds an element of ambiguity to a female identity that already feels itself a bit untrustworthy. Eve is always at work to undermine Mary's dedication to good. Mary is never going to let Eve enjoy herself without waking up to a guilty morning after. The practical effect is to weaken still further the capacity of any woman to act in her own interest: She cannot be sure what her interest is. Eve cannot trust Mary, nor Mary Eve. A state of civil war becomes endemic.

The disciplinary matrix of feminist studies allows us to understand that this war is not a product of female being but of male psychology reacting to male experience of the world. The nineteenth century offers a fully developed exemplar from the great Victorian era of sadistic sentimentality. Having spawned its tens of thousands of prostitutes (Walter Houghton estimates 50,000 "known to the police" in England and Scotland in 1850),[3] the Victorian age simultaneously created a compensatory legend of "the angel in the house," whose dazzling purity was able to counter the lure of license in the dark streets. Love, married love, was exalted as a means of saving men from "the sensuality that threatens society." It was seen as "a great ethical force which can protect men from lust and even strengthen and purify the moral will."[4] The angel was a kind of moral muse, whose duty was

---

3. Walter Houghton, *The Victorian Frame of Mind, 1830–1870* (New Haven, Conn.: Yale University Press, 1957), p. 366.
4. Ibid., p. 375.

to inspire male virtue. Were she to try to act independently, she would mistake her proper role.

We direct our attention today to the negative side of the paradigm, to the condemnation of freedom of action and choice that acting the part of moral muse laid on our foremothers. But we would be wrong to underestimate the positive attraction exerted by the angel in her own time, a time when the either/or choice between Eve and Mary was threatening and extreme. Mary was not only the guardian of a place supported by Victorian social values, she offered the only accepted role in which sexual activity could be undertaken by women at all. In addition, the legitimate outlet that the role offered to male sexuality could (it did not always) make her the object of devotion. Virginia Woolf remembered her own struggle to slay the angel, and well she might. Before her parents married, Leslie Stephen wrote to Julia Duckworth in true Victorian exaltation: "You must let me tell you that I do and always shall feel for you something which I can only call reverence as well as love. . . . You see, I have not got any saints and you must not be angry if I put you in the place where my saints ought to be."[5]

What is being romanticized—or rather sentimentalized—here is a male vision of the ideal mother. There is a mythic attraction to the figure. She is imagined as a moral force that works by inspiration, persuasion, charm, enchantment but never by threat or force. Male fears of the powerful first parent, who later turns out to be female, are undergoing denial by sublimation. The angel in the house is exalted in order to give her sufficient power to order her children (including her husband, whose original identity was learned as a son) in the way they should go. Her duty is to socialize them to norms of affection and restraint, natural for daughters, difficult for sons, who require repeated "exemplars." It becomes an easier task, however, if some supernatural agent can be invoked. If one can just believe in magic, morality becomes easy, the superego is a source of pleasure, and we choose to do what we must do. It is a vulgarized, Bowdlerized version of Dante's vision: Mary, Queen of Heaven, ruling a happy family of six sisters and seven brothers, enshrined in a plush and mahogany parlor. She must stay there, however. The Mary half of the feminine image is invested with moral authority at the cost of giving up any active intervention in the world of events. The angel in the house must not leave the house unchaperoned.

---

5. Noel Annan, *Leslie Stephen* (Cambridge, Mass.: Harvard University Press, 1952), p. 75.

Is Mary wife or mother? She is both; hence the oedipal conflict. The Victorian view of "wife"—and let us not imagine that it has vanished—is of a domesticated mother. The duty of the angel in the house is to accept and sublimate the male sex drive by transforming it into procreation. She allows her husband to fulfill God's commandment to be fruitful and multiply. She will then raise her children according to the norms of male society, and in the process her sons will acquire the double vision of women to which the angel owes her existence. They will experience the classic fears invoked by the myth Freud formulated in the name of Oedipus, whose purpose is the structuring of the psyche into id, ego, and the internalized social-parental deterrent of superego. Meanwhile her husband, also once a son, has the opportunity to assuage his own early fears by the control, in maturity, of a tamed mother figure. If she can be contained within a mythic structure, playing out her family role of inspiration and muse but forced to limit her power to this sphere, his primal struggle and its accompanying guilt can be resolved where it began. Mother and wife are aspects of the same image of female sexuality. If they compete with each other in real life, it is for the same position of moral authority: the role of saint for those who have no saints but still feel the need for a domestic shrine.

The real opponent to Mary the pure mother figure is Eve. While Mary's ascendance both derives from and is limited by her long investment with moral authority, Eve's power arises in the invitation she offers to unlimited sexuality, that is, immoral authority. For Eve is a goddess too. Her representatives, the whores in the street, can be bought and the serving girl debauched. They yield to male demands and vanish. But Eve symbolizes the temptation to which men yield in seeking them out. In this aspect she is very clearly a projection of male desire. That is why she is dangerous to men, why she can gain the upper hand, catch True Thomas within the fairy ring and transport him to Elfland. She is a dream figure who commands the power of "primary process" feeling because she comes out of the internal realm where it rises. Her power can subvert society, and the superego too, for it is rooted in the unacceptable yearnings that antedate the oedipal drama lived out by children being socialized to patriarchy. To stay for a moment longer with the Victorian confrontation, turning away from the angel in the house and giving oneself to Eve invited damnation even for those who had no saints, damnation via a choice of intemperate pleasure over the challenges of achievement and position in social life.

During the deep Christian centuries it meant damnation in a more vivid sense, and so Eve's lure had to be offset and the perils of yielding to her spelled out by underlining the dangers inherent in female sexuality. Eve the temptress was pictured not only as impure but as filthy. Her needs were declared to be excessive and disgusting, thus sparing the pride of any man who might not be able to satisfy her flesh-and-blood surrogate. Beware of her! say the legends, and not only the legends. Henry Kraus, in *The Living Theatre of Medieval Art*, describes a sculptured relief over the door of a monk's cell in the Chartreuse-du-Val-de-Benediction near Avignon, "a warning against woman's bestiality, meant to rally the monk's resistance at faltering moments. . . . The subject . . . is wild and obscene, representing a recumbent woman in a scabrous position with a goat. 'The old hag is letting the goat do to her,' the concierge commented disgustedly."[6] And when Lady Alice Kyteler was tried for heresy in 1324 at Kilkenny in Ireland, the accusations included copulation with her private demon named Robin who "appeared sometimes in the guise of a cat, sometimes of a shaggy black dog, and sometimes in the guise of a Negro." Robin was, he said, one of the "poorer demons in Hell," but his influence persuaded Lady Alice and her friends to anathematize their husbands, or so said the charge. Copulation with demons (and Robin once appeared in triplicate as three Negroes "bearing iron rods in their hands")[7] thus carries the message that female sexuality stamps women as being not just out of control but inhuman in their desires, more demanding, less fastidious than men. It is not only rape that they really want, but rape by goats and cats and shaggy black dogs and three men carrying iron rods.

All these masculine visions of female sexuality, embodied in the paradigms we know, are attempts to manipulate woman's vision of herself. Historically the purpose has held firm while the image has been touched up to conform to contemporary reality. When the power of the Church was great, as in these instances from earlier stages of our culture, chastity was enforced by relating it to the sacred authority of the Mother of God, while the unchaste were condemned for consorting with demons. Protestant, bourgeois Victorian England found Mary a niche in the parlor as the angel in the house. At the same time a new element was added. The dogma of women's excessive sexuality

---

6. Henry Kraus, *The Living Theatre of Medieval Art* (Bloomington: Indiana University Press, 1967), p. 41.

7. Norman Cohn, *Europe's Inner Demons* (New York: Basic Books, 1975), pp. 199–200.

began to give way to a quite opposite view: women were, on the contrary, passionless, "less carnal and lustful than men." Nancy F. Cott's analysis of this reversal, in a recent issue of *Signs,* ties it to "the rise of evangelical religion between the 1790s and the 1830s." As women became a majority in the Protestant churches, and as the bourgeois revolution proceeded, moral authority was increasingly assigned to women. But this superiority needed a rationale. It was found in a conviction that the female sex was by nature modest and virtuous. "Passionlessness was on the other side of the coin which paid, so to speak, for women's admission to moral equality."[8]

Cott's views are convincing. The glueyness of women, it would seem, is being called on to promote order in society as an age of change begins. I suspect that the concept of female passionlessness found further support in the Victorian fascination with new, and frequently pseudo, scientific theories. Now the old idea of female chastity can be connected to physiology, and any deviation be declared not just immoral but abnormal. We see here how a shift in the rationale of a continuing social mythology enlists a novel causality as a means for sustaining a desired behavior pattern. As the threat of scientific challenge clouded simple religious belief, chastity acquired an up-to-date reason for being. So two centuries ago the Protestant churches, shaken by the Great Awakening, found female chastity and morality to be a valuable resource in their work. A century ago, it was still important enough to be shored up by some clever pseudoscientific bricolage.

Why, then, is that not the case today? We seem to be looking at a major change in the structure of our shared beliefs. How has this come about? The question lies at the heart of our current paradigm shift in female sexuality. Let me say at once that I do not believe it can be answered solely on psychological grounds. It is due, rather, to a remarkable alteration in the dynamics of our society. The male fears that produced our images of female sexual being cannot be dismissed or glossed over, but the male experience of life that shaped those fears has somehow been changed. Chastity in women is no longer important to individual men because it no longer serves a necessary social function. Either that function has ceased to be necessary, or it can be serviced by other means. We are not wrong to say that definitions of women's proper behavior are the product of masculine psychology,

---

8. Nancy F. Cott, "Passionlessness," *Signs: Journal of Women in Culture and Society* 4, no. 2 (Winter 1978): 227–28.

but we must add that male ideas come out of lived experience in the real world of events, even though they are shaped by mythic desires.

Historically speaking, the function of chastity, once great, has now declined sharply. Let us consider the glueyness of women, which in fact antedates history. The exchange of women among groups and individuals, wrote Lévi-Strauss, establishes basic kinship systems, which are elementary social structures. "Kinship systems, marriage rules, and descent groups constitute a coordinated whole, the function of which is to insure the permanence of the social group by means of intertwining consanguineous and affinal ties. They may be considered as the blueprint of a machine which 'pumps' women out of their consanguineous families to redistribute them in affinal groups, the result of this process being to create new consanguineous groups, and so on."[9] The matter of chastity enters the picture obliquely. Obviously the children of one woman form a kinship group whether they have the same father or not, and matrilineal descent is a feature of many social systems. Chastity became important only when society began to worry about legitimate male descent. That concern appears to be linked to the ownership of individual property, as Engels remarked a century ago; or, more specifically, to the inheritance of property or status, or rights to both, by children of one father, as opposed to clan or extended-family rights in the use of territory and prerogatives. The peaceful passage of inheritable property from father to son, from brother to brother, from uncle to nephew, demanded that the legitimacy of the heir be accepted within the social unit; and the chastity of the wife-mother thus became a prerequisite to maintenance of social order in a patrilineal descent system.

All this sounds very ancient and prehistorical. In fact, shifts in inheritance customs were taking place in Western Europe at the time that our own society was being formed, and their effects are easily traced. True, inheritance customs play something of the same role for medieval historians that kinship systems do for anthropologists, and the lay person had better walk warily among questions of partible versus impartible inheritance, preciput, the joining of conjugal property, and the like, just as with cross-cousin marriage and its rules. But certain general observations can be made. The exchange of women in order to form new families is now explicitly linked to the passage of property no matter what rules may guide the division or validate the entitlement to property. David Sabean, discussing "the ways in which

---

9. Claude Lévi-Strauss, *Structural Anthropology* (New York: Basic Books, 1963).

households regulate their holding of property and the passing of property to the next generation" in rural Western Europe in late medieval and early modern times, begins just as did Lévi-Strauss with the need "to insure the permanence of the social group by means of intertwining consanguineous and affinal ties." It is now inheritance of property that conveys permanence. "In this context (i.e., inheritance) establishing a new household is itself a fundamental aspect of the process. In passing wealth on to the next generation the parents ensure continuity of social arrangements and provide for their old age. Passing wealth on to the next generation must always be seen in the light of setting up new households or the establishing of new conjugal funds."[10]

Legitimate descent was particularly vital in the case of land. Goods and chattels, like the second-best bed that Shakespeare left to his wife, while the real estate went to a daughter, could be and were disposed of by will, at will; but the pattern of land inheritance was controlled by custom. Customs did indeed differ, and under the manorial system, minor variations could be sanctioned on payment of a fee to the lord in return for his consent.[11] But, though traditions could be modified to meet particular circumstances, they were the norms. They assumed—indeed, they validated—the existence of the legitimate heirs, whose peaceful right to take over property was unlikely to be challenged.

In addition, a good deal of property tended to be passed from older to younger generations while one or both parents were still living. Elders would hand over active operation and management of family land to an heir, who would in return (by custom and/or agreement) provide the former possessors with a living. Parents thus had a continuing stake in the legitimacy of the passage of property. Reinforcing their concern was that of the lord of the manor, who desired continuity of tenure and service among those who worked his land.

I bring in these mundane matters to illustrate the grounding in daily living of the patterns of female sexuality which Western society recognized and prescribed. Masculine psychology certainly elaborated and fantasized these patterns, and women's lives were indeed distorted by them. But the statics of social structure and the dynamics of social change both come out of customary reality. That is what we expect

---

10. David Sabean, "Aspects of Kinship Behavior and Property in Rural Western Europe before 1800," in *Family and Inheritance,* ed. Jack Goody, Joan Thirsk, and E. P. Thompson (Cambridge: Cambridge University Press, 1976), p. 103.

11. Eleanor Searle, "Merchet in Medieval England," *Past and Present* 82 (February 1979): 3–43, see esp. p. 7.

to put up with whether we like it or not. But when the old customs shift a bit, some of those who have been disadvantaged will try to improve their lot, seizing on opportunities offered by such changes. How far they can get depends on an underpinning of support in the world of events, and perceptions of that support can be slow in coming and, indeed, resisted. Socially speaking, accepted inheritance patterns are desirable precisely because they are accepted and do not demand time, money, and energy to enforce them. Shared beliefs and values will tend to keep them in place, for once a paradigm of governance has been established, it will not be changed by psychological divagations alone. Changes in paradigms become necessary, says Thomas Kuhn, only when existing rules fail to operate, when anomalies can no longer be evaded, when the real world of everyday experience challenges accepted causality.

The accepted causality enshrined in the customs that directed patterns of inheritance began to be challenged in medieval England by the extension of royal power. The king's law, his courts and their rulings, impinged on daily life and the "custom of the manor," and in so doing they offered an alternate system of causality. Some of the disadvantaged at once rushed to seize on these new opportunities. Among them were younger brothers, denied equal inheritance with the firstborn, who applied for writs of bastardy claiming that their elder siblings had been born or conceived prior to the rite of marriage.

These challenges clearly cast doubt on the chastity of the mother, but noninheriting younger sons seemed unconcerned about morality as long as a writ of bastardy against an older brother gave them title to the land in question. In the event, female purity was regarded as just a fulcrum on which the passage of property turned. Chastity, it appears, ties into the economic substratum of daily life by way of inheritance patterns. It is the glueyness of women, linking generations in the interest of the peaceful passage of property, that matters more than their morals or than filial respect. Lady Alice Kyteler did not face a charge of heresy because of spiritual outrage. Her stepsons and daughters objected to the disposition she made of the property that came to her from their several fathers, for, not content with demons, dogs, and Negroes, Lady Alice had married (and survived) four husbands.[12]

Our sexual paradigms were shaped by the daily existence of our ancestors as that experience filtered through the belief structure of the

---

12. Cohn, p. 200.

male power elite. But existence changes, and as it does, beliefs adjust themselves to what is becoming customary. In Western society, property can still be inherited. What has changed is the *importance* of inheriting it. Customary reality, in medieval Europe, did not include a cash economy. Today most of us can sell our labor for enough cash to keep ourselves in reasonable comfort; in the normal course of events, we live on the wages and salaries we earn, independent of inherited wealth and therefore indifferent to it. It is true that this normal course does not apply to everyone in our society. The fact of a self-perpetuating class of disadvantaged poor, an internal Third World, still shames us. But the existence and extent of such a class in the past was exactly the "normal course of events" that forced our ancestors to clutch so frantically at any chance to inherit the goods of this world. The landless and the rootless were a majority and likely to remain in that position, as were their children after them. In such a world the question of who had a legitimate right to inherit a claim on ownership worked out as meaning, who can expect to live with some barrier against the worst of hunger, disease, drudgery, and disaster? It was not only property that was inherited, it was the circumstances of life and, quite possibly, life itself.

Even when external disaster broke up inheritance patterns and offered a chance for the redistribution of land, few of the rootless were able to profit from the opportunity. Cicely Howell has undertaken a study of landholding in one English village, Kibworth Harcourt, over a stretch of four centuries, using court rolls and periodic lists of rentals. There was, she writes, a "remarkable continuity of tenure between 1280 [her starting point] and . . . 1340; everyone of the 1280 surnames is featured on the 1340 rental without exception." Only five new names were added over sixty years. Even this modest increase was remarkable for, Howell notes, "in other parts of England village populations were already in decline." Then in 1348–49 came the Black Death. Out of fifty-odd names on the rental rolls, forty-four died. And yet by the end of 1349, 80 percent of these holdings had passed within the accepted pattern to sons or brothers or nephews. It took another sixty years, during which the plague returned every decade or so, to bring about real changes, and the end result was not to broaden tenure but to narrow it. Smaller households each held more land. It would seem that the rich got richer, whatever happened to the poor.[13]

---

13. Cicely Howell, "Peasant Inheritance Customs in the Midlands, 1280–1700," in Goody et al., eds., p. 123.

My point is this: The chastity of women is an ideal enforced, not simply by a patriarchal social structure but also by a society in which legitimate inheritance of property is a matter of enormous economic importance. It is the latter factor whose significance has waned. Patriarchy is still with us, but the economic function of chastity is vanishing. A century ago, the linkage between financial comfort and inherited property was still strong enough to ensure that the paradigm of female sexual purity was kept in being as a guarantee that legitimate heirs would not find their claims disputed. When fifty years ago Virginia Woolf declared that, for independence, a woman needed an income of £500 a year on which to get on with her life and her work, she could not imagine that such a sum could be routinely earned in the marketplace and posited an inheritance from an aunt. Only in the recent past has earning capacity, even for women, risen to make wages or salary the chief component of income. Adding to the lessened significance of property, inheritance taxes have joined in from the other side to whittle away the value of family holdings. With it has gone a major reason for the emphasis our forefathers placed on the chastity of our foremothers. Thus a deepening shadow of unconcern has fallen across the image of Mary, for the female virtue that she symbolizes, the purity that guaranteed peaceful passage of male-held property from one generation to the next, has become of small account in our lives—so small, in fact, that curiously little resentment accompanies the loss of what was once a potent and influential paradigm.

That would seem to offer women much greater freedom to imagine a new paradigm, out of authentic female experience. I believe that such opportunities exist; but in working toward them, we have to take into account not only the fading ideal of the angel in the house but also the opposing image of Eve the temptress, insatiable, multiorgasmed, bound to no continuing relationships, at large in the male psyche as a threatening mythic figure, uncontrolled and inviting the loss of self-control and of command. Eve is still with us. Tricked out in polyester, her doll-sized simulacrum presents herself as the *Cosmopolitan* girl. Other diminished versions appear in popular novels, movies, and of course on television, Charlie's fallen angels. It would be pleasant to think that these superficial puppets could operate as a kind of killed vaccine that would immunize patriarchal society against the mythic terror of Eve and the revenge it invites, but I am afraid that is overly optimistic. Since Eve is the projection of masculine emotions onto the outside world, her influence is not easily affected. She is a figure of patriarchal myth, and only a drastic change in the world, comparable to that which dethroned her polar counterpart, can serve to keep a superficial image from growing into a dream ogress. Eve existed and endured in a balance with Mary, who limited her power. Now the balance has ended. Between Mary and Eve there was a polarity. Within Eve, there can exist only unresolved ambiguity, dread and desire in the same figure.

She is also more private, more emotional, and closer to the inner world of fantasy. Mary, pure mother and wife, served a significant social function, pumped out of her consanguineous group to form affinal ties with the family into which she was married. Her presence was public, legal, and an essential part of a system of kinship and governance. Eve, on the other hand, is subversive and disruptive to social man. She represents passion and forgetfulness of duty, place, and public obligation. She is the body, she is physical nature, she is the darkness where the proudly erect penis satisfies uncontrollable desire and collapses, "spent," in the vivid Victorian word. She is the fatal woman, and her legend is still alive, carried over from the Christian centuries with little change of feeling tone. It was she who seduced Adam, from whose body she had been taken, and so set in motion primal sin and the fall of man, with which it was punished. Not until Mary's son was sent to offer the hope of salvation could Eve's act be redressed.

These teachings shaped the sacred myths in which our Western culture took form. As the Mary myth dims, the Eve figure loses the opposing force from which were derived the social limits that controlled her attraction and her menace. What does this shift in the weight of our paradigms of sexuality mean for women? Is it good news or bad? Certainly Eve represents freedom, an explicit denial of the shackling lessons of chastity that forced us to reject the reality of our own feelings. Eve is undomesticated; the doll figures of the media are just attempts to draw a tamed version. She invites us to enjoy our own pleasure. Freedom, delight, wildness, a dionysian testing of edge experience—all this is alluring to those who were not permitted them in the past. With that attraction goes justified anger against a society that denied us autonomy and action. Women feel that change is "right," both personally and politically. We want to stretch ourselves to extremes, and we deeply want to overthrow the social structure and challenge the social myth that bound us to positions defined and enforced by others, for others. For us Eve stands not just as a trickster but as a heroine too, challenging the gods and disrupting propriety and social controls. Where Mary embodied the superego, Eve represents the force of id.

But that is not all the news there is. We must also take account, first of masculine myth and the weight it carries, and second of the fact that woman does not live by id alone. Instinctive revolt will not do away with patriarchy or create a human society based on other values. The strength of the Eve figure, in the world as it is, still carries its legendary meaning. In that legend, Eve introduced Adam to sexual pleasure, but in the course of doing so she made a fool of him and then brought down on his head the wrath of a righteous God. To the extent that the legend still persists in male imaginings, Eve stands as the source of trouble and the root of desire, and therefore as a cause of guilt. Should she not be punished for provoking sin and muddle-headedness and pain and humiliating need? And the pleasure she offers, is it not unlimited, and therefore excessive, and therefore dangerous? Can a man satisfy her? Somewhere on the edge of that last speculation lurks Robin the demon, a shaggy black dog, and three Negroes bearing iron rods. And for this too should she not be punished? For the fury and fear she provokes? In patriarchal myth Eve the temptress is guilty of inviting the very pornographic violence and sadism that punishes her, of forcing men to yield to the filth of their emotions. A patriarchal social system cannot accept her without seeking to offset the threat that she represents, a threat of dissolution, anarchy, and antisocial disorder. If Mary cannot balance her, more direct means will be sought.

Beyond this, and more important to women's own inner reality, is the fact that Eve is not our own creation. We find license for pleasure within this paradigm, but that cannot disguise the clear evidence that *our* pleasure is not primary there. In the Eve image of female sexuality there is no true sense of internal experience, no vision of a female self choosing, enjoying, directing, and controlling her own pleasure. Eve's sexuality is not related to other female interests and activities, it is not part of a complex individuality, it is most immediately the door to a loss of self, not by transcendence but by the destruction of coherence. Eve does not serve women, but patriarchy. The media representations of her image do not show us woman as sexual being but as sexual object. They are intended to teach us how to behave in a "sexy" new way not because that will be liberating or rewarding, or even just fun, but because with Mary gone, men are now free to forget about chastity.

Such a vulgar distortion of women's potential for joyous and free interaction in sex can be seen as another patchwork emendation of the old paradigms. It reverses the attribution of "passionlessness" with the same purpose in mind. Sexual activity is being offered as an up-to-date opiate of the female masses. It is designed to buttress old patterns of male dominance: Somewhere in the background of the *Cosmopolitan* girl there exists job continuity, at times elevated to the status of career. But her real status derives from her ability to attract males even though she must combine this with work for pay (the most important males, of course, being those who buy advertising space). A tamed Eve pleases men, a wild one frightens them, but in neither aspect does she serve the needs of women. The message she conveys is, Keep your sexual needs and pleasure at modest levels, where they will flatter your male partners. Passionate or passionless, you are still an object. Become something more and mythic terrors will rise like smoke around you.

This is not only divisive to a felt identity, it is extremely isolating. The Eve figure can never stand level with Adam. In her wild condition she is his nemesis; tamed she becomes a convenience. Needless to say, many heterosexual relationships grow past this dilemma into true human sharing. But to achieve that, the paradigm must be first denied and then overcome, and that is a barrier, even if it is one that affection- ate intimacy breaks down in daily life. In addition, Eve presides over a world in which sexual coupling between male and female stands as an isolated peak of pleasure; and affection is not a normal, expected accompaniment of intimacy, but something to be won. That not only devalues female/female relationships, it also devalues any bonds of warmth and affection that are not specifically sexual. The effect is to assign primary significance to a relationship in which a male is neces- sarily present and which he can control.

In the past, kin connections, local friendships, and shared experi- ence of place and labor were usually a large part of the human environ- ment in which people lived. Urbanization, geographic mobility, and job shifts now combine to make such connections matter for conscious effort. They do not happen by themselves. The female self is thus placed in a more precarious position than in earlier times. This is, of course, part of the decreasing glueyness of women represented by the Mary role, whose chastity legitimized male descent lines; Mary's di- minuendo is a psychological reflection of the loosening of social ties. The freedom we gain is accompanied by the loss of social support, and if we want the first we must prepare to cope with the second. Freedom to invent new roles does not just allow innovation, it demands it. The failure of old paradigms forces the search for the creation of new ones.

How are we to do that? As yet no specific answers are possible. We have not had time to live as free people in shared authenticity, though beginnings are being made. But we shall need time, not just to experiment but in which experience can accumulate and form the basis for judgment so that we shall be able to assess the value of our experiments. There is a process here that must be lived out—judgment of emotional values, the transfer of these values to the human environment, the growth of new sorts of connections that will inevitably affect the grounding of the self and bring about changed relationships developed among changed selves, with other human beings of various ages and sexes and conditions of life. Sexual connections are never only personal. They are always shaped and used by other social imperatives at the same time that they influence the form these imperatives take. The freedom we now feel for the creation of new paradigms of female sexuality is not total freedom. If it were great enough to allow us complete control over sexual relations, we should simply be inventing anew the kind of dominance that has crippled human beings of both sexes during the long reign of patriarchy.

In such circumstances the old paradigms can be used best as guidelines to what we do not want to do. We do not want to remake a Mary figure that has simply been updated to suit current male mythology. We do not want to reglue ourselves into a social structure that is still patriarchal. We do not want to accept the mothering function as central to our true identity, and we should certainly be wary of the attempts now being made to make us chief, if not sole, child raisers, attempts that in the fifties enjoyed a relative success. Mary was revived as nurse instead of legitimizer, with poor results all around, for the important task of raising the next generation is a social duty that cannot possibly be carried by one adult alone. Nor do we want to agree to current efforts to frighten us back into the domesticated version of the Mary role as supportive wife or live-in partner. The proliferation of novels and films featuring deserted husbands, aghast at having to manage personal lives, stunned with self-pity, has this as an end. We certainly do not want to find ourselves split in two between polar roles. Nor do we want to succumb to the lure of patriarchal myth that appears to honor female being but does no more than set up mirrors for projected images of male desires. The myth of matriarchy, in which female authority replaces male, is simply the flip side of one-sex dominance, and it is attractive in bad times to a male power elite that faces problems it cannot solve by its own old paradigms. The re-creation of mother goddesses would condemn us to a continuing displacement of self in favor of some version of the Mary role. And, while the freedom and daring that are part of the Eve image are surely needed in a new paradigm, in Eve they are pushed past intensity to excess.

We are indeed in a situation that differs from the realm of science where Kuhn's analysis of revolutionary process took place. His investigation is useful as regards the past, but he assumes that new paradigms will have begun to take shape as old ones lose their ability to explain relevant problems and suggest means for testing them. Independent scientists have a longer history than free women, it seems. We are not in a position where we have been able to imagine new structures of belief and behavior. We have to invent not only new paradigms but new selves, selves capable of working out the significant generalizations that will make our existence coherent and structure our purposes. It is not my task to consider the creation of new paradigms of female sexuality. But as the Mary image fades, like the smile of the Cheshire cat, it is clear that her loss can influence our vision of the future. The patriarchal grounding of the Eve figure marks her as dangerous, even though she can offer valuable strains of daring, of freedom, and of enjoyment; but she is insufficient for our needs. And yet we would do ourselves great harm if we were to try to cure this insufficiency by dreaming up a replacement for Mary. Any polarity is dangerous to creative thought. Thesis and antithesis claim to sum up the world and resolve our puzzles by merging into a synthesis, but what, we should ask, has got left out because it did not figure in either thesis or antithesis?

We do not know; or rather, we know some elements but surely not all, and we cannot yet be sure of relating them properly (functionally) to each other or even of weighing their importance sensibly. We need a period for self-analysis without pressure. That is rather unlikely, but we must try for it. It will take time to reach the deep layers of repressed and denied mind and feeling, and the shadow of ages of patriarchy still influences our perceptions and our standards. What we could use best would be a time for experiment and play in which alternatives could be tried out in a spirit of lighthearted joy and in which elements from other cultural traditions, newly available, would have a place. Unfortunately the emphasis that our male-oriented society places on sex as achievement or feat is not conducive to an atmosphere of affectionate play. It is easy enough to register a vote for alternatives and options, but not at all easy to assume that we shall have time and space to weigh and judge the value of these alternatives without being frozen into some of them before they have been sufficiently explored.

Let me say tentatively that I think our best chance of finding our way toward new paradigms of female sexuality would be to widen the range of personal connection, from which we draw the values we use in assessing interpersonal relations, beyond the strictly and narrowly sexual. For women, heterosexual coupling has been held to outweigh any other affection by far; even mother-child love has been seen darkly as crippling to children while it is still offered women as a valuable reward. Male friendship is taken seriously, that between women is regarded either as trivial or as abnormal by our social definitions; antilesbianism is certainly the popular anti-Semitism of our day. But taking lesbianism to be an instant cure for male sexual dominance seems to me dangerously reactive and therefore superficial. Can woman-to-woman affection be free, as yet, of the distortions forced on us by patriarchy? So much combat and contest has gone on in our experience of sex, and so much pain has resulted from it; so much denigration of women has been absorbed into our sense of ourselves, and yet so many of us, over time, have been able to approach reciprocal affectionate valuation with men; none of this experience can be ignored or denied or solved in one equation. Merely to reverse our old paradigms leaves us still bound to them.

The "casual" sex of today is much deplored, but it seems to me that if we could be *truly* casual about it—enjoying self and other, noting trauma, rejecting it, and choosing pleasure—we might be on the road to getting over both the binding chastity of Mary and the excesses of Eve. Then the female self, the ego-person who has never figured in past paradigms, might be able to find her way to a valid sexuality that would grow from herself and her own needs and urges.

What will she be like, this uncreated demiurge with "eyes at the back of [her] head," this diver into the wreck, this sleeping fury, this "Psyche, the butterfly out of the cocoon . . . whose attention is undivided . . . [whose] book is our book; written or unwritten"? Our poets are feeling and thinking ahead for us, but a new Eve will have to be tested in reality. Her myth will grow out of dailyness, finding there both the common experience and the deep significance that will shape itself into symbolic generalizations that express shared beliefs and values. Who is Sylvia, whose name carries an edge of wildness and a hint of unexplored memory? We do not know, but we will surely recognize her when she comes.

LITERATURE

WOMEN WRITERS were the first female colonists to settle and survive in the territory recognized by male authority as belonging to the fine arts. A lot of reasons for that: Language use is a common, popular craft as well as an art, and mothers are adept at using words flexibly and creatively with young children. Women, that is, can't be kept from knowing about succinct and telling communication. Then writing requires very little in the way of apparatus; lyric poets don't even have to be literate. True, work by pioneers or marginal creators is easily appropriated by others. "Anonymous was a woman," the old tag runs. But Anonymous is so deeply involved in communication and turns out such a bulk of it that not all of it can be taken over. In addition, her skill increases with practice. Women as child raisers and teachers become women as memorializers of life changes and life cycles and then as preservers of great events by way of legends and folktales. At the same time, in the dailyness of life, women function as purveyors of gossip, which illuminates great events and illustrates life cycles, gossip in which fiction finds its roots. Scheherazade left her shadow as teller of tales; Sappho left actual words and a dangerous reputation—one wonders if the latter was added as a deterrent. Perhaps labeling a great poet with disapproved sexuality was meant to frighten other female creators back into anonymity. Or is lesbianism in woman writers a special, gender-related form of the penalty of the artist, which Edmund Wilson explored in *The Wound and the Bow?* Of course as lesbianism loses its stigma, it is seen rather as a place on which a creator can stand in freedom from orthodox conventions of vision and speech, one of those peaks of marginality-to-an-established-society that provide a wider view. In any case, if much of what women have had to say has been masked and sibylline, so has the writing of other groups whose center lies outside traditional creeds and ideologies. It's easy to bury a nugget of gnomic truth in a swaddling of myth or apparent muddle, so that the meaning is there to be heard by those who speak one language of experience, and the muddle distracts those who are ignorant of it; witness thieves' jargon and canting slang.

That keeps channels of communication open for followers of Hermes Trismegistus (for example) or other alien deities, but it has the effect of excluding such texts from the major canon of any culture. Often such exclusion is not only assumed but desired. What a deviant group has to say could hardly expect a fair hearing from traditionalists and might, in fact, be so dangerous that any hearing must be avoided on pain of persecution for heresy. Private literatures have abounded in the past, leaning on secret books and shrouded in shimmering, misleading myth. The journey of women toward recognized person-hood—citizenship—out of the specialized place that Western civiliza-tion has provided really began when female writing turned away from reliance on private language and started to use the common diction and syntax of literature-as-written. True, as Virginia Woolf noted, literature-as-written employs a masculine style and will not attain humanity until women have worked its metal in our own fires. But a beginning was made when Anonymous dropped her cape and took off the mask of a male pen name.

Because the physical instruments of writing are so few and so simple—a little paper and some ink—the wall fencing in the realm of literature is low. Women had long kept accounts, daily records and diaries, and to write a novel instead of a journal was not a large change. The equipment was at hand and only the purpose had to shift, and that shift could be made inside one's own head. An aspirant painter, on the other hand, would have had to lay claim to canvas, paints and space, a room with a north light and a door that could be shut on the children who would otherwise surely take over the palette themselves for smeary fun and games. Most of all she would have needed license to take on such an occupation, to go through an ap-prenticeship to a craft that was not, like language, a part of everyone's daily life, and to reserve the time to work at it steadily. Instrumental-ists need instruments and training, and in order to compose as well as to perform, they too need time and quiet. As for a woman aspiring to a block of marble and a studio in which to attack it frontally, God help her. Doubtless her inspiration produced some elegant pots.

But if women writers were the first practitioners and creators (rather than performers) in the arts, the path to authority has not been

easy. Determination, a change of purpose and product, don't guarantee that the result will be a work of art. Nor does "the dream of a
common language," to adapt Adrienne Rich's lovely phrase, make the
struggle with conventional masculine diction easy and inviting. It is
hard to give up the old vernacular that conveyed meaning by hiding
it. The effort to speak openly in a human language requires that such
a language be invented. That won't be a short process for it asks for
speakers to accept the expression of female experience as being "of
comparable worth" with that of men and to do it in the minutiae of
daily speech. We all know what a vein of heavy-handed satire has been
exploited—still is, in fact—over the use of Ms., or "person" instead
of "man," and so on. Hostility to change spurts up like a sour-smelling
geyser; this reaction is really worth studying at length by interested
linguists and psychologists for it evidently syphons off some underground pool of angry unease. Nonetheless, the first steps in a revaluation of women's writing and a concurrent change in its direction, a
broadening of its subject matter, have been taking place. Some major
work by women has of course been taken seriously through the years,
even by traditional standards of Western culture. But one of the
remarkable shifts of the last ten years has been a growing awareness
of women's writing as being not just occasionally important but as
representing a body of experience that is both coherent and valuable,
a women's literature.

When I finished the article included here that carries this title, in
the spring of 1977, two fine studies of women's writing had recently
appeared: *Literary Women* by Ellen Moers, in 1976, and *A Literature
of Their Own* by Elaine Showalter, in 1977. But two and a half years
before, when I began to search out American women writers publishing after 1945, there had been no guides to turn to at all. Since 1977
a cornucopia of feminist criticism has poured out. Novels, stories and
nonfiction by women authors that the male canon could not encompass and thus consigned to obscurity have been rediscovered. Major
monuments by women and men have been surveyed again, factoring
in the significance of what they said or neglected to say about the
presence or absence of women and about the gender orientation of the
philosophy embodied there, both on the surface and hidden. Particularly exciting is the freshness of feminist criticism and the vitality and
daring with which it casts up, and investigates, wide-ranging new
hypotheses. It's as if a sleeping Muse (Anonyma?) had suddenly
waked from centuries of slumber, stretched, lit a lamp and revealed

a room piled with treasure. Who could have imagined that such richness was there, unknown?

Well, to be mundane, all of us who were involved in any way in the renascence of women's writing during the seventies can imagine it. Of course the past achievements of women could not be utterly ignored, but the room that housed this material seemed at first glance to have little to show. There were old trunks in corners, magazines were stacked in dusty and toppling piles, a couple of open drawers were stuffed with manuscripts (mss. by Mss. you might say), but there was little order in this lumber room; no card catalogues, no neat bibliographies existed. One winter at the beginning of the seventies, when I found myself lecturing on college campuses about women's affairs with some regularity, I functioned as a carrier pigeon, conveying bibliographies used in a course on women's literature given at a college in the Northeast to an English professor in the South, and adding another picked up there to carry on to the Midwest. When I started to search the libraries for women's writing from 1945 on (the span I was charged to cover in the essay I'd agreed to do), I was reduced to hunting through weeks of Sunday book reviews for titles. Actually it was an interesting, even a revealing, quest. The number of books by women deemed worthy of praise or even notice that were not fiction, poetry or biographies of other women (plus autobiography) could be counted on the fingers of one hand in almost every year. Women wrote, yes, but the material allowed for this enterprise was still very much the "domestic sphere"—emotional life, family concerns, personal morality. Large-scale social matters had to be translated into their secondary effects in personal relationships if they were to be discussed by women writers; I should know, that's what I did myself—though at least the social and political context was always present and influential.

I wonder now, looking back, whether this emphasis on the personal was seen, interpreted, as giving women's writing a kind of timelessness, an existence outside of history. I suspect this is the case. As a result, women's work could all be bundled up together. It did not have a progression, it did not have a causality. It did not have an inner drive. (It did have, of course. I am simply describing the perception of it by the critical establishment that began by seeing it as occasional and peripheral to the masculine progression.) And so it could be carted off to that neglected dusty room, adorned with a few steel engravings of recognized matriarchs: Mary Wollstonecraft was hung too high for the viewer to make out the features; George Sand had been taken down and stood in a corner, face to the wall; a color snapshot of Colette was tacked up by the door where it could quickly be moved outside to the corridor of popular literature.

Things are different now. There is no way that women's work will ever be crammed back into an obscure corner. The critical establishment hasn't found this out yet, but women know, and the establishment will either learn or be left behind.

In addition to several papers dealing with women's writing, I have included a few discussions of work by other members of the human race. Two of them stretch the time span bounding the rest of this collection back some years. Hobgoblin consistency protests, but I see these reviews as analogous with the search and analysis on the human condition, and human errors of understanding, which underlie other studies in the book. If I haven't added more, it's not a discriminatory decision but a desire to avoid straying. Those printed here touch on many of the same questions considered by women and central to women's writing. Nabokov, for example, delighted in talking across boundaries of language and of background and loved to wrap up truth in elegant tricks. He liked the game, but—more important—it was a way of saying new or odd things accurately. And he was a maker or finder of legends who wrote on the edge of one culture as he moved into another. He knew a lot about shifting identities, mirrors and doubles, all of them motifs in women's experience. My review of Norman Cohn's study of the medieval definition and exploitation of witchcraft, *Europe's Inner Demons,* has, I think, something timely to say about paranoia in a ruling oligarchy and intellectual elite, about structured, self-defensive victimization, and licensed persecution of the weak in the name of theocracy. It also argues against the lure of magic solutions to problems, both "their" solutions and "ours." The paper on "The Family in American Literature," given at a Smithsonian Institution conference on Kin and Community, both is and is not about women's experience. Or is the need to interpret that experience and confront the social meaning of women's existence always present in American literature? Has it, perhaps, shadowed the whole body of classic literature, presenting itself as an absence or a darkness, a seeming mystery that is really chosen self-mystification? Does the exclusion of women's experience from serious consideration in classic literature and philosophy (and it goes back to Plato at least), while the day-by-day existence of women can hardly be ignored, does this purposeful double-mindedness give rise to the greatest problems that literature and philosophy find it necessary to address? To classes, to castes, races and differences, to inner duality, to the impenetrability of "others," to conflict, loss, fear, and the needed, reciprocal hope of love and finding a world in which to live happily ever after, an eternity of grateful forgiveness and satisfied desire? Which reality a divided society must inevitably deny?

Women's Literature

THE FIRST CONCERN of anyone writing about women's literature must be to establish that it exists at all. A number of women who write would declare that they are writers who happen to be women and that the accident of their sex does not influence either the subject matter they treat or the forms they use. In the past "women's literature" has been a pejorative term, and its rejection by women writers today is a reaction against automatic disparagement of their work. Serious professionals in any field do not welcome assignment to a subcategory, out of the mainstream and yet measured by mainstream standards. If an entity that can be called women's literature exists, it will have to be defined in a way that is mindful of its authentic value as a creation with its own laws and essential identity, not as a dialect version of high culture.

Any literature, that is, must have a base. If there is a women's literature, it will derive from an area of experience, worthy of exploration, that is known pretty exclusively to women and largely overlooked by men or, at the best, described in terms of alien standards. Female patterns of living and dealing with the world have produced in women a point of view different from that of their brothers. This point of view will not be easily accessible to men because it is conceived by them as being either odd or unimportant, since the norms of our culture are based on masculine experience and adapted to male roles and behavior. Even when the literature of revolt attacks, or condemns, orthodoxy, it does so in a masculine voice, using male formulations to express ideas grounded in male experience. Significant areas for discussion and study are thus always perceived in masculine terms, the assumption being that truly important subject matter and truly important literary forms will be found in their purest state only in literature created by men or attuned to male norms. An unnoticed exclusion of female lives and female judgments results.

Literary production by women and women's literature are not, of course, coterminous. It is quite possible for women to write successfully, by masculine standards, just because these standards are omnipresent in our society and so are part of the cultural background of women as well as of men. Still, doing so demands an adjustment for women. In some fields, certainly, the substitution of other experience for one's own as a basis for literary creation must hamper the process. (Analogously, though on a smaller scale, homosexual writers have had to transmute their erotic experience into heterosexual terms.) In a much-quoted text, from *A Room of One's Own,* Virginia Woolf commented on difficulties of composition at a basic level:

> All the great [nineteenth-century] novelists like Thackeray and Dickens and Balzac have written a natural prose, swift but not slovenly, expressive but not precious, taking their own tint without ceasing to be common property. They have based it on the sentence that was current . . . at the beginning of the Nineteenth Century . . . It is a man's sentence; behind it one can see Johnson, Gibbon and the rest. It was a sentence that was unsuited for a woman's use.

This unsuitability, Woolf held, was owing to the fact that "the weight, the pace, the stride of a man's mind are too unlike her own for her to lift anything substantial from him successfully." This is untrue; women authors have of course learned much from the great male tradition. It is not, however, what the tradition has sought to teach them: They have been subjected, Woolf notes, to the "perpetual admonitions of the eternal pedagogue . . . now grumbling, now patronising, now domineering, now shocked, now angry, now avuncular." She supplies a few examples: "Women rarely possess men's healthy love of rhetoric . . . a strange lack in a sex which is in other things more primitive and materialistic." Again, "Female novelists should only aspire to excellence by courageously acknowledging the limitations of their sex." Two generations later this sort of condescension seldom surfaces so overtly, but the scholarly estimate of women's writing does not grant it full equality, for a glance at the canon of literary works judged as excellent and significant by today's critics reveals it as very largely masculine.

This may be a correct judgment. If that is the case, revaluation will not alter it; but works once deemed major do drop out of the mainstream or find themselves placed in new relationships. New genres appear, marginal at first, but some of them move toward the center, often gathering existing works to themselves as they go by a sort of gravitational force. Where individual writers used to appear, one can discern a new entity. This essay, then, attempts to discover what can be included in a field called women's literature if it is defined *not* as an adjunct to normal, masculine writing but as an equally significant report from another, equally significant, area of existence.

Various guidelines have been used. A most helpful one is supplied by T. S. Eliot in his discussion of a similar question, the identification of something called American literature. Eliot changed his mind about this matter. In 1924 (*Transatlantic Review,* January issue) he held that "there can only be one English literature . . . There cannot be British literature or American literature." Later however, in "American Literature and the American Language" (1953), he found himself able to observe "what has never, I think, been found before, two literatures in the same language." He went on to provide some identifying marks of a definable literature: "Strong local flavor combined with unconscious universality." Such a literature "comes to consciousness at the state at which any young writer must be aware of several generations of writers behind him, and amongst these generations, several writers generally acknowledged to be of the great."

It is possible to discern Eliot's criteria in the case of women's literature. For some generations women novelists and poets, following on an earlier tradition of diarists and memoirists, have drawn their material from the local experience of the female sex, as the writers of a native vernacular did in other times and places. Among these authors are some "generally acknowledged to be of the great." A sense of "unconscious universality" is perhaps less easily seen, but its locus lies in the steady growth of importance and centrality attached to women's activities, which, in turn, encourages women to take knowledge gained here as emblematic of common experience. It is not the specialness of women's lives that is being sought in the explorations undertaken by many contemporary writers. The intent is, rather, to enlarge our understanding of the human condition by adding to it what has been excluded in the past, namely, women's experience, which is now perceived as humanly, "universally" valuable. On this point we might recall Henry Adams's observation, in *The Education of Henry Adams,* that "the study of history is useful to the historian by teaching him his ignorance of women. The woman who is known only through a man is known wrong."

These analogies and suggestions must be pulled together into some sort of core definition of women's literature, preliminary though it may be. The women writers treated here, then, will be those who deal with women's experience from within; but clearly not all writing by women, about women, can be called women's literature. The touchstone used is the author's vision of the experience treated. Is this experience described and judged in terms that can be various and individual but that are inherently the product of women's lives, or is it judged by masculine principles and values? This system of evaluation may sound arbitrary; in fact, anyone mapping new territory must be arbitrary. In practice it is easy enough to sense the difference between a study of women that regards them and their activities from the standpoint of an objective, supposedly neutral, outsider and one that rejects the assumptions on which such neutrality is based as being false.

An advantage in this approach is that it gets rid of such "political" considerations as the conscious, stated views of any writer on the position of women today. I would (for example) reckon Jean Stafford as an author of women's literature while noting with respect her rejection of the tenets of the women's liberation movement. I would exclude Lillian Hellman's plays and Mary McCarthy's fiction because these writers base their interpretations of women's needs and desires on standards that are essentially masculine even if they are not conventionally so. In the same way, the literary criticism of Susan Sontag and the political thinking of Hannah Arendt use traditional criteria with great force but do not call on that special existence of women that feeds women's literature. The authors of this literature sense that women's lives run a different course from those of men, and they want to investigate the difference. Subliminally, at least, they know that one needs a different lens to see them clearly and a different semantic set to express them truly. The task seems worthwhile because it identifies unknown areas and seeks to relate them to the total human condition.

The effort to determine new values by which to judge any area of life is sometimes seen as a rejection of existing values, and by extension, of values per se. This need not be the case. It is not the idea of standards that is being questioned, but current limitations in orthodox standards. Imagine, if you will, that Western composers had been confined to writing music in a major key. What would happen when they suddenly discovered the minor? Not a rejection of major harmonies, but an extension of the range in which composition could take place.

The sources of women's literature stretch back in time, but the period from 1945 to the present is certainly that in which it has begun to come together as a coherent body. The impulse to create an identity, however, draws on a wide context that is not only literary but also historical. An authentic literature reflects actual life. It pulls events together into comprehensible processes and patterns, and the patterns reach back, for the question "Who am I?" implies another, "Where did I come from?" In the same way, women's literature finds useful clues to identify in psychology and the social sciences: Reports on behavior in the real world diminish the restrictive force and the misdirections of old ascribed images of femininity. A new literature is open to influences. It will try out ideas and images and ways of speaking, and its practitioners may write in several forms or graft one form onto another. It is characteristic of women's literature, then, to be open and rather fluid. Common female experience can all but obliterate national lines, so that European writers like Simone de Beauvoir, Virginia Woolf, and Doris Lessing seem generically related to contemporary American women's literature.

Another tendency is a concentration on lived experience, often presented confessionally—or, better, as a testament to "the way things are." Women poets report on bouts of madness and on suicide attempts. Men have written in this vein too but in rather a different emotional tone. There is more distance between the male poet-as-writer and the suffering human creature whose experience is being discussed; artistic control is stressed. Women poets of madness and suicide give an impression of being raped by life, drowning in an overwhelming sea of sensation, though they do not welcome this fate in self-pitying, masochistic fashion. They appear, rather, to make a choice—and a daring one—not to resist. They seem to be putting themselves at risk purposively, *in order* to penetrate to the heart of the mystery of being, as if this were one way to discover the origin and meaning of their lives. Powerlessness means something different for women; it has been a constant and profound part of their lives, not chosen but assigned.

For a woman to look at her life, she must look at powerlessness; she must, that is, choose decisively to confront what has been happening to her as a passive creature and try actively to understand what it means and has meant. Often she must choose to give up known means of control and the accepted logic of causality in search of the inner reality of her experience. If this is a choice of madness, it is a special kind of choice. The closest analogy to such a quest is the mythic or legendary journey to Hell of the hero of the epics, taken from the role of the shaman of primitive religion, who puts himself and everyday sanity at risk in search of the healing truth that lies behind accepted structures of belief. It is possible to see this kind of interior journey, which is very much part of contemporary women's literature, as a counterpart to the masculine drive to physical journeying, to "the road" of Kerouac and the Beats.

Very often these interior journeys turn up annals of victimization. These stories are confusingly familiar. They form the traditional matter of "women's literature" in the pejorative sense, where betrayed heroines abound. How does such present-day documentation of deception and suffering differ from the illegitimate Gothic descendants of nineteenth-century romances? Here again, standards of judgment are arbitrary. The depth of involvement of the writer cannot in itself extend her skill, but it can increase the daring with which she explores the territory of terror. Then, having chosen this area for study, she is prepared to judge it, not to accept its existence uncritically. Looking at a faded convention in a new way can revivify it. The trivialization of women's lives has been typified by the judgment that writing about them is trivial. Much of it has been, but if the same material is written about seriously, it yields a different result. Charlotte Brontë has been faulted for the soap-opera element of that mad woman in the attic who concludes *Jane Eyre* by setting the mansion afire and handing Mr. Rochester over to Jane. Jean Rhys, in *Wide Sargasso Sea* (1966), turned her into an unforgettable tragic figure. She is still "seduced and abandoned," in the conventional mode, but she is significant. A trivial form is being used to convey something important. Such a development is not unique, but it is always confusing to the critic, just as the use by serious writers of science fiction forms has been.

The form may in the end strangle the content, or squeeze it back toward triviality, but contemporary novels of victimization are too various and lively to suggest such a fate. Still, the close involvement of many women writers with their material seems to minimize their interest in form itself. The novelty in this work lies in a new vision of experience, not—or rarely—in its expression. The innovation most often seen is a mingling of fiction and autobiography. This is a dangerous combination in traditional work, but intensity of emotion and involvement holds it together more effectively than might be expected. In addition, the need for women to exchange information about their lives and thus to arrive at shared judgments and conclusions gives such reportage a particular interest in this period of growing awareness of identity.

These special characteristics of women's literature mean that orthodox standards of evaluation do not quite fit. Familiar material—the experience of powerlessness, betrayal and victimization—which was once presented to show how limited were the lives of women and how vulnerable is now being used for a quite different purpose, as notes from an underground. The fragile creatures who once lived there have decided to get up and leave, en masse; and as they do, they express some quite violent opinions about the experience. A great deal of what they have to say concentrates on mundane details, which they appear to find at least as important as metaphysical hypotheses. They are, moreover, personally involved with the material of their books and poems to the detriment of aesthetic distancing, as well as objectivity. Even Virginia Woolf was worried about the way that Charlotte Brontë's "indignation" at the narrowness of her own fate "deformed and twisted" her work and "interfered with the integrity of the woman novelist." Orthodox criticism would normally condemn the reworking of familiar, trivial material, the absence of serious reflection about abstract principles, and the failure to set one's work off from one's own emotions; and yet these books speak with great force to their audience. Is it not, then, the duty of the critic to try to see past the orthodox criteria to whatever new elements this writing brings to light? Perhaps in time women's literature will produce changes not only in literary forms of creation but in forms of criticism as well. After all, the Romantic revolt against the standards of the Classicists did something of the kind.

Any survey of contemporary women's literature will be somewhat subjective. As yet we have no standard canon and no accepted measures for judging this writing. Later, more refined, studies will certainly alter some of the views expressed here and add to the authors considered. This is not an apology but a necessary statement of fact, inviting the reader to disagree and to supplement the writers discussed. Changing social circumstances will also influence this literature more strongly than other fields because changes in the position of women and in the importance attached to their experience will produce shifts in point of view. In 1945, thus, America was at war, a war that was drawing to a close. Not surprisingly, the vision of woman projected in some contemporary writing was of a mother figure who might, by her "selfless love . . . inspire the leaders of nations to forget their own political ambitions, petty hatreds and selfish interests," and lead the world toward peace (quotation cited in Mary R. Beard, *Woman As Force in History,* 1946). The social questions that publishers felt to be of general interest dealt with returning war veterans. What happened to Rosie the Riveter when she went back to woman's place at home was of as little moment as what happened to the blacks who had moved from the rural South to the industrial cities of the North.

Predictably, the best-selling book of the year by a woman about women's experience was *The Egg and I* by Betty MacDonald (1945). It is a long, humorous dissertation on putting up with things, in this case life on a chicken farm with an inarticulate and self-centered husband; in short, a traditional study of female victimization that is deliberately stamped "Not to be taken seriously" by its humor. It is quite good humor: "According to Mother," writes MacDonald—the book is presented as a memoir—"if your husband wants to give up the banking business and polish agates for a living, let him. Help him with his agate polishing. Learn to know and to love agates (and incidentally to eat them.)" One may see this as an underground statement on the plight of women, distress made bearable by the laughter that declares it to be unimportant. Such an attitude is the ground base from which a serious and considered women's literature has had to detach itself.

Gertrude Stein's *Wars I Have Seen* (1945) is a very different study of powerlessness. It abstracts from the feminine situation (Stein recalls her life history in terms of wars she remembers) to that of a civilian population in occupied territory. Powerlessness invites boredom and lethargy: If one cannot change anything, one does not plan a future. It invites treachery and distrust. It produces a sense of unreality, when decisions are forced upon one. With distrust at large in the world, on what bases can judgments be taken? The feminine/civilian view begins to surface, contradicting an orthodoxy that no longer predicts events in a trustworthy way: "I have said so often between 1939 and 1943, I cannot understand why men have so little common sense why they cannot understand when there is no possibility of their winning that they will lose, why they cannot remember that two and two make four and no more." They "have nothing to do with the business of living," she adds, "because they believe what they are supposed to believe." In such a situation a tart contradiction to received ideas is welcome, as this from Alice B. Toklas in reply to some conventional statement about forgiving but not forgetting: "I cannot forgive," said Miss Toklas, "but I do forget." We might also note how effectively the tendency of women's literature to use banal, everyday events is demonstrated here. By reproducing these details Stein comments continually, though seldom explicitly, on the ways that war, repression and the abandonment of political common sense distort existence. *Wars I Have Seen* illustrates the positive force of women's literature at the opening of the postwar era, just as *The Egg and I* embodies the negative tradition of self-deprecation that this literature has been determined to overcome.

Two books of nonfiction from the immediate postwar period offer a much more explicit confrontation between positive and negative images of women. Mary Beard's *Woman As Force in History* appeared in 1946; *Modern Woman: The Lost Sex,* by Ferdinand Lundberg and Marynia Farnham, in 1947. Beard was anxious to disprove the idea that "women had been nothing or next to nothing in the long course of history" prior to the rise of feminism in the nineteenth century. Her data have been challenged in part by recent feminist historians, who believe that she overestimated the status and the activities of women in the Middle Ages and Renaissance. But her thesis was advanced at a time when the public estimate of the value of women's efforts, in spite of their record of wartime employment, could be expressed (in *Life* magazine, January 29, 1945) as "simply ridiculous." *Life*'s proposal for the reform of women was to draft them, in order that they could be taught responsibility by the men who would exercise authority over them. More respected figures avoided such discourteous suggestions but found it easy to overlook the contributions made by women and even, it might seem, their existence. Allan Nevins and Henry Steele Commager, for example, discussed the settlement of the American continent as if it had been effected by the male sex alone, while Christian Gauss of Princeton considered the possible future of civilization on a similar premise.

Beard's questioning of received historical tradition must itself submit to being questioned, but it points toward the re-examination of the past that is now so central to feminist work in the social sciences and the humanities.

The collaboration of Farnham and Lundberg, *Modern Woman: The Lost Sex,* embodies another trend in thinking about women that has produced some recent examples. Women are here seen as a problem, indeed, "as one of modern civilization's major unsolved problems ... on a par with ... crime, vice, poverty, epidemic disease, juvenile delinquency ... racial hatred, divorce, neurosis and even periodic unemployment." Not only that, because they live "in an emotional slum," they are themselves "principal transmitting media of disordered emotions" that affect others. Neurotic mothers create neurotic children.

Although (in the view of Farnham and Lundberg) history is largely responsible for the plight of these unfortunate women, they cannot be absolved of guilt because their own response has been destructive, not positive. They have listened too readily to the siren songs of the women's movement, learned to hate men while, at the same time, they seek to achieve maleness. A dizzyingly bitter attack on feminists—grim-faced and sadistic, they are moved by a deep, raging hostility that leads them to seek to castrate men and go back to primitive promiscuity and communal ownership—does not spare other women who may have shunned these carryings-on, but have "acted out their discontent in the home, with disastrous consequences to the rising generation." In addition, by "denying their femininity" the poor creatures have sentenced themselves to frigidity.

The diagnosis suggests the cure: "Women who experience sexual difficulties, with some exceptions [but we hear no more about these], are women who consciously or unconsciously reject the idea of motherhood." Let them, then, select a new goal, that of the Feminine Mother who "accepts herself fully as a woman [and] knows . . . she is dependent on a man. There is no fantasy in her mind about being an independent woman, a contradiction in terms." Once cured of neurosis, she "can tell, without reading books on child care, what to do for the children by waiting for them to indicate their need." Indeed, much of formal education should be returned to her, while spinsters should be barred "from having anything to do with the teaching of children on the ground of theoretical (usually real) emotional incompetence." At the same time, negative propaganda should direct women away from "male areas of exploit or authority—law, mathematics, physics, business, industry, and technology." With such measures taken, the nation may yet be spared the fate of ancient Rome.

It is worth dwelling on this intemperate treatise in order to make clear some of the popular assumptions about woman's role that were prevalent as our period opens. *Modern Woman: The Lost Sex* was widely read and discussed. The malice of its attack on women's natural aspirations is masked throughout by pietistic assertions that it supports true femininity, which is equated with passivity and subordination. Still relevant is the technique of argument that awakens self-doubt and guilt in the reader by suggesting that inevitable mischances or occasional disabilities are her own fault, thus promoting the fear of autonomous action and so reinforcing its thesis. Later volumes of feminist philosophy should be seen against a background of this kind of propaganda, which masquerades as analysis. Statements from the women's movement are often emotional and tendentious, but it is this manipulatory sermonizing that provokes such reaction. We should not imagine that it has ceased to exist.

The period under consideration is sharply divided by the rebirth of conscious feminism in the 1960s, a process that has had the general effect of shifting the view of women's intentions and accomplishments even among those who have reacted very little personally to its advent. It seems best, therefore, to treat the topic of this essay historically rather than simply by sorting out the work and careers of individual authors. The break is not complete. Distinguished women writers at work in the two decades following World War II did much to express the matrix of feeling and judgment from which sprang the renewed self-consciousness of women that is typical of the later sixties and seventies. Katherine Anne Porter, Eudora Welty, Christina Stead, Jean Stafford, Zora Neale Hurston, Caroline Gordon, Kay Boyle, and Hortense Calisher were all publishing fiction as the era opened. None of them, of course, was dealing consciously with feminist issues, but in their work can be found a steady, unromantic concentration on the immediate lived experience of women.

This was, in fact, the continuation of earlier trends; as T. S. Eliot suggested, a literature needs roots. Kate Chopin, Emily Dickinson, and Edith Wharton have supplied recent American women writers with a sense that they have indeed been preceded by some authors "generally acknowledged to be great" who wrote out of feminine experience. Though Dickinson's sensibility was confined, for its data, to the private world of women, it reached far beyond this in its expression. Chopin, long overlooked and reclaimed only recently by feminist critics, touched a note that has become increasingly significant when she described the heroine of *The Awakening* as a family prisoner. Not just her husband but "the children appeared before her like antagonists who had overcome her; and sought to drag her into the soul's slavery for the rest of her days." Edith Wharton, placing her women in society, still found a major theme in the limitations that society laid on them as prisoners of a slightly larger world. Willa Cather and Ellen Glasgow continued the serious exploration of women's lives, extending the range covered both socially and geographically. The contribution of women writers of the forties was a reinforcement and an enlargement of the realization that what women know and do and think, of and by themselves, is worth writing about.

Certainly moving and vital female figures are not absent from the work of men, but there they seem to serve different purposes. They create crises for male protagonists. They illustrate aspects of life in a symbolic fashion. They are instruments for social criticism. What distinguishes women's literature is that the everyday existence of women is being investigated for its own significant value. This examination of unexamined lives may well have been influenced by the proletarian novels of the thirties; but whereas these were laden with a political message, serious women writers of the forties and fifties were not trying to convey an explicit moral. The romantic love story does not vanish, but it becomes increasingly problematic. There is little suggestion that any couple lives happily forever after a wedding. Much more frequent is the assumption that couples do not. Indeed, some of the characters in these novels were already making statements that would be echoed in the later writing that reflects the conscious feminism of the sixties and seventies. As early as 1940, Christina Stead had already caught the festering, ingrowing fury of frustrated housebound women. *The Man Who Loved Children* precedes the period dealt with here, but it was reissued and read later as a forerunner in much the way that Kate Chopin's *The Awakening* has been, though to a lesser extent. Here is its heroine:

> Henny was one of those women who secretly sympathize with all women against all men; life was a rotten deal, with men holding all the aces . . . Against [her husband] the intuitions of step-mother and step-daughter came together and procreated, began to put on carnality . . . This creature that was forming against the gay-hearted, generous, eloquent goodfellow was bristly, foul, a hyena, hate of woman the house-jailed and child-chained against the keycarrier, childnamer, riothaver.

Later when Henny is thinking about her children, it is only in her sons that she can take pleasure: "About the girls she thought only of marriage, and about marriage she thought as an ignorant, dissatisfied, but helpless slave did of slavery."

Caroline Gordon, in *The Women on the Porch,* gives us a softer heroine, less brutal in her condemnation of marriage but far from content with it:

I was married young, [Catherine] thought. Maybe I've only begun to live now and it seemed to her, looking back, that her marriage had been only a long straining to live up to what her husband demanded of her. She recalled evenings when she had sat silent for hours while two men, or half a dozen, conducted a conversation of which only an occasional phrase was intelligible to her. It had always been like that. When she had the opportunity of making new friends—and she rarely had that opportunity nowadays—her first thought was not whether she liked the new acquaintances or whether they liked her but whether they would be acceptable to her husband. Even now, after fifteen years of married life, she could not tell what would bore him.

Zora Neale Hurston, in *Their Eyes Were Watching God* (1937), moved beyond personal introspection to generalize: "De white man throw down de load and tell de nigger man to pick it up. He pick it up because he have to, but he don't tote it. He hand it to his woman folks. De nigger woman is de mule uh de world so far as Ah can see."

Again and again in women's writing of this era we note, first, descriptions of the dependence of women on men; second, their anger at their situation and, at the same time, their acceptance of their lot. Rebellion is private. Sometimes, as with Katherine Anne Porter's heroines, it gives women inner strength. They endure their fate because they are capable of separating their inner selves from it sufficiently to judge it, as with the grandmother in *The Old Order* (1944). They acquiesce in what seem to them demands of necessity but hold back some part of themselves from complicity in the bargain. The condition of Jean Stafford's heroines is influenced by their age. Her tomboys enjoy their freedom; so do her domineering old women who have lived past the years when they are expected to submit to the traditional role of Happy-Wife-and-Motherdom. Young women fall in love, and their emotions push them toward the conventional (the only "normal") choice, though this is not all that happens to them, nor is it all that is possible. But the area outside the conventional role is bleak. Those who do not accept it must expect to experience varying forms of disaster, running from social disability to the death by fire of the heroine of *The Catherine Wheel* (1952). If happiness still goes with marriage, there is nothing automatic about it.

Eudora Welty's heroines are more likely to find happiness following on conventional marriage in the conventional way; but when they do, they either belong to an earlier period or they live in a time warp that casts back to an older system of life. The mistress of a large delta plantation is "happy" because she is so engaged in multifarious activities that she has no time to reflect on her emotional state. Those who live narrower lives in less affluent conditions cast doubt on the validity of the conventional role by their tendency toward the eccentric. There seems to be some connection between feminine contentedness and the preservation of the life-style of an earlier day.

Two other southern women writers go further in presenting characters whose oddity dissociates them from contemporary values and norms of behavior. In the work of Carson McCullers and Flannery O'Connor eccentricity is so general a state that it can no longer be seen as odd. Instead, these oddities merge to express a state of alienation that breaks through any gap in the accepted pattern of life. Another reality is being reported on: isolation, a frantic search for relatedness without any real knowledge of relatedness. McCullers still gives us innocence embodied in children and occasionally in adults who carry some stigma or handicap. O'Connor's people have moved further away from any settled structure of belief and behavior to live like weeds in a stony desert. Innocence has been distorted by ignorance and malice; but ignorance and malice are the result of a bad fit between the inner experience of life and the symbolic actions available to express it publicly.

The interest of southern writers of both sexes in eccentric characters corresponds to the social and economic circumstances of southern life at this time—"backward" in material matters and still shadowed by memories of defeat, occupation and powerlessness. An analogy can be drawn between these conditions and the normal subordination that has been the ordinary lot of women and that was becoming, increasingly, the subject of literature. It was natural for southern women writers to feel this connection. The idea of another sort of life, tangent to that of the mainstream but running its course according to different rules, is familiar to literature: Pastoral offers an example in which such a different life is idealized. It would seem that the life black people led might have presented itself for such use, as peasant life was used by the novelists of nineteenth-century Russia; and indeed, Faulkner did attempt to employ blacks as a means for commenting on the norms of white society. But black existence was less amenable to manipulation for aesthetic purposes than were the peasants of Tolstoy, Turgenev and Chekhov, because it possessed a structured "other" culture of its own that resisted the effort. Eccentrics and misfits, however, were merely individuals who could be exploited as examples critical of the standards of white middle-class society.

Flannery O'Connor and Carson McCullers, while in no way specifically feminist in their work, are critics not just of society but of its
premises. Thus they help to legitimize a fundamental challenge to
mainstream values and to orthodox roles, including gender roles.
They have moved further from the past than did Faulkner, for whom
the old myth of honor still colors the sky, still provides a contrast to
the dislocation and disorder of life in the present. For O'Connor and
McCullers, this order is not there at all, might never have existed. The
lens through which their books present a world to the reader is set to
a different focus from the expected. The distortion of view is expressed
through the disturbing characters who swim before our eyes—crazy
curios of old men and women, obsessed children, young people inap-
propriately in love or devoting their lives to impossible endeavors—
but this material could not be seen at all if not for the distortion
of the lens. Their writing authenticates the use of this skewed view,
just as Gertrude Stein's writing-as-speech-pattern put forward the
legitimacy of using repetitions and hesitations to get under the skin
of formal communication.

In poetry the forties and fifties sometimes seem to be reversing
expected gender roles, which assign the personal voice to women and
the abstract idea to men. Perhaps the attention to classic craftsman-
ship found in Marianne Moore, Elizabeth Bishop and Babette
Deutsch represents a reaction against the personal poetry of Edna St.
Vincent Millay and Elinor Wylie with its emphasis on romantic love
in a fairly familiar mode, which the previous decades had taken as
prototypically feminine. In any event, while the Beats plunged into
self-exploration, Moore created brilliant tesselated surfaces that seem
composed by utmost adult skill married to the intense ageless vision
of a child but that offer no guidelines to an interior world. These poets
hardly say "I," and it is rare for them to speak of particular experience
and its intimacies. Their poetry reinforced a growing acceptance of
serious writing by women into the critical canon, but it did not challenge the canon.

The experience of passion and attachment between men and
women does not disappear from the work of women poets in these
years any more than it does from fiction, but certain changes take
place. First, it is de-emphasized, becoming one among other themes.
Then it is abstracted and subjected to questioning. What does the
experience of passion mean for a woman? writers are asking. They find

it less and less possible to accept the traditional significance of romantic passion as a supreme and unique emotional event.

One way of dealing with these personal storms of feeling is to generalize them by sinking them into myth so that they may be identified as more than individual, as part of "what happens to women" typically and recurrently. Sometimes (as with the novelists) mythic symbols are introduced to reject traditional feminine virtues of gentleness and passivity in an oblique way. Louise Bogan puts the intenser forms of female experience into mythic figures under the names of Medusa or Cassandra or the Sleeping Fury, while still assuring us that this "wilderness" is not to be found in women—that is, "normal" women living ordinary lives. The split between life-as-woman and life-as-a-creator-of-literature is clearer in her work than in that of the novelists then writing, no doubt because the demands of poetry on the author are more intense and less easily diffused. Writers of fiction can turn a double awareness into different, disputing characters; poets need a single eye. In Bogan's work the most powerful emotion is found in poems that use myth or dream as mask: "Tears in Sleep" and "The Dream" can be added to the mythic figures used, as cited above. A woman's consciousness, it seems, must put on fabulous form before it can speak fully and openly. In some poems this pursuit of outward symbol illuminated by inner passion becomes so intense, its meaning knotted so tightly, that we receive the impact with a kind of magical force. Nothing is explained. The words are utterly simple and yet profoundly mysterious, falling on us like a spell. Who is it speaking in "The Crossed Apple"? Is she Eve, who offers temptation with fruit from her orchard, the "lovely apple" that can breed "wood for fires, leaves for shade, apples for sauce"? It is the product of a new cross, "a tree yet unbeholden," and thus it represents the promise of an unknown, unpredictable future. Certainly some power of enchantment sounds through the female voice!

> Eat it; and you will taste more than the fruit:
> The blossom, too,
> The sun, the air, the darkness at the root,
> The rain, the dew,
>
> The earth we come to, and the time we flee,
> The fire and the breast.
> I claim the white part, maiden, that's for me.
> You take the rest.

Something is being said here that we feel with an intimate frisson, but it is masked behind the conscious verbal form like a dream message behind the dream work. A female voice is speaking, but to whom? Is it to a lover or, perhaps, to an apprentice sorceress whose turn it is to learn both to use and to hide her power at a time when committing the act of poetry is held to turn a woman into a fabulous monster since in humans the split between woman and poet remains unhealed?

The use of myth, archetype and dream by women poets may create new symbols, but it also revivifies the old ones. H.D. (Hilda Doolittle) seized on the apocalypse of destruction that overtook wartime London, where she was living, to probe the meaning of catastrophe as a recurrent event in human life. In the opening lines of "The Walls Do Not Fall" (1944, reissued in *Trilogy,* 1973) she is asking why humankind still survives although the flesh "was melted away, the heart burnt out," and "husk dismembered." Now that we have "passed the flame: we wonder / what saved us? what for?"

To answer her question she sieves through myth and history looking for instances of wholeness and continuity in dismemberment and fragmentation and finding symbols of rebirth that are archaic but protean. These she reproduces with the force and intimacy of dream. Indeed, she incorporates dreams in her work. They are bits of experience that our minds have tied up into symbols for our private selves, ordinary everyday touches of myth:

> this is no rune or riddle,
> it is happening everywhere. -

Among these dreams is an explicit figure of the New Eve, seen first in terms of the past, as coming to "retrieve what she lost the race," but then discovered to partake of the nature of Demiurge, genetrix of a new future; a vision found again by later women writers. This Eve will bring with her a book not "of the ancient wisdom" but containing "the blank pages / of the unwritten volume of the new." She can no longer be seen imprisoned "in a cave / like a Sibyl"; she is instead "Psyche, the butterfly / out of the cocoon." ("Tribute to the Angels," 1945; reprinted in *Trilogy*)

At the opening of our period Muriel Rukeyser is already demanding self-determination in "Beast in View":

> I want to speak in my voice!
> I want to speak in my real voice!

But the images of women that exist in men's eyes, and have been accepted as limiting definitions, cannot be ignored; they can only be transcended. In "Wreath of Women" (from *Beast in View,* 1944), she explores the process as it takes place among the "women in my time," for whom "Choice is [the] image; they / Choose the myth they obey," a myth that had once seemed to limit choice to "Whores, artists, saints and wives." The best that could be hoped for was some composite life, whose diversity might at least give the spirit some inward, motive, vitality, but whose task was always "to give / Weakness its reasons / And strength its reassurance." Each of us, and the poet too, have taken gifts of life, grown in the narrow gardens where these women have had to live. To honor these gifts is to see clearly the choice they now offer: to accept the past of "interminable girlhood," or to venture on "the free pain and terror" of life truly imagined and lived in full.

The enlarged possibilities of life are reflected in a loosening of the rhyme scheme as Rukeyser looks toward a future where reconciliation of the self with the undertaking of a vocation is finally feasible. Even so, it has not happened yet and the landscape retains a tinge of the fabulous, a dream scene where our gaze finds:

> Three naked women saying Yes
> Among the calling lakes, the silver trees,
> The bird-calling and the fallen grass,
> The wood-shadow and the water-shadow.

The use of myth to express the condition of women is ambiguous, incorporating both the image that has been imposed from without and the aspirations that stir within. As feminist awareness dawns and grows, myth and fable are more and more intertwined with the everydayness of women's lives, which is now coming to symbolize a connection to reality instead of the triviality of their existence. In the title poem of her book *With Eyes at the Back of Our Heads* (1959), Denise Levertov writes of a mountain "not obstructed with woods but laced / here and there with feathery groves." Before we can reach it, however, we must find our way through "a facade / that perhaps has no house back of it" and where in any case the doors "are too narrow, and one is set too high / with no doorsill." What is to be done, faced with this mean entrance to a desired future? Instead of accepting a distorted facade as a barrier, one remakes it:

> The architect sees
> the imperfect proposition and
> turns eagerly to the knitter.
> Set it to rights!
> The knitter begins to knit.

Fairy tale or parable, the passage through the distorted "house" of the present is made possible by means of an ordinary female skill, the knitting that corrects proportions at the behest of the architect-professional.

A movement toward common speech that is yet charged with symbolic significance can be seen in the poetry of Adrienne Rich during the decade of the fifties. Like Rukeyser, who interpreted the few roles allowed women as condemning them to an "interminable girlhood," Rich sees masculine protectiveness turning them into spoiled children and chronic invalids. They are granted the "blight" of a "sinecure" in which their work is judged by degrading standards, so that "mere talent is enough for us— / glitter in fragments and rough drafts." By such condescending judgments, "we hear / our mediocrities overpraised . . . / every lapse forgiven." Things change, however, if masculine protection is refused. Then those "who cast too bold a shadow / or smash the world straight off " face another fate, "solitary confinement, / tear gas." Writing in 1960, Rich remarked wryly that there were "Few applicants for that honor."

But she too foresaw a future of change, mediated by a female creator even though

> she's long about her coming, who must be
> more merciless to herself than history.

At her advent, when she plunges "breasted and glancing" through the air, we shall see her "beautiful as any boy / or helicopter"

> poised, still coming,
> her fine blades making the air wince
> but her cargo
> no promise then:
> delivered
> palpable
> ours.

During these years the earliest instrument of women's writing, the journal, was being put to exhaustive use by Anaïs Nin. Though not published till the sixties and seventies, Nin's experiment in seeing the world through the network of her own nerves and emotions gives us invaluable news of how, in the thirties and later, a sensitive female consciousness perceived the messages that reached it from life. The use of oneself as a measuring stick leaves the writer open to charges of egocentrism and self-aggrandizement, and Nin, like Norman Mailer, has not been spared. Indeed, the reader sometimes feels that one more reported compliment on the author's unique sensibility from one more great man will be the last straw; but there is something else at work here that contradicts, or overrides, the impression of vanity or silliness that swims off Nin's pages at times. This is a commitment to an honest and to a full, complete revelation of lived experience in the conviction that this experience is not that of a special, treasured, rare female creature but that of someone whose quirks and faults and insights and joys and dislikes are of value because of what they show that is common to other human beings. Like Whitman, Nin is not afraid of contradicting or making a fool of herself, and as a result we get from her fresh, salty tides from a wide sea, even if rubbish sometimes floats on the surface.

Other conventional volumes of memoirs by women of course appeared at this time, usually by those who had attained some degree of distinction in one field or another and whose lives could thus be seen as examples of success within society-as-it-is. But these chronicles all include some difficulties, and almost always they are those of women forced to choose between the accepted pattern of femininity and whatever it is that brings them to success. Most widely read was Eleanor Roosevelt's simply written story of growing up an ugly duckling in a famous, if uneasy, family and of her life-long struggle to find a mode of life that accorded with her own standards and her own moral imperatives.

Two autobiographies by close contemporaries of Eleanor Roosevelt may be cited to indicate the tensions inherent in the lives of successful women. In *Many a Good Crusade* Virginia Gildersleeve documented (with circumspection) the life of an early career woman in academia. Unrivaled administrative skills and single-minded dedication to her work established her as dean of Barnard College of Columbia University, one of the Seven Sister schools, a post she held for nearly forty years, retiring in 1945 to become the only woman on the American delegation to the San Francisco conference that set up the United Nations. The cresting of the first feminist wave was played out in the everyday events of Dean Gildersleeve's life. Very much part of the New York Establishment, she accomplished political feats that thwarted the conventions of the Establishment: The admission of women to Columbia's graduate professional schools is one that she notes with carefully repressed pleasure. In her life we see one aspect of the split between old roles and new realities.

Ellen Glasgow's very different story of the life of a highly success-ful woman writer appeared in the same year, 1954. *The Woman Within,* being a posthumous work, could afford to be more intimate and revealing, though, even so, names of the men closest to Glasgow are suppressed. Here, the emotional crises almost overwhelm the liter-ary success that Glasgow enjoyed. This is the account of a desperate, indeed an unrelenting, struggle with the context of life, outwardly pleasant and inwardly murderous. She was the ninth of ten children, with a patriarch worthy of Roman antiquity for a father, and her every effort to reach autonomy required the courage to attack, not simply the stamina to endure. "Looking back on my life," she wrote (and it was a life marked by milestones of tragedy), "I can see that a solitary pattern has run through it from earliest childhood. Always I have had to learn for myself, from within . . . To teach oneself is to be forced to learn twice." The family romance that she lived out in an old-fashioned extended household was a Senecan tragedy, where death and desertion became commonplace. She and her sister, she records,

> lived and breathed and moved for months at a time in the atmosphere of despair. The very bread we ate tasted of hopelessness . . . And then, in the midst of it all . . . I was seized . . . by a consuming desire to find out things for myself, to know the true from the false . . . I flung myself on knowledge as a thirsty man might fling himself on a desert spring. I read everything in our library . . . I was devoured by this hunger . . . to discover some meaning, some underlying reason for the mystery and pain of the world. [She was only in her teens but] I had ceased to be a child . . . I had entered the long solitude that stretches on beyond the vanishing point in the distance.

This stoic determination to outlive tragedy—and the catastrophes that befell her included the early death of her mother, of her favorite brother, of the brother-in-law who had become a friend and mentor, of the lover she could not marry, plus the advent of deafness that increasingly cut her off from the world—was not unique to her in her time. But of all her generation of writers—and it included Colette and Willa Cather as almost exact contemporaries as well as Virginia Woolf, eight years younger—Glasgow speaks most forcefully of the saving grace to be found in work, work as a continuing, demanding presence that bestows an identity on an individual even while it stretches her past known limits. Women had certainly lived such lives from the beginning of time; now they were looking at them consciously.

Other kinds of nonfiction were being written beside the diaries and memoirs that have long been occupations of women. Lillian Smith took up the century-old concern among southern women for an end to black oppression, which she saw (like the Grimkes before her) as causing a self-inflicted distortion of white identity and moral ideals. In her novel *Strange Fruit* (a best-seller in 1944 as our era opens) and in the essays collected as *Killers of the Dream* (1949), she described the pain and the crippling of human relationships that our society has suffered as a cost of racial bigotry. Her condemnation of prejudice was based on a moral stand and did not challenge the social and economic structure of which discrimination was a part. In this way it was both limited and made acceptable by its fit with the old female image where womanly concern for others was felt to be proper. But in a period when few black voices could yet speak strongly for themselves, her work, insisting on the moral obligation to live out actively a commitment to equality, affirmed the old connection that women have felt between their own position and that of black people from the days of Abolition on.

This connection, very naturally, is more readily seen by women than by black writers, whose experience of oppression by all whites does not invite sympathy for those who are perceived as belonging to the oppressors, even if oppressed themselves. But as an element frequently found in women's literature, it extends the realization of one's own experience toward metaphoric universality. Older southern women writers, like Katherine Anne Porter, Eudora Welty and Caroline Gordon, could, on occasion, draw black characters who are far from being stereotypes. Though the everyday events of experience recorded in women's writing often reflect the traditional submission and outward humiliation of blacks as facts of the life then being lived, there is also evidence of respect for emotional qualities that are not the banalities of the black stereotype: endurance, stamina, wit and deep resources of strength and dignity.

We see examples in Eudora Welty's story "A Worn Path" (in

Selected Stories, 1954) a spare report on the arduous trip to town made by "an old woman with her head tied up in a rag" determined to get her grandson the medicine he needs but also to beg, borrow or steal the few coins that will buy him a toy, a trip made on the knife edge of physical strength. It is not just Granny's compassion but her cunning that Welty admires. In *The Women on the Porch* (1944) Caroline Gordon moves into the mind of Maria, a black cook, and establishes her commitment to grief for her son, jailed for two murders. She is able to make comprehensible the black woman's conviction that the crippling and distorting restrictions of the white world have produced black violence and will continue to do so. Black fury is seen (and it was a rare vision at the time) as the product of a society that maintained the logic of white law at the price of violence among its black subjects. Katherine Anne Porter describes the surfacing of true identity, hidden for a lifetime but still alive, in the old black woman Nannie, who insists, in her old age, on moving into a cabin of her own away from the white family she has raised and tended. To their astonishment "she was no more the faithful old servant, Nannie, a freed slave: she was an aged Bantu woman of independent means, sitting on the steps, breathing the free air."

Authentic black experience from within was coming from Gwendolyn Brooks in the forties and fifties, in poetry and in autobiographical fiction. It is interesting, and typical of a new literature, to note how we find a continuing loosening in Brooks's work of the elegant and rather formal style used at first, as if it were necessary to prove her mastery of Mandarin before she could feel free to use demotic language. This kind of breakthrough indicates not only the growing courage of the first substantial writers in a new field but also their sense of having an audience tuned to a new idiom. These writers discover that they are speaking not just *for* a people but *to* them. Brooks has emphasized her consciousness of race above sex, but the content and the feeling of her writing fall within the bounds of women's literature. We see black aspiration and women's use of everyday experience combined in part II of "The Womanhood" (in *Annie Allen,* 1949), a poem about her small son. In it she describes how "we both want joy of deep and unabiding things, / Like kicking over a chair or throwing blocks out of a window." But this transitory delight symbolizes something more: the courage to experiment, reach out and try new experience. The chair may fall with "a beautiful crash," but the child "has never been afraid to reach. / His lesions are legion. / But reaching is his rule."

* * *

Other women writers combine the experience of working-class backgrounds in ethnic and minority groups with that of growing up female. Tillie Olsen uses the minutiae of obscure lives to pose and reflect on major metaphysical questions. Such abstract questioning, as has been noted, is rare in women's writing of this period. When it occurs it is apt to be associated with the socialist or anarchist doctrines that were very much a part of working-class life among these immigrants. Olsen goes far beyond ideology, however. What meaning can be found in life at the end of life? she asks, in the prose of *Tell Me a Riddle* (1961), as Yeats asked in his poems of old age. Here these are questions put in a female voice, questions that value the high creeds of revolutionary self-sacrifice in terms of "one pound soupmeat, one soupbone . . . bread, day old" and "cheap thread." These cares are what the old woman remembers in her mortal agony, and they overwhelm memories of dedication to the movement, marriage, children born and laboriously raised. Love, anger, frustration, hope, the fellowship that endured poverty—all fall away before the inescapable chores of living, relieved only by a sudden echo from music heard in childhood. To her husband the old woman becomes an astonishing, disturbing stranger:

> It seemed to him that for seventy years she had hidden a tape recorder, infinitely microscopic, within her, that it had coiled infinite mile on mile, trapping every song, every melody, every word read, heard and spoken—and that maliciously she was playing back only what said nothing of him, of the children, of their intimate life together.

He is right. What she hoped for was a patch of life of her own, completely to herself; and then death intervened.

The full weight of consciousness is present and expressed in the simple events of life for Olsen's women. "I stand here ironing," begins a woman in the story of this title (in "Tell Me a Riddle"), and weighing out the inescapable failure of her care for her child, raised without her father, passed to a neighbor in order that the mother could earn enough to keep them both, a little girl who had to be good and was; of whom too much was demanded. Reflection can find no cure, no solution, only note again how childhood loneliness was matched with adult anguish and balanced against what the other children needed, "that terrible balancing of hurts and needs I had to do . . . and did so badly, those earlier years." Awareness of what we owe each other and cannot give, of what humanity might become if love could be unrestricted, shapes this story, though "I will never total it all now," the mother tells herself. "My wisdom came too late . . . Let her be. So all that is in her will not bloom—but in how many does it? There is still enough left to live by. Only help her to believe—help make it so there is cause for her to believe that she is more than this dress on the ironing board, helpless before the iron."

Grace Paley's short stories come out of much the same background, but they are told with wild humor. It is not the humor of earlier women's writing, which served to trivialize the experience recorded, but a humor of attack and mockery. Life is absurd and Paley's women are caught in its irrational trickery, but they may well be less deceived about events and causation than the men who work so hard to fit these tricks into the patterns of received wisdom. These women are swinging into a future. Like Gwendolyn Brooks's little boy, they are "not afraid to reach." They are moving beyond victimization, acting out changes in ordinary relationships that underlie the conscious revaluation of women's experience that appears in the latter part of our period.

These observations of life, like the notations of eccentricity that appear in the work of Flannery O'Connor and Carson McCullers, differ from the eccentric symbols used by such male writers as Pynchon, Barth and Barthelme in being less willed and worked, more *objets trouvés,* odd pebbles turned up on the path of one's daily walk. Certainly as women writers begin to turn into feminist writers, a systematic criticism of the orthodox structure of ideas manifests itself. But it stems from, and often harks back to, the contradictory details of "what the woman lived," to use the title given to Louise Bogan's published letters. Like the diaries of Anaïs Nin, this and other collections of casual writing by women authors serve to validate for other women the commonality of their experience. Such validation is a central purpose of feminist writing, as it is for any national or ethnic literature in its first, formative stages. Those who are shaking off old standards of judgment need to compare what they have in common and so establish an essential indwelling identity, which will give coherence and vitality to the negative identity defined by differences from the past model that is in process of being replaced.

In the early sixties, two major nonfiction works illustrated the growing ability of women to criticize cogently the taken-for-granted approaches to methods of modernizing our society. Jane Jacobs's *The Death and Life of Great American Cities* (1961) attacked the mindless acceptance of "urban renewal," which destroyed old neighborhood patterns of life and networks of community support for families and individuals. In her view, a commitment to architectural design and essentially academic (therefore masculine) principles of development was winning out over the intimate knowledge of human interaction, which only those who lived by these interactions could value properly. Even more influential, Rachel Carson's *Silent Spring* (1962) attacked the suicidal use of technological methods for controlling the natural environment by pesticides, with little or no prevision of the results. Both books can be seen as examples of an extension into the public sector of the kind of care for individual human creatures that is traditionally assigned to women. Both testify to the dangers of downgrading "housekeeping," in these cases social and ecological housekeeping, in favor of uncontrolled experiment. In a strict sense these books may not be countable as "literature," but they evidence a growing breadth of mind among women writers as to the subject matter on which they felt themselves able to speak with serious weight. Thus they contributed to the increasing confidence that women were feeling in their capacity to judge not only their own lives but also the dynamics of social process. It is another step toward the "unconscious universality" that T. S. Eliot noted as a prerequisite to a true literature.

Betty Friedan's *The Feminine Mystique,* published in 1963, is the document that is most often taken to signal the appearance of a new wave of feminist self-consciousness. Friedan's book is important as a social statement rather than as a literary text; but its anger and its enthusiasm evoked a response from a widening circle of readers that has made it a classic of movement writing. Ten years before, the American edition of Simone de Beauvoir's *The Second Sex* had received praise from critics (some as unlikely as Philip Wylie) and had been widely read; it is still a source of intellectual stimulation, but it did not produce the public reaction that welcomed Friedan's examination of the frustrations plaguing American middle-class women. Readers of *The Feminine Mystique* found their own malaise tellingly described and identified as originating in a social context, not in private neurosis.

Previously, orthodox wisdom had been assuring them that happiness and fulfillment were to be found only in self-abnegation, nurturance of others, and the acceptance of a subordinate role, a doctrine put forward overtly in such works as *Modern Woman: The Lost Sex* but also implicit in much other writing, both serious and popular.

Talcott Parsons, for example, took it for granted, in his studies of the function of the family, that the most important choice of a woman's life—almost the only important choice—was her selection of a husband. Once married, she took her status in society from him, as she had previously done from her father. Independent action on the part of a woman was conceded to be possible but neither frequent nor significant enough to offset the influence exercised by the "male head-of-household." This assumption was now being challenged. Friedan's achievement was to assert convincingly that female reactions that had formerly been seen as "deviant" were, in fact, signs of normal resentment against disabling restrictions. For any woman, social permission to respect one's own opinions and rely on the validity of one's own perceptions was liberating, but surely for none more than for those who undertook creative work.

During the late sixties and, even more, the early seventies, feminist polemical writing began to proliferate. Much of it was ephemeral, but a considerable body of serious literature and valuable scholarship was accumulating. It is beyond the scope of this essay to consider the latter in any detail, but its purpose and its approach parallel that of women's literature and thereby provide scholarly support. Indeed, the underlying premises of what can and should be studied and taught in the humanities and social sciences have been altered as the women's movement extended the range of material deemed worthy of study. Historians, sociologists, anthropologists, psychologists, theologians, and students of comparative religion, critics, philosophers and theoreticians have found their disciplines linking themselves to form a new area of women's studies. Mary Daly, in *Beyond God the Father* (1973), explores the significance to Christian thought of the absence of a female principle. Jean Baker Miller (*Toward a New Psychology of Women,* 1976) and Dorothy Dinnerstein (*The Mermaid and the Minotaur,* 1976) discuss sociopsychological changes in family structures, both past and potential, and the profound impact on social values they are having and will have. Elizabeth Janeway in *Man's World, Woman's Place* (1971) and *Between Myth and Morning* (1974) has taken women's lives as a field in which the effect of shifts in social and cultural directives on behavior patterns can be observed. How does the experience of women reflect and respond to historical trends? How does it illustrate the process of psychological adjustment forced universally by major alterations in the context of life? Historical research into women's lives has enlarged and enriched the fund of information available to economic historians and demographers. The tendency in sociology and anthropology to concentrate on material dealing only with males and to base general conclusions on these observations has been to some extent countered by research that draws on feminine experience as well: Man the Hunter is now granted a partner in prehistory, Woman the Forager. Such activity, quite apart from the information it turns up, points to the increased importance attached to women's perceptions and judgments. It thus authenticates the trend, already noted in women's literature, to take seriously what women think and do. Since this has seldom been the case in the past, such authentication adds to women's confidence and enlarges the area of study or of literary endeavor that they feel is open to them. Thus recent polemical writing and continuing scholarly research have had direct and indirect effects that cannot be ignored on the range and the seriousness of women's writing.

Scholarship in the novel field of women's studies has of course added breadth to common knowledge, with the result that more of women's lives can be taken for literary material. In addition, the exaggeration typical of polemics has functioned in a positive fashion in this new area. To think or to say the unthinkable may be absurd or false in a period enjoying great homogeneity of style and culture; but when the "thinkable" becomes stale—or false to reality—exaggerated, angry questioning can initiate productive thought about alternatives. Thus when Kate Millett, with *Sexual Politics* (1970), and Germaine Greer, with *The Female Eunuch* (1971), set out to attack on a dozen fronts what they saw as outmoded patterns of patriarchal thought, they might be faulted here or there, but they were providing evidence that received ideas were ripe for rethinking. Polemical writers also showed up the irrational connections contained in accepted systems of thought about the sexes. Even when these radical attacks have little literary value in themselves, they act as manifestos that diminish the force of obsolescent assumptions attuned to an old system but becoming alien to the growing structure of thought that informs a new literature.

More closely related to enduring literary style than to exaggeration is an element widely present in feminist writing of the sixties and early seventies: the resort to immediate autobiographical experience, which is not, however, offered as merely individual. Rather, "what happened to me" is presented as a parable of what has happened, or may probably happen, to other women. Sometimes this reporting is fictionalized, but it does not detach itself entirely from the writer's impressions or from her didactic purpose. It does not aim at true fictional distancing but keeps a connection with fact and a handhold on personal emotion.

This intrusion of the "I" as both author and character is typical of any movement literature in its early stages, when a need to testify to newly discovered truths looms larger than aesthetic rules. We find it, during the early seventies, in *Combat in the Erogenous Zone* (1972), where Ingrid Bengis reports not only on her experience of male/female relations but also on what she has learned from them in a general, philosophic sense. We find it in the rather more conventional reportage (of high order) in Vivian Gornick's *In Search of Ali Mahmoud* (1973). Gornick's journey into Egyptian middle-class life was set off by the sensation, disturbing to a woman conscious of her Jewish background and its valued culture, that she and her Egyptian lover have a great deal in common. To discover what this is she undertakes a journey to his country and a visit to his family, which must at all times be checked against her own sensibility, so that her book gains value from both objective reporting and subjective feeling. Kate Millett's *Sexual Politics,* passionately felt but presented within a conventional scholarly frame, was followed by *Flying* (1974), an intimate report of the crises and interior tensions created by her unexpected rise to fame as a heroine of the women's movement. Such writing can be called confessional, but the guilt usually associated with that term is seldom present. The intention is, rather, to bear testimony to aspects of life that have been overlooked or misinterpreted.

The impulse to report on personal experience is clearest in the work of poets. The earlier use of mythic or fabulous figures does not disappear, but its purpose begins to shift. These figures cease to serve as a mask for profound feelings and become, instead, a setting-off place for an examination of ordinary experiences; or they are used as metaphors to identify the significance of an emotional event. Old symbols may be retained, but they are given a new content that grows out of daily existence. In *To See, To Take* (1970) Mona Van Duyn responds to Yeats's poem "Leda and the Swan" with two of her own, "Leda" and "Leda Reconsidered." Yeats makes the moment of union between god-bird and woman an epiphany of transcendence and terror, taking place outside imaginable life. Van Duyn, on the contrary, introduces the rest of life. In her "Leda" we are given a vision of Leda grown old, not so much rejecting as never having conceived the "men's stories (in which) her life ended with his loss." This Leda "was not, for such an

ending, abstract enough . . . She married a smaller man with a beaky
nose, / and melted away in the storm of everyday life."

But this picture did not exhaust the possibilities of the scene for
Van Duyn. In "Leda Reconsidered" she replaces it with that of a
woman who can anticipate the future and imagine the reality of others, even of the god:

> She had a little time to think
> as he stepped out of the water . . .
> She sat there in the sunshine . . .
> watching him come,
> trying to put herself
> in the place of the cob, and see
> what he saw . . .

To see what he saw, she looks at herself and finds a woman with
a sense of the context of life; indeed, one whose presence and emotional force influences the mythic encounter. She is an accepting participant who considers the meaning of what happens and chooses to be
chosen.

> She waited for him so quietly that
> he came on her quietly,
> almost with tenderness,
> not treading her.

Yeats's Leda is overcome:

> How can those terrified vague fingers push
> The feathered glory from her loosening thighs?

But Van Duyn's is present and conscious:

> Her hand moved into the dense plumes
> on his breast to touch
> the utter stranger.

In this recent poetry, myths are constantly transformed by the
content of everyday life that is poured into them. When Carolyn Kizer
declares herself to be "Hera, Hung from the Sky" (*Midnight Was My
Cry,* 1971) she is not masking emotion but illustrating it:

In an instant of power, poise—
Arrogant, flushed with his love,
Hypnotized by . . .
. . . the dream
That woman was great as man—
I threw myself to the skies
And the sky has cut me down
I have lost the war of the air:
Half-strangled in my hair,
I dangle, drowned in fire.

In "A Voice from the Roses" (*Halfway,* 1961), Maxine Kumin takes an old myth, that of Arachne, transformed into a spider by an angry Athene for her impudence in challenging the goddess to a contest of weaving, and uses it to illuminate the ambivalence of a mother-daughter relationship; but she can also, in "The Appointment" *(Halfway),* cast up a new anonymous symbol for some as yet unnamed disturbance: a wolf, "my wolf," who settles like a pet at her bed's foot to watch the night through,

> breathing so evenly
> I am almost deceived.

The nightmare-wolf, calmly in possession of his accustomed place, looming out of dream into daylight, increases further the uneasiness his presence causes because he arrives with no mythic identity, has slipped loose from any established order of myth or folktale. Similarly, Sylvia Plath's "Disquieting Muses" (*The Colossus and Other Poems,* 1962) gain no reassurance from bearing a familiar name. "Mother, mother," asks the poet,

> what illbred aunt
> Or what disfigured and unsightly
> Cousin did you so unwisely keep
> Unasked to my christening, that she
> Sent these ladies in her stead
> With heads like darning eggs to nod
> And nod and nod at foot and head
> And at the left side of my crib?

Like Levertov's knitter, setting things to rights with her needles,

Plath's muses with darning-egg heads translate us to a world of female perceptions and skills. Each illustrates the trend toward altering the effect of symbols by shifting their content and replacing stale references by others that are immediate and intimate.

Plath's poetry, and her life, were completed before the new feminist consciousness had begun to find expression, but her work has become a touchstone for the women's movement and is best considered in this context. She and Anne Sexton represent a poetic current that is central to the cultural identity of the first phase of the movement. Both women use personal material that is at once the stuff of daily life and the expression of despair and dislocation. The exhaustive exploration of this material should not be misunderstood as masochistic or narcissistic. Its readers do not find it so. They are not looking for Gothic horrors but, first, for reassurance that their own similar sensations have been shared and, second, that someone has faced them and struggled to understand them.

It is difficult for critic, as well as reader, to separate this literature from its experiential context. On purely critical grounds, one cannot judge this writing successfully without understanding that part of its impact comes from its intimacy and that this impact derives also from a shared moment in time. To say that this poetry deals with pain and frustration is not enough. One must add that it could not have been written at all, and this novelty is part of its force, unless a particular kind of pain and frustration *could now be perceived as ending.* The ability to look openly at humiliation and degradation and to testify to the profound emotional confusion that arises when the presence of these emotions is first brought to light depends on a sense that such a state need not continue. If there is no choice open but pain or numbness, the human creature will try to be numb and shield the pain with self-deprecatory laughter—as we have seen. Even when earlier writers of fiction expressed resentment at the fate of women, it was tempered by awareness that there were few alternatives. Plenty of bad marriages and disoriented wives can be found in novels, but as long as marriage remained a prerequisite for normal female life, it was seen, perforce, as something that women had to put up with; and the worst and most crippling of its disorders went unmentioned or were disguised. When a life without marriage, or without the traditional form of patriarchal marriage, became socially and emotionally feasible, what had been hidden began to emerge. The atmosphere of exposé increases the impact of these revelations.

Plath and Sexton function not just as authors but also as exemplary figures for their readers. They act out familiar scenes, but they carry the action beyond what is expected. Both of them married and had children. Both of them went through episodes of madness. Marriages broke up. Each killed herself, succeeding in this act after earlier attempts had failed. Their struggles and tensions are recorded in their work, and their lives reinforce their words. Each endeavored to combine a life in the traditional mode with a career as a writer, and each broke down. For their devotees, reality gives the writing a weight that goes beyond merely literary statement.

This is not meant to belittle the value of their work. Plath's novel, *The Bell Jar* (1963), is episodic and uneven, but that could be said of many poets' novels. From a rather formal beginning, her poetry grows steadily in intensity and power. In "Edge" (*Ariel*, 1965) we see her death previsioned, but the strength of the poem lies not in our knowledge of the soon-to-be-accomplished event but in her transformation of the simple data of life into chilling symbol:

> The woman is perfected.
> Her dead
>
> Body wears the smile of accomplishment,
> The illusion of a Greek necessity
>
> Flows in the scrolls of her toga . . .
>
> Each dead child coiled, a white serpent,
> One at each little
>
> Pitcher of milk, now empty.
> She has folded
>
> Them back into her body as petals
> Of a rose close . . .
>
> The moon has nothing to be sad about . . .
>
> She is used to this sort of thing.

Sexton's poetry, like Plath's, is much involved with the tensions between rules about motherhood and daughterhood and the realities of obligatory relationships. These poets are constantly forced to con-

sider such noble symbols in terms of dailyness. Plath, both in imagining her death and in actually going to it, thought of her children.
Though she saw them dead in the poem, drawn into "perfection" with
her, in real life she left them sleeping with bread and milk beside them.
Sexton, put to writing her first poems as a therapeutic task set by her
doctor, dates the bout of madness that hurled her out of normal life
by remembering the illness of one of her children and times her return
to sanity by encounters with the child and with her own mother. These
poets need and use immediacy, taken (writes Sexton) from the "narrow diary of my mind / (and) the commonplaces of the asylum."

For Plath and Sexton and for other women writers as well the
experience of madness is neither shunned nor sharply divided from the
rest of life. It is, rather, seen as a metaphor for the absurdity of the
rest of life, absurdity brought to light in newly felt contradictions and
frustrations. In literature of this period, madness becomes a limit
toward which victimization and powerlessness push women; but there
is also a sense in which madness is chosen as a revolt against normality
when normality can no longer support a life that includes joy, freedom
and imagination. Like the eccentric characters of O'Connor and
McCullers, those who have fallen into madness measure and criticize
the values of orthodoxy.

In one year, 1970, several books by women writers made serious
attempts to understand situations of alienation and madness that
seemed to grow out of traditional roles. (Toni Morrison's powerful
The Bluest Eye appeared at this time but will be discussed later with
the novels and memoirs of other black writers because the experience
called on differs from that used by white women.) In *Play It As It Lays,*
Joan Didion chronicles the disintegration of her heroine, Maria, into
numb despair. Maria has been separated from her small daughter,
who is institutionalized for some mental or emotional disturbance. She
takes this as evidence of total personal failure and incapacity to act
in any way that can produce a positive result. She is hopelessly at odds
with what is required of her by social expectations: If they are right,
she must be wrong. But if they are right, there is no impulse of hers
that she can trust; and that must mean that she is evil, beyond redemp-
tion. It is a vision of Hell after Judgment Day, when no remorse, no
penance, can buy salvation. There is no help for Maria; Didion is not,
however, directing us to drown in fruitless pity for her heroine but to
consider the unbearable weight that a traditional role can lay on an
ordinary person.

Gail Godwin, in *The Perfectionists,* gives us a heroine, Dane, who has not just fallen into a traditional role but has chosen a particularly difficult version of it. Dane is determined on the self-abnegation and denial of will that have been celebrated as female virtues because she sees them as something more: doors to transcendence of selfish involvement in the world. She marries an unorthodox psychologist and takes on his strange, probably autistic, little son. The marriage choice she makes is a bid not for safety but for the challenge of a demanding existence. It is not, however, an existence over which she can exert control: Ordinary life continues to make its own ordinary demands for proper behavior and day-to-day management, even though this behavior runs counter to her own emotions. It is not enough to devote herself to the silent, secret child; she must cope with him. She is not very good at it and begins to see him as an antagonist. Her affection does not reach or alter him, and Dane then finds herself striving to penetrate his identity by force, whether that hurts him or not. The role of nurturing, self-denying woman, even when chosen by the woman herself, turns out to be inappropriate and ineffective. It offers guilt instead of the promised fulfillment.

In the same year Nancy Milford published her biography of Zelda Fitzgerald, where we find a close reading of the advent of madness in real life. A talented woman lives out a role of subordination to a talented man. Zelda too made a daring marriage choice, which preferred challenging experience to safety, and unfortunate results followed. This marriage takes on aspects of a *folie à deux,* but it is Zelda who is judged as mad, not Scott. His talent is admired and exploited, insofar as his drinking and eccentric behavior permit. Her talent is actively discouraged. Scott feels her writing as competition so unfair that it amounts to betrayal, and her attempt to become a dancer is dismissed as utter foolishness. There is no way to tell, now, who should be "blamed" for these conclusions, and Milford is not really trying to do this. Like Didion and Godwin, she is describing the rules of the game. But all these books point out how the rules can work to move women, by way of powerlessness and victimization, into a state that is then diagnosed as madness.

During the seventies a revaluation of traditional marriage proceeded apace. Different aspects are examined: Marriage may be repudiated entirely, it may become the scene of a struggle, it may be left behind and life alone tested, but it ceases to be taken for granted as inevitable in and/or necessary to normal life. The equation of marriage with fulfillment is rejected, but the rejection is still seen as difficult. Heroines do not leave or refuse marriage and go calmly on to some other sort of average living. Having feared flying, they burst out of wedlock and try to soar on their own. Divorce leaves them threatened as well as isolated: Who is friend, who is enemy? Familiar figures change shape; loss of status (no male head of household to define one now!) plunges ex-wives into vulnerability. Alternative relationships must be improvised, and within them even accepted friends may become strangers. Autonomy carries a component of loneliness: These women lie alone at night thinking about unmarriageable lovers, or they take on partners whom they would, in earlier days, have reckoned highly unsuitable. There is little or no disposition to return to the orthodox matings they found crippling, unless, as in Alison Lurie's *The War between the Tates* (1974), the tone of the novel is satiric. But there is not much joy offered these departing heroines. Their lives are fragmented.

And yet the old bargain has become impossible. The wives who go back feel themselves to have redefined their identities so completely that the marriage will be taken up at a new point, in a new way. This will include the details of living; it is not simply an abstract aspiration. For these heroines, whether they try to salvage an old relationship or hang onto the new status of woman alone, it is often the strand of dailyness that holds things together. The shift within the self is endured and made permanent by keeping in touch with a chain of minute-to-minute sensations. One of the most dramatic moves into isolation is described by the Canadian author Margaret Atwood in *Surfacing* (1972). Having broken with her lover and escaped from the friends who had come to share some time on a wilderness lake where she had lived as a child, this heroine undertakes an explicit and conscious re-enactment of the mythic journey to the interior, including a deliberate search for sacred images painted by Indian shamans and a repetition of their imagined ritual of denial and destruction. But the fantasy is embedded in the immediate. We are given minute details of the ritual: What is to be worn, what can be eaten, what must be destroyed and thrown away. There is no blurring of experience in these books; when the past is rejected and the future not yet invented, one holds fast to the present.

There appear, then, to be two major elements at work in women's literature as it moves beyond the phase in which it is simply in search of an identity. First is the insistence on looking at the data of ordinary life and on using the occupations of women, overlooked by high culture, as trustworthy evidence in which some kind of significance can be sought. While a structure of values that was formed elsewhere, by others, and matched to other needs is being abandoned, one clings to felt reality, even if this reality can be described as mad, under the old system. Second, there is an urge to create a new set of values that will suit the lives and purposes of women as seen by women: a system of authentic emotional relations and interconnected beliefs drawn from lived experience that will develop the force of social myth and thus explain the workings of the world and direct appropriate behavior.

At first blush, this grandiose program may seem to conflict with the emphasis on minutiae of living; and, indeed, some feminist writing does rush toward utopia, indulge in fantasies, and imagine future societies so doctrinaire as to be hardly habitable by human beings. But this is typical of any movement writing in its early days. Generally in women's literature, and certainly in most effective writing, whether it is fiction or nonfiction, the drive to create a new world of symbols does not separate itself from dailyness. Instead, it works within everyday experience, looking there for clues to a new interpretive paradigm that is already taking shape. Its first manifestations may be felt merely as disturbances in orthodox theory; but as they increase, they point to the existence of an alternative world view that will in time stand forth in its own essential identity. This quest for a new symbology respects the real and refuses to assign an arbitrary value to it, preferring to let its own significance illuminate it from within. We can even find a description of this search in women's writing. Adrienne Rich's image of a future female explorer, quoted above, seen to "plunge breasted and glancing through the currents" recurs a decade later as the poet "diving into the wreck," not only for herself but as a being who is more than a single individual:

> We are, I am, you are
> by cowardice or courage
> the one who find our way
> back to this scene
> carrying a knife, a camera
> a book of myths
> in which
> our names do not appear.

And in "The Long Distance Runner" (*Enormous Changes at the Last Minute,* 1974) a fantasy that is held down to earth by immediate details of objects seen and scenes traversed, Grace Paley writes of a

woman revisiting the neighborhood where she spent her childhood
and feeling the changes that have taken place by living them out. In
the end this "Long Distance Runner" sums it up: "A woman inside
the steamy energy of middle age runs and runs. She finds the houses
and streets where her childhood happened. She lives in them. She
learns as though she was still a child what in the world is coming
next."

The future can best be foreseen by looking at what goes on under
our noses, these writers say. Ideas of a different world—and if this
literature rages at the past, it is hopeful about the future—tug us
toward imagining new systems. Nonetheless, they declare, all our lives
remind us that one cannot make bricks without straw or a society
without considering who gets meals, cares for children, looks after the
old, mourns the dead, and keeps the wheel in motion. In the past and
still in the present, these tasks were and are done by ubiquitous,
irreplaceable female creatures, loving, marrying or not marrying,
earning as well as spending, and always tending to the recurrent,
necessary processes that go on below the level of attention and bind
communities together.

The work of Joyce Carol Oates, a writer both prolific and wide-
ranging, illustrates a number of these themes and the devices used to
communicate them. The eccentricity of Oates's characters is sometimes as great as those of Flannery O'Connor, but they are always
placed within the framework of society. Sometimes they are part of
an elite whose actions show up the workings of a shaky and inhumane
social structure. Sometimes they are conscious rebels struggling for
change even though they are not certain that any change is really
possible. Or they may be puppets of social forces, but if so they are
feeling puppets. They may reject the whole world as it is and be
defined as mad. Oates refuses to vouch for any alternate system of
morals even as she discloses the immorality of the one that exists. Her
protagonists are not conventionally good, though some of her rebels
try uneasily to be. But her central characters have been too mishan-
dled by life for goodness. They are selfish, if not greedy, and yet they
are conscious that something has gone very wrong. They do not, like
the rebels, aspire to make a better world of community and connection, they are concentrated on saving themselves; but they tend to
posit a better world or at least to hope for one because they sense that
it is only in such a place that they could be saved. They differ from
the manic, driven automata who have achieved fame, success and
money in the artificial world of the present, because they are still

capable of natural feeling. Oates's protagonists may try for the goals that are held up to them as desirable, but they sicken on the way.

"Success," then, is equated with sickness. Oates's rebels know that; they appreciate the overwhelming need to substitute a healthy society for the way we live now, but they cannot imagine a substitute that is persuasive to those who are infected with sickness. As with Mered Dawe in *Do with Me What You Will* (1973) the attraction they exert is lunar, spectral. Typically, Mered is victimized—arrested, beaten, declared mad, driven mad. But he is simply the most obvious victim. The society described here is a madness-inducing machine. No fully human relationships are possible within it, though the rebels somehow keep the hope of them alive in others. These people are fetishists; they can love only in part, feverishly. They are themselves only present in part, able to exist only by not looking at the world, like Elena in this book, or, like her mother, Ardis, able only to leave an earlier persona behind like a snake shedding its skin. We come to know Ardis quite well before she marries off Elena (beautiful, biddable, dreaming) to the famous, monstrous lawyer, Marvin Howe. When Ardis reappears later she is someone quite different, a television personality with a new name and a new appearance. She is not just willing to deny her past identity, she insists on it. Her motherhood, she tells her daughter, must be a secret between them.

To be successful, says Oates, one must give up any stable identity, which implies giving up the ability to establish authentic relationships with others. But this demand creates a great malaise in the bulk of Oates's folk, for though they long to be successful they want an identity too and shrink from the sacrifice of self made by the great. Who am I? they ask. What can I believe? They stare at minor events, trying to assess them. Are they important? There is no way to be sure. Without continuing identities there can be no sharing of experience, no validation by others of what has taken place; and so there is no assured causality. Oates's characters are tossed about, their lives out of control, whether they come from the working class, as in *Them* (1969), whose dreams and hopes are token gifts from advertisements and commercials, or have climbed to be the amazing powerful men of *Expensive People* (1968) and *Do with Me What You Will,* whose wives, nevertheless, run off with other men, whose children turn against them, and whose powers wane with age like those of anyone else. Desperately they attempt to find their way into the alternative reality that must exist somewhere, in a universe of truth—or why do we live? Why do we dream up such a word as *truth?* The hero of the short story "An American Adventure" (in *The Seduction,* 1975) walks uneasily through a familiar neighborhood: "What worries me is that there is a world beyond the world I see that is simultaneous with it." But it is a world where "nothing is human. There are no rules or laws or chemical 'truths' . . . (It is) a hard, vivid world . . . emptied of people and therefore permanent."

Such alienation slips into madness. Again, it is a condition conceived of not as essentially different from the state in which we live most of the time but as a limit, or a metaphor, for our present case. Oates's characters are pulled two ways, looking for a natural identity in a permanent world (though then it would have people in it) but bemused by injunctions from the chaotic present that hold up to them the gaudy goals that authority tells them to value. At the same time, their natural sense assures them that these goals are irredeemably false. Caught in this tension, they move easily to violence, which has its own validating force, so that murder becomes a kind of reassurance: If one could do something as extreme as to kill, one must surely be in possession of a truth important enough to kill for. Action authenticates meaning. Or does it? Murder is not difficult at all, Marvin Howe assures Elena. He could have had her lover killed at any time; it would have been cheap, since the man is so unimportant. He is rather astonished that he did not.

It is an unwelcoming, indeed a terrifying, world. And yet these characters, confused, obsessed, on the verge of slipping from one persona to another, rage through it in so violent and lively a fashion that they redeem it. Against its expressed pessimism they assert the value of life: a life that refuses to accept falseness as truth, that searches for something better, is fobbed off with a new falseness, recognizes it, and goes on searching. "If you woke up one morning and ran outside and ran away from your life, wouldn't you come into a new one?" asks a young girl in the story "Where Are You Going, Where Have You Been?" (*The Wheel of Love,* 1970). "Only into a life that is worse!" says the author, already laying out the trap into which the girl is to run. But the hope and the question are not presented as foolish. An active drive toward something better is everywhere; it is what these people live by. Oates will not hand us a positive answer about the future, show us that simultaneous universe where we could find new lives and understand their meaning. What she does is report an omnipresent urge to discover or make such a universe. Her characters look for clues to such a place in the events of their lives, desperate to find a world with a coherent structure, where human beings can live with dignity.

Such an assessment of humankind is nothing new: Dostoevski offers a familiar example. What Oates adds is the flavor of women's testimony on their experience, whether she writes of their interior lives or of the actions of men in a world deficient in feeling. Her women feel themselves directed from outside. They lose spontaneity and autonomy and take on instead tasks of consumption that they are instructed to find central to their lives. The maintenance of art and high culture is assigned to them, and because they are subordinate, art is trivialized and loses its power to heal and communicate. These are failures of the overall system of our society, but they are acted out by women. These women, like those of Dostoevski, tend to hysteria; but where Dostoevski takes this for granted, Oates shows us how and why this happens. Typical of women's literature is her analysis of what even the great male writers have presented as simply "female traits of character." Women writers are splitting open the atom to show us the mechanism inside. It is not a mechanism special to women. Understanding it enlarges our knowledge of psychological causation—another contribution to universality.

The process of discovering new symbols in everyday life is apparent in Oates's work. She is, for example, vastly interested in houses: in how they are furnished, what they cost (usually in rent; her characters are too mobile to buy property), and what sort of neighborhood they occupy. Her restless, formless people are defined by the living space they settle in briefly; they establish a temporary stability for their uncertain identities in terms of monthly rent or social position of neighbors. But houses, like personalities, are subject to co-option: Marvin Howe, a lawyer whose fees can bankrupt the clients he represents, owns houses all over the country, taken in part payment from those he has "saved." He fattens on these legitimate victims like a fairy tale ogre, and the social approval he enjoys suggests that in the world Oates portrays this ogre-victim relation is central.

The telephone has long been a symbol in women's writing. Stubbornly silent, it signifies a lover's rejection, and its rings will as often as not be deceptive, nursing false hopes. Even so, it speaks of the possibility of communication and connection with another. In Diane Johnson's novel *The Shadow Knows* (1974), however, the telephone is a channel for inchoate, violent intrusion. Her heroine, N., has left her husband—the change in her life is symbolized by a change of housing, moving herself and her four children from a comfortable middle-class home to a unit in a housing project—and the telephone sometimes brings her a call from her lover, one of those unmarriageable men, married to someone else. But more often the message is menace: from an anonymous phantom; from an ex-nursemaid raving revengefully of terrors to come; from an ex-husband, her own or that of her current baby-sitter, expected but ambiguous. If there is a connection via phone, it is with a world that is no longer understandable, a world where tires are slashed, doors bashed at, and women attacked in the dark. "You are vulnerable," says the telephone. N. knows that is true but feels it is a price she is willing to pay, for vulnerability is how one stays human and responsible. The toughness she hopes to achieve is that not of a hardened surface but of interior survival strength.

Relationships too are reassessed for their symbolic significance. Marriage is one, as we have seen: Is it a necessary part of life? If it is undertaken, what weight should be allowed each partner? What demands should be accepted? How can it be enlarged, if it can be? What is the place of children and their needs? Less explicitly stated, but running through memoirs, poetry, and fiction, is an effort to take this last question by itself and rethink the parent-child relationship, especially that with the mother. Sylvia Plath's furious attack on "Daddy" is one of her best-known poems; but in "The Disquieting Muses," cited above, she blames her mother for the disturbing presences that shape her work and haunt her life. Her mother "meant well, her witches . . . always got baked into gingerbread," and she saw that the proper arts were taught to her daughter. But the daughter found herself unteachable in these disciplines. She learned from other muses, and if they were "unhired by you, dear mother," still, "this is the kingdom you bore me to."

Here, and in much other writing by women, the mother is seen not only as source of life but as source of knowledge. Even when life is good, the knowledge that women have had to learn has been painful: an awareness of secondary status and limited living space. Yet within this process of learning, one has learned oneself how to deal with the world and to engage oneself with others. When women begin to question traditional truth about such arrangements, they find themselves questioning what their mothers taught them. No wonder, then, that painful and ambivalent attacks on mother figures are so common in women's literature and not only in the writing that comes out of a white middle-class background.

In *The Woman Warrior* (1976) Maxine Hong Kingston remembers her growing up in California as "a girlhood among ghosts."

Strictly speaking, the "ghosts" are the white Americans as seen by the Chinese community, but the confrontation of cultures affects her Chinese family too. The force of their beliefs and behavior is drained away by the society they have come to live in. Kingston's mother, who had qualified as a doctor at home and lived independently, still followed her husband overseas when he sent for her, and she tries to preserve old ways and to raise her daughters in proper submission. The girls, caught between the California in which they go to school and the "talk-stories" that strive to preserve the Chinese past, hardly know whether their fate directs them to leave the whole ancient tradition behind or to conform to the role of daughter-slave, according to the harsh rules laid down by their mother. Kingston rebels. Yet, returning home years later, she hears the driven tyrant of a mother moan, "How can I bear to have you leave again?" and herself feels the tug to return to her roots, even though "my mother would sometimes be a large animal, barely real in the dark; then she would become a mother again." It is only when her mother allows affection to show, and gives permission for her to go, that she feels free of a weight of obligation that matches her anger. The book itself is the gift given in return for this freedom. It is not grateful, expected affection that it offers, however, but a strict analysis of what can be preserved and what must be left behind in order that affection may be possible between mother and daughter.

Black women writers have produced some of the most intense and revealing studies of the strains that a madness-inducing society puts on its members. History is always present in these books, fiction or no; and it is a history of daily inescapable assault by a world that allows so little room for a continuous coherent self to grow that one wonders how survival is possible at all. In *The Bluest Eye* (1970) Toni Morrison weaves together scenes from an underground whose inhabitants suffer as much from confused social directives as they do from abysmal poverty. The exploration of this world of victimization gains from the fragmented form of the book, for life is essentially fragmented when seen through the eyes of any single individual. Bad as oppression was in the rural South (and other writers, like Sarah Wright in *This Child's Gonna Live,* 1969, tell us about that), life there had some sequence. In the northern cities, powerlessness is made worse by the unpredictability of events: Anything can happen, and those who have climbed a step out of chaos fear nothing so much as falling back into it.

The seductive tug of white standards and values adds to the disorder of mind. A black woman servant will find the only safety and order she can expect while she is at work in a white woman's home, will taste power there, find tradesmen polite, and her work valued. She will also, before the eyes of her own child, seem to prefer the white child she looks after: Society tells her the latter is more valuable. Morrison's stunning insight reveals the disrupted emotions produced by living in a world where white standards and goals are presented to blacks as uniquely important and, at the same time, impossible for them to achieve.

In Morrison's work and in that of other black women writers we find examples of how women's literature can extend itself beyond women's experience. A life without power, known to black women ("Everybody in the world was in a position to give them orders," Morrison writes, echoing Zora Neale Hurston a generation before), produces an astonishing capacity to see into other, similar conditions. Morrison, Toni Cade Bambara, and Nikki Giovanni not only write of women, proud of their vigor and ability to survive, but also understand the frustrated fury of black men, whose identities are falsified and torn apart because the masculine ideal of power and control is both presented to them and denied. Morrison does not excuse, but she comprehends, the inverted, desperate, rejected search for affection and closeness that can produce violence, even violence as extreme as the rape of a man's own daughter. To communicate such understanding leads us, again, toward universality.

In writing of their own lives these women both question and affirm the importance of the mother link to the past and of the knowledge that society directs and permits a mother to pass on to her children. Maya Angelou's memoirs, beginning with *I Know Why the Caged Bird Sings* (1969), give us a split mother figure: her own, and her mother's mother, Momma. Momma was a storekeeper and a proud landholder in a small Arkansas town who knew her place and kept it with disdain but defended it with fury. Maya's mother was a sophisticated woman, on her own in great cities. When the child, at seven, was sent to her, she decided that her mother was "too beautiful to have children, that's why she sent us away." The care she gave seemed to demand gratitude in return, and Angelou, like Maxine Kingston, found she had to rebel. Reconciliation came only years later, when seventeen-year-old Maya, having concealed her pregnancy until the last moment, turned to her mother for help and the help was given.

Other black women writers cast back to strong women through a matrilineal connection. In *Generations* (1976) Lucille Clifton recalls the legend of her great-great-great-grandmother, Caroline, born free in Dahomey in 1823, captured and enslaved as a child, and at age eight marched from New Orleans to Virginia. She survived to raise a great-grandson and assure him that he could be proud of coming from "Dahomey women." A strong and intransigent grandmother, Louvenia, lives in Nikki Giovanni's memory, a troublemaker who had to be smuggled out of Georgia in the dead of night to the comparative safety of Knoxville, Tennessee. Giovanni and Toni Cade Bambara bring the tradition of autonomous black women up to date, remembering themselves as tough, fighting little girls, though both see the deliberate undermining of the self in black men by white society as a hateful part of the causes for women's strength. But though they deplore the pressure on black men, they still celebrate the daring and the adventurous spirit of black women. Some of this celebration creates icons: The legend of Harriet Tubman makes her a fabulous figure. Indeed, Tubman and Sojourner Truth are cited as myths to be honored by white as well as black women. The spirit of these myths is re-created in images of black women who invent and labor for change in the present.

Alice Walker, in *Meridian* (1976), gives us a black heroine who has some of the strangeness and even the physical disorders that mark significant figures in Flannery O'Connor's work. Meridian, however, has a conscious purpose in her life that is presented as both realistic and hopeful; she is not merely an eccentric instrument for criticizing the deficiencies of society. Meridian has a long journey to make out of privacy and ordinary life, out of early marriage and motherhood, that seems like a dream, out of an existence that hardly belongs to her to a large involvement with the world. If she becomes a figure of myth, she does it before our eyes, not in the memory of some descendant. Instead, she carries and transforms the weight of the past, for her awkward choice of independence distresses a mother who has accepted, and been broken by, ordinary life, though Meridian's choice also expresses the ambition her mother could not fulfill herself.

It is Meridian's destiny to act out, and to analyze for herself and for us, the social forces that produced the civil rights movement of the early sixties and the revolutionary violence that succeeded it among the urban guerrillas of the North. Meridian cannot give herself over totally to this violence: She is willing to die for the changes she believes in, but she cannot state her willingness to kill for them. Disowned, she returns to the South alone, to gestures of confrontation that seem minor and a bit ridiculous—to a dailyness of struggle. Yet we feel that something profound is working itself out within her. She too has undertaken an interior spiritual voyage, searching for essential meaning by exploring the data of life, present and past. At the end of the book Meridian is emerging as saint and heroine. She stands inescapably askew to contemporary life, very much as Dostoevski's Myshkin does in *The Idiot*; but Meridian, we guess, will not end in complete madness and withdrawal, as Myshkin does. Meridian, says Walker, has imposed on herself the sentence of bearing the conflict of our time in her soul. She has lived through it. Now this sentence "must be born in terror by all the rest of us." Not privately but publicly Meridian becomes a progenitor. Perhaps the creation of a figure through whom we are invited to look to a future society that is no longer a madness-inducing machine points to still another sort of universality of imagination that has grown out of the experience of black women.

The passage of women from daughterhood to motherhood, whether it is private or actual or, as in the case of Meridian, symbolic, appears to be replacing the rite of marriage as indicator of maturity in women's writing. No doubt, union with a male is the symbol most apparent to male writers and is naturally the one chosen by a male-oriented society. The act of sex that transforms a virgin into a woman will take precedence in masculine literature, as it necessarily does in time. Women's experience, however, suggests that the more essential change is from the role of daughter to that of mother and that the two conditions illuminate each other. Anne Sexton struggles with her "desertion" of her daughter during her stay in an asylum by matching it with her mother's "desertion" of herself by death. "The Double Image," in which this comparison is made, refers less to individuals than to relationships. Sexton remembers how her mother had her portrait painted soon after she had left the asylum. It seemed to the poet that the image of herself was to replace the reality, the actual daughter whose attempt at suicide could not be forgiven. At the same time, in the same poem, she finds herself doing something similar. When her own daughter was born, she recalls, she had hoped for "a small milky mouse of a girl," not a boy; for she, too, needed an image.

> I who was never quite sure
> about being a girl, needed another
> life, another image to remind me . . .
> I made you find me.

When we extrapolate from Sexton's words, we find her private search for an image to explain herself to herself reproduced in women's literature, where the quest for a new image with which to explain life is central. Women are writing in order to assess what life has taught them, what it has made of them; and, indeed, the work of any new literature concentrates on forming a new identity out of an overlooked, or misunderstood, past and a turbulent present. The search covers many areas, the images are various, the voices that describe them diverse, but always a grasp on daily life supplies both continuity and commonality. Susan Griffin gives us poetry, in *Like the Iris of an Eye* (1976), where unfinished phrases express the disjunction and interruptions of everyday life. She also writes a minute-to-minute, nursery-level account of experience that is shorn of obvious feeling. Yet out of this building-block architecture is constructed the shape of a life.

> This is the story of the day in the life of a woman trying to be a writer and her child got sick. And in the midst of writing this story someone called her on the telephone . . .

There follows a record of interruptions, some of them interesting, and concerns, many of them traditionally a part of women's lives in the age-old mode: fixing meals, sewing curtains and pillows, watering plants, and, pervasively, anxiety over the sick child, all mingled with exasperation at one's inability to center on one's work. The whole conveys the flavor and scent of a representative, even symbolic, life by means of bits of commonplace brilliantly selected and joined together to make a coherent statement. Of course, it is an old story. Very few women have not lived through such a day, whether they were trying to write a story or to complete any other undertaking. But Griffin is not simply living this, she is thinking about it; thinking about it not angrily or with self-pity, not as an irritating example of how women's lives are trivialized—though humanly speaking all these factors are there—but fundamentally as a clue to the nature of life itself. One's identity is precious, one's work demands to be done, and yet one exists in a network of relationships—there is no way out. They cannot be denied anymore than Diane Johnson's N. can refuse the vulnerability that goes with keeping herself open to the world.

Naomi Lazard's "Ordinances" (1978) has something of the same flat tone, but the irony is overt. These are direct messages from Authority in a madness-inducing society. They direct the reader to stand in one line or another, which should be chosen with care and which will then move, or not, toward a goal that will be the opposite of what is desired. Or they offer

> Congratulations.
> The suspense is over. You are the winner.

But of what dubious contest the reader, and the winner, too, are completely unsure, while the prize may or may not turn up, in which case "do not bother to inform us."

A more passionate view of dailyness declares the need to transcend it. Marge Piercy in *Woman on the Edge of Time* (1976) both describes details of living and provides a visionary future with which to contrast the present. Piercy is imagining an alternative reality, a science fiction utopia. She is offering it not as an escape from the present, a fantasy into which we can retreat, but as an injunction to invent a future that will meet our needs better, both emotional needs and social urgencies, a way of living not guaranteed to drive us crazy. In *Speedboat* (1976) Renata Adler holds tight to the present, but she abstracts from its flow moments of strong feeling that seem to belong to another pattern, clues in a different language. The current pattern is disintegrating; and if we are to construct another, we need material with which to work. Adler's flashes of "found" meaning judge the present and its ridiculous associations by setting themselves off from it, while at the same time they ask to be joined in new ways that will create new styles of living, serious and feasible. They speak of true feeling and relational reality that can still be found and preserved in the surrounding falseness.

Other novelists use more conventional techniques, but one finds in them the same major themes: exploration of the experience of powerlessness in an effort to understand the past and its effects, revaluation of familiar relationships, both that of marriage and sexual connection and that between parent and child, and a search for symbols expressive of authentic present reality that can be joined together to build a new structure of beliefs that will match contemporary human needs and show us the way to a livable future. Paula Fox's sharp eye and daring mind rummage through recent history, reviewing our path to the present. Like Alice Walker (and Doris Lessing, in England), she considers the movements of rebellion and revolution that have engaged Americans during the last generation, seeing them as another sort of attempt to establish an alternative reality; they are failed attempts, but they indicate a need. The communists of the thirties and forties furnish a model that, in *The Western Coast* (1972), is interwoven with the California culture, so different from that of the more rooted East. Annie Gianfala comes to a hard-won maturity in the years of World War II, moving from a passivity almost as complete as that of Oates's Elena, in *Do with Me What You Will,* to a considerable command of her actions and judgments. Again, the immediacy of experience provides Annie with learning tools: poverty, violence, unpleasant ailments, hunger, grubby jobs, a succession of men who are in some way deficient and who see Annie as an answer to their problems but not as a person whose autonomy must be allowed for. Only Max sees her so, and Max, who loves her, is another unmarriageable married man, committed to other responsibilities. Max and Annie avoid a traditional love affair, but a larger relation between them supports them both in trust and respect, disproving easy, belittling judgments on human life.

The complicated tugs of motherhood and daughterhood, which have to do with the passage of values as well as with the establishment of identities, are absent in this novel, but they are dwelt on in Fox's *The Widow's Children* (1976), where we see women so overwhelmed by the disruption of patterns of living through social change that they are unable to pass on values. Raising children is itself a process of inventing a future, a process long handed to women as obligation and vocation. The weight of this responsibility is central to female feeling. Consequently, the stunting of growth by a disturbed society is felt in a personal way by women and expressed in their writing with immediate anger. Men may see, and detest, the loss and distortion of human potential, but they are usually spared the burden of dealing with the details. In *The Abduction* (1970) Maxine Kumin gives us the example of a black man, Dan, who is truly concerned for the deprived "inner city" children that a government program is trying to help; but it is the white woman, Lucy, who acts at a moment of crisis. By Dan's lights, and indeed in the reality shown here, she is wrong to flee the riots that follow the assassination of Martin Luther King, taking with her the small, brilliant black boy, Theodore, who stands as a symbol of hope for black and white teachers alike. Dan knows that Lucy is in the grip of fantasy, imagining a new sort of family, with Theodore as her son and Bey, the head of the project and her lover, as the father. Lucy does indeed feel herself a failed mother in her own marriage, one beloved daughter dead in a car crash and the other abandoned to an unsympathetic German lover, while she nurses a guilty sense of delinquency because she has not "given" her husband a son.

But though Lucy's action is irrational and Dan is right to step in and reclaim Theodore, we are seeing here a new sort of heroine. If the absurdity of our world has driven her to unacceptable action, at least it is action, not passivity. And her dream of a kind of family connected by conscious affection that is broader than blood kinship is noble. It may perhaps point to some sort of future where isolated individuals reach out to each other and where true concern and mutual help extend past orthodox family bonds to a wider community. The madness-inducing machine has caught sensible, capable Lucy, but the fantasy with which she reacts points to a felt need—one that is widely seen in women's fiction of the seventies as an urgency to find better ways to raise children, not just because this is part of women's traditional occupation but as a matter of grave social policy.

Adrienne Rich turns her attention to this question in *Of Woman Born: Motherhood as Experience and Institution* (1976). The shift of genres in which a poet discusses the social machinery that directs maternal behavior and shapes emotions is not unusual in contemporary women's writing. Rich sees the current mother role as one of collaborator and co-conspirator with patriarchal society. Women's vital need to remake images of themselves can begin here in reality, as well as in literature. Explicit in the book is evidence that feminists are far from rejecting motherhood, as some propagandists claim. What they reject are inhumane distortions of the affectionate pride in and hope for one's children that should be allowed to nourish the process of mothering. Says Rich:

> If I wish anything for my sons, it is that they should have the courage of women . . . who, in their private and public lives . . . are taking greater risks, both psychic and physical, in the evolution of a new vision . . . acts of immense courage (which can involve) moments, or long periods, of thinking the unthinkable, being labeled, or feeling, crazy; always a loss of traditional securities . . . I would like my sons not to shrink from this kind of pain, not to settle for the old male defenses . . . And I would wish them to do this not for me, or for any other woman, but for themselves, and for the sake of life on the planet Earth.

Critics of women's literature are still few, but in some recent books we begin to find the sort of re-examination of old texts that can provide a basis for thinking about the human condition in a way that includes women's situation. The mid-sixties shift in their perception of themselves shows up later in critical writing than in poetry, autobiography or fiction, as is only to be expected: Writing criticism demands the existence of a structure of beliefs on which judgments can be based, and such a structure is formulated slowly for any genre in any art. Without it, criticism tends to be anticriticism, which takes the existing apparatus and reverses it, pointing out how falseness has engendered defects in insight and failures of discrimination; but without a doctrinal system there can be no positive statements.

We see this effect in such a preliminary work as Mary Ellmann's *Thinking About Women* (1968). Ellmann's title is misleading, perhaps purposely. Her topic is male thought about women, with masculine criticism of women writers as the field of study. Women's writing is thus at a remove from Ellmann's text, which is mainly an analysis of how the acceptance of stereotyped views of women has distorted masculine perceptions of their work, their worth, and their very nature. Ellmann documents a history of what must be called massive male stupidity, if we define stupidity as the deliberate choice of ignorance and comfortable prejudice. Her insight is penetrating. The chapter on phallic criticism is a graveyard where can be found generations of self-deceptive, self-congratulatory opinions on women writers, still not unknown but increasingly embarrassing to read. It is worth being reminded of how widespread and how respectable has been the unquestioned assumption of women's inevitable, innate, and significant "otherness," and Ellmann here collects utterances on the subject not only from those we might expect (Norman Mailer, Leslie Fiedler, Anthony Burgess) but from Robert Lowell, Malamud, Beckett, and Reinhold Niebuhr.

Useful as this is, however, Ellmann, writing in the middle sixties, had little to go on in offering an alternative. Her own style is not free from the self-deprecation she deplores in other women writers, and she is put to it to point to creators of women's literature whom she can really admire. She finds no continuing tradition in women's writing, and her recommendations are limited and limiting: reliance on wit and mockery and the rejection of a tone of authority, which she sees as a masculine trait, thereby confusing, it would seem, social and political authority with knowledgeable force derived from lived experience. But she perceives well how the attention women writers pay to details of existence contributes to their strength and that such interaction is not trivial but evidence of their engagement with reality.

Another transitional work is Patricia Meyer Spacks's *The Female Imagination* (1975). Though Spacks does not limit her observations to male thinking about women, she seems uncertain of what her material does consist of. The first task of criticism is to frame relevant questions, and that is hard for early practitioners to do: The old questions still distract them. Spacks gives us a number of sharp insights on particular writers. She is sensitive, for example, to the special quality of outlook shared by Lillian Hellman and Mary McCarthy that sets them somewhat apart from ordinary female experience and legitimizes for them the use of masculine standards. However, her exclusively literary criteria do not allow her to see how women involved in left-wing political thought of the thirties became able to use these alternative realities, which broadened orthodox standards for a time. Overall, Spacks is uncertain about major themes to be explored and major questions to be asked in approaching the work of women writers.

Elizabeth Hardwick's *Seduction and Betrayal* (1974) stands by itself. It does not need, nor take, a place in a historic transition of thought but comes straight from a critical and imaginative intelligence of such a high order that one feels it stands outside of history. Of course, this is too sanguine a reaction. A serious examination of writing by, or about, women undertaken in the fifties would have had to excuse or justify itself in some way. Writing in the seventies, Hardwick manages to reconcile the sound standards of the old critical canon with the insights given women by shared experience that differs from that of men and to explicate in a straightforward way the effect that living as a female has had on those who also wish to live as writers.

Seduction and Betrayal includes essays on male writing about women, on women writing about their lives both as fiction and biography, and on women who were not authors but who stood close to the careers of men: Jane Carlyle, Dorothy Wordsworth, Zelda Fitzgerald. At first view, this looks like a heap of material without structure, but Hardwick knows the right questions to ask. This is about relationships: How can men and women live together? What have they felt about this, and how have they expressed their opinions and hopes? Where have things gone wrong, where do misfit images fail to match reality? Hardwick is quite aware as Ellmann (or Kate Millett, for that matter) of the indignities that have been the lot of women writers, but she is not just calling angry attention to them, she is considering how they have affected the work of these women. This is a central part of the essential business of criticism, and when it can at last be undertaken, rancor falls away.

Her short essay on the Brontës, for example, draws far-reaching conclusions from the familiar details of the restrictions laid on

poor and talented women. It is, so to speak, a sequel to Virginia
Woolf's famous vision of what would have happened to a sister of
Shakespeare who possessed his genius. The Brontës lived on a cresting
wave of change when it was just becoming possible for women to write
seriously as professionals, but when the social disabilities of doing so
were still high.

> The worries that afflicted genteel, impoverished women in the nine-
> teenth century can scarcely be exaggerated. They were cut off from the
> natural community of the peasant classes. The world of Tess of the
> D'Urbervilles, for all its sorrow and injustice, is more open and warm
> and fresh than the cramped, anxious, fireside-sewing days of the re-
> spectable. Chaperones, fatuous rules of deportment and occupation,
> drained the energy of intelligent, needy women. Worst of all was soci-
> ety's contempt for the prodigious efforts they made to survive. Their
> condition was dishonorable, but no approval attached to their efforts
> to cope with it. The humiliations endured in the work of survival are
> a great part of the actual material in the fiction of Charlotte and Anne
> Brontë.

Hardwick sees her subjects as figures in a landscape, and she under-
stands what this landscape offers and requires if one is to exist there
by using the view as material for fiction. What one sees, of course, is
individual: Emily Brontë gazed at a lonelier, stonier, more dramatic
range of country than that of her sisters. Perhaps truth was more
important to her than survival. Charlotte and Anne reworked the drab
humiliations they had known as teachers and governesses to suggest
that defeat was not absolutely necessary, even though the suggestion
was not entirely justified; defeat had to be expected. Hardwick under-
stands well the process of making heroines out of sour scraps of
memory, so that survival could at least call on imagination for the
right to hope:

> Most governesses in fiction are strangely alone, like sturdy little female
> figures in a fairy tale. They walk the roads alone, with hardly a coin
> in their pockets; they undergo severe trials in unfamiliar, menacing
> places and are rescued by kind strangers. Shadows, desperations, and
> fears are their reality, even if they go in for a litany of assurances of
> their own worth and sighs of hope that their virtues will somehow
> . . . stand them in good stead.

Hardwick's comprehension of what it is that authors are doing is equally helpful in her chapters on men writing about women. The title essay in *Seduction and Betrayal* deals with ravished heroines, from Clarissa on. It is the heroism of these female figures, Hardwick finds, that is essential in the minds of their creators. Their moral stature and human dignity must be beyond question. For such a character, "her fall or her fate can only be truly serious if a natural or circumstantial refinement exists." Indeed:

> In the novel, when the heroine's history turns about a sexual betrayal, it matters whether she is the central figure in the plot or a somewhat less powerfully and less fully considered "victim" on the periphery. If she is the central figure, psychological structure seems to demand a sort of purity and innocence. Not physical innocence, but a lack of mean calculations, of vindictiveness, of self-abasing weakness. Sexual transgression loses its overwhelming character as a wrong or as a mistake when the persons have virtues of a compelling sort, or spiritual goodness, or the grandeur of endurance. The inner life of the woman matters, what she feels and has felt, the degree of her understanding of the brutal cycles of life.

Hardwick lays her finger here on one of the perennial problems that rise when we compare the female figures of classical literature with what we know from history about women's actual lives: How can Antigone or Lysistrata be derived from the uneducated, housebound women of Periclean Athens? These grand heroines, projected from men's minds, are clearly designed to inhabit an alternative reality: They reflect a male need to value women as equal and worthy, in order to authenticate an order where honor and dignity rule. There is surely nothing wrong with such projections, if we see that the question they pose (social, not literary) becomes how to alter current reality toward this ideal. If we assume that these heroines typify existing reality, we are guilty of a literary blunder: We are falsifying what exists. The impulse of women writers to immerse their characters in a soup of everyday annoyances is an effort to avoid this falsification.

The decade of the seventies saw a growing acceptance of the idea that a women's literature exists and is a proper field of study. Two solid critical works illustrate the change that has taken place since Mary Ellmann, scouting about for exemplary authors, found them thin on the ground. Ellen Moers in *Literary Women* (1976) concludes with a fifty-page bibliography (and there are still omissions). Elaine Showalter provides one nearly as long, combining primary material and critical estimates, in *A Literature of Their Own: British Women Novelists from Brontë to Lessing* (1977). Both books do much more than list and describe. Some of the themes that have been touched on in this essay are examined in depth. Moers opens with an example of dailyness in a writer's life that more than matches Susan Griffin's: a letter from Harriet Beecher Stowe to her sister-in-law, dated 1850, where cooking, cleaning, negotiations with a plumber, a long bout of household sewing and the birth of a child ("I was really glad for an excuse to lie in bed") are supplemented by the report that "I have employed my leisure hours in making up my engagements with news- paper editors"; that is, she met her deadlines. Perhaps the most valu- able product of Moers's researches is the sense she gives us of a conscious continuity in women's literature: the influence of Jane Aus- ten on George Eliot; the admiration that Emily Dickinson felt for Elizabeth Barrett Browning's poetry and its effect on her own work; the use Gertrude Stein made of George Eliot.

Relevant to this continuity is Elaine Showalter's remark:

> Criticism of women novelists . . . has ignored those who are not "great," and left them out of anthologies, histories, textbooks and theories. Having lost sight of the minor novelists, who were the links in the chain that bound one generation to the next, we have not had a very clear understanding of the continuities in women's writing, nor any reliable information about the relationships between the writers' lives and the changes in the legal, economic, and social status of women.

The effect of this, Showalter notes, is that "each generation of women writers has found itself, in a sense, without a history, forced to redis- cover the past anew, forging again and again the consciousness of their sex."

Women's literature is at last developing the history and traditions that validate it as an entity. It is doing this by questioning time- hallowed assumptions that grow both from literature and from life: Showalter's analysis of Virginia Woolf subjects her marriage to scruti- ny for the light that it throws on her work. Like Hardwick, but in greater detail, Showalter explores the opening up of a literary career as an alternative to being a governess for nineteenth-century women. The price that the copyright of a potboiler could bring tells us some- thing about the reasons why talented women wrote potboilers. In male criticism of women writers of the period we discern an element of financial fear: May they not drain off the audience that supports the male boiler of pots? All this insistence on seeing literature in its social context is typical of current critical writing by women. It is another mode of hanging onto reality.

Carolyn Heilbrun in *Toward a Recognition of Androgyny* (1973) goes beyond the (much needed) effort to establish definitions of women's literature and to examine its origins. Heilbrun is looking toward a future in which the old tradition and the new will have become one: "Androgynous" in her terminology can be equated with "universal" as used in this essay. Heilbrun looks back to myth for examples of common feeling between men and women, for fully shared and valued experience. She takes the heroines of Greek drama as expressions of a male need for women who can act with full human responsibility and traces this hope through the works of the accepted critical canon. It surfaces in unexpected places, not simply in the heroines of Henry James and Ibsen but in D. H. Lawrence's *The Rainbow*. These women heroes are removed from immediate life, but, in Heilbrun's view, they represent models that can facilitate the coming together of male and female ways of looking at the world. Such writers as Virginia Woolf and Colette, Heilbrun suggests, give us a preview of an androgynous literature that could help to create affectionate understanding between the sexes.

This is hopeful; perhaps it is also true. Still, one feels that the range and power of women's writing are growing and deepening in a way that will, and must, send it scouring through the experience that has lain unexamined until now. If this happens, it will pour into the mainstream, bearing its full freight. There is a body of women's literature still to be written and a tradition still to be forged before this segment of human existence will be open to exploration by all.

Public and
Private Space

LIKE SO MANY THINGS in wo-
men's lives today, conferences tend to connect with each other and
form linkages, as if they were part of a continuing conversation. Your
discussion leader and I shared a conference recently, and the topic
we're talking about tonight came up there too. The conflict between
private responsibility and the public demands of a career was raised
in an academic setting by a political scientist. How was she to reconcile the standards set by her feminist beliefs, she asked, with those held
up to her by masculine-oriented scholarship? She is now at work on
a biography of an interesting political figure—I hardly have to say that
he was of male gender, for political figures rating biographies are
seldom feminine. For practical reasons, she naturally wants to produce a piece of work that will count favorably in her record when the
question of tenure arises. It must, therefore, fit the standards of the
male academic world reasonably well. Can she do so without violating
her own, feminist perceptions, which have in fact led her to question
orthodox values?

That is both an extreme and an everyday statement of the dialectic
between "public and private spaces." How can women who are scholars, or artists, stay whole if they must judge their work by two sets
of values—one of them public and taken for granted, founded on the
experience and judgments of a masculine elite that regards female
being and doing as idiosyncratic, trivial, or both; and the other a
private set of values rooted in a centered female self, which, therefore,
comes out of a contradictory base?

I came away remembering this question and remembering also the
response of a much respected older woman scholar who declared that
she herself had never been troubled by the problem. Was this, I asked
myself, a matter of age? Have older women simply bought the aca-

demic standards of the masculine elite as not just orthodox but properly so? If that's the case, I thought, I'd better pay attention since I'm
a good deal closer in age to the untroubled scholar than to the young
questioner, and it therefore behooves me to ask myself whether my
generation may not be guilty of large-scale denial of reality. Or was
there another possibility? Was the difference actually due to other
factors, such as the institution where one works and the content and
context of the work done? In fact, the older woman's career has been
made at a woman's college, and her work has long dealt exactly with
cross-gender relationships. Her material itself, that is, addresses the
very question that was being raised, and her tenured position is on a
faculty much more balanced sexually. That observation made me feel
less anxious about my own situation; although, it is true that I have
almost always been able to write out of my private space what I felt
to be true to my own standards and to find an audience that appeared
to understand what I was saying.

Since I don't approve of what public space and social mythology
deem appropriate for women, am I kidding myself when I say that I
can write truly out of my private experience and that readers and
listeners are not deceived and betrayed? Am I kidding not only myself
but them too?

I guess that's a question that all women writers and painters and
creators of whatever branch of the arts ought to ask ourselves every
now and then. If we can't keep ourselves honest we should cease and
desist. My answer, like most answers today, is somewhat ambiguous:
I don't think I'm kidding myself too badly. The reason I am able to
think that is not based on anything personal. Just as with the two
women scholars at the conference, I think that the difference in work
context matters and that such a difference now that gives women
artists an advantage over women scholars.

Our first advantage derives from the nature and demands of our
labors. Artists are required by their work to approach the question of
public and private space in a fashion that's different from that of
scholars. For us, the two fields interact more strongly and closely and
must do so inevitably, for creation and criticism go hand in hand. The
self, the dweller in private space, has to function as a channel into
public space, and her knowledge of the outer world also shapes the
form of her creation from its inception. We simply can't operate if the
split between public and private is too deep. The artist's opinions and
judgments—the deep ones, that is, conscious or not—are always present in the evaluation of reality, and our experience influences the

vision of a finished form. We work where public and private meet and mingle.

Another sort of advantage comes from the sheer presence of earlier women artists who broke trail for those of us alive today. They, of course, did not have this advantage. How much we owe them! It is good to see respect and gratitude being paid in recent works of feminist criticism. For women in Academe, however, the situation has not yet changed all that much. It resembles that of our literary predecessors. The critical canon, in the humanities as well as the sciences, is a possession of the masculine sex. Naturally enough the possessors see no reason why that should change, which doesn't do women much good, whether they agree or not. Women who want to change the canon must approach like invaders attacking a buttressed citadel. If they are going to find a way in to where the defenders may be willing to listen, they are going to have to disguise their persons, lower their voices, learn male gestures and explicate their positions via male rhetoric. The woman who can do that without suffering co-option, not to say exhaustion, is a heroine. And women who share the masculine mystique are hampered too, of course, by the sense—conscious or unconscious—of their own personal, inescapable otherness.

It's true that there still exists a citadel of male criticism in the arts. It is not as uniformly strong as in Academe, though it has strengthened a bit recently simply because so many critics in the humanities and the arts are now keeping body and soul together by teaching; the weltanshauung of Academia encroaches on the world of the arts and literature more strongly than it did a generation ago. This is somewhat offset by the birth and healthy growth of an audience that is attuned to the internal standards of feminist scholars and artists. It is also offset by the fact that criticism and sales are not tied together as tightly as scholarly production and the path to tenure. Women writers particularly can be crassly, commercially successful in the same way as male writers. We can also fail to make a living. Would so many teach if they had a real choice?

Just the same, we are nowhere near so hard-pressed by the economic tie between our pay, our status and male opinions as are women scholars. I know that is not nearly so true for visual artists as for writers, but it is for us, and it has been true long enough for us to live away from the most dangerous phase of invasion of the private mind by heroic images from outer space. Male standards do indeed prevail there; they reach us with every intake we make from the whole culture we live in. But we are not only aware of the fact, we can now do our work without having to ask ourselves, in accurate fear, with each sentence, whether this one violates male myth so dangerously that we may be risking unemployment. We have thus created something of a public space of our own in which we are increasingly free to experiment with different frameworks of significance and causality that (we find) explain outer reality better than do orthodox male conceptions.

Women have been able to write well—brilliantly—in the past, but to do so we have had to take male symbols and transform them, use them to convey in covert style whatever we knew that differed from male knowledge, hinting and suggesting, using mythic figures when we needed to generalize, sliding around orthodox interpretation in graceful arabesques, and congratulating ourselves on the feminine cleverness that enabled us to get away with what we were doing. That's not really a good way to work; though God knows it's better than not being able to work at all. But it does ask the strong, centered self to deny some of its own intensity, some of its force and value, as it sets to work to speak the truth; and it limits what we can talk about openly and without apology to what Establishment thinking would accept as "women's issues."

For writers, at last, this transitional phase is beginning to pass. The interior journey into our own deep consciousness of being is not new or confined to the literary arts; it is and always has been where any creative artist begins. But women writers are now increasingly able to speak straightforwardly of these explorations and discoveries; that is, in so far as art itself speaks straightforwardly. The arts are symbolic languages; the statements they make are multivocal, multisignificant, necessarily mysterious if scanned by logic alone. But now we can at least create our own symbols. In the past, we did communicate with each other, but our language was impoverished, both by the need to translate it from the masculine and also by our inability to test our insights through action. The imagination finds it hard to soar if what it envisages will never affect the world out there. Private space draws in on itself if it's cut off from the public arena of action. Women will stand silent guard, their visions will rise, but they will go only into enriching dailyness by permitted crafts and skills and stop there. I honor that daily beauty of our ancestors—but I want our creativity to have no such limits. I want our private wisdom to break through in our own symbols that establish our own community and assert our own strong presence in the world.

And that is happening. Today the woman artist is finding an audience that does not have to be addressed in male rhetoric; she need no longer disguise her person and lower her voice if she wants to say something serious. She can even speak of her own weakness and know that her hearers or readers or viewers will understand that in so doing she celebrates the courage to confront weakness and so affirm the strength that will be used to move away from weakness. She can make jokes that don't have to be explained. She can record her discoveries with some sense that they are going to remain discovered and not be consigned to odd corners of male maps among the anthropophagi, the mermaids and the monsters. And of course as she does this she not only strengthens her audience, she starts to alter the whole of public space.

What we are doing, as you all know, goes far beyond the limits of feminine cultural activity; or *any* cultural activity as defined by contemporary male dominated society. We are inventing a future. We are creating a community that didn't exist before. It is rooted in women, and it will need to have a very strong sense of those roots for a good long time to come. We are only beginning to explore the wealth of women's experience of the world, to turn it over and put it together and consider its meanings and discuss them with each other. We are a long way from throwing the door open and blithely asking all our male friends to drop in so that they can tell us what we've got here and how to hook it up together. Androgyny, in my opinion, is rather a makeshift concept—at least it is a preliminary one, if it's used to mean the wholeness of humankind. I think both sexes need to look hard and long at themselves in search of the essential qualities of humanness they possess behind the distorting limitations of gender that have polarized our past existence. Only then, I think, can there be real healing, at every level.

But in the long run, as we reach down to dredge up what we know, examine it, and fit it into a new framework of understanding, on which we can build alternative methods of judging and acting and managing relationships—well, this knowledge I am sure is going to reveal itself as connected to that public space out there. Not as part of what already exists in a set structure, but as an equal component of something larger that will manifest itself when the future we are inventing begins to take shape. Frankly, I've no idea of what that shape will be. I know that any future will have to call on the neglected creativity of the people who have not been in command up to now and to draw upon their memories and habitual responses for valuable but neglected data.

It seems to me inescapable that women artists will play major roles in this new act of creation. Susanne Langer long ago overwhelmed me with a conviction that art is indeed the language by which authentic feeling is conceived and communicated through the creation of a many-phased virtual world that parallels and illustrates the emotional truth of lived experience. Very well. To whom has been allotted the preservation and nourishment of authentic feeling and of emotional language? To women; and because emotion and its expression were then devalued as being inherently feminine, the outer world of male activity was despoiled. Rationality has been allowed to reign alone, served by logic and mechanical reasoning and unrefreshed by the intuitive inner sense that can penetrate and comprehend the emotional identities of other human creatures. Those are useful forms of thought, but they don't make up all of mental activity. Now it is time for those who were entrusted with the interpretations of feelings to move out of the private place where we have been waiting and to intervene in the public arena, where our masters are finally starting to notice that rationality, left to itself, has achieved a record of notable disasters. Please—I don't suggest that women are going to tidy up the world for them, using the supportive feminine skills made familiar by standard patriarchal thinking. No. But I believe that history has finally reached the point where we are aware of our own strength and at last able and ready to trust it.

Art, it seems to me, is a kind of public dreaming—not a matter of fantasy and wishing but the sort of dream that Martin Luther King spoke of, a dream that prefigures a future that can be made actual, just as the sense of the finished art object offers itself to the vision of the practitioner and shapes its own creation. In art, then, I believe we can find and use the symbolic language that will teach us the connections and the concerns of our own community of women and will then prove itself to be a shaping tool for building the larger community of humankind in which the future we invent will be made real for interventions in mainstream—that is, public—activities.

Family Themes in American Literature

THE IDEA THAT literature can tell us a good deal about the way our ancestors perceived and acted upon their social situations is one that gets overlooked too often in favor of oral history or social investigations whose conclusions can be expressed in chi squares and graphs. I'm sure these are valuable instruments for exploring our world, but they do not command the range of subtle expression that literature has at its disposal—nor its ability to bring naked emotional force into the picture as it occurs in the real world; nor the ability literature enjoys of combining judgmatically causal pressures, inhibiting factors and the tug of desired goals in order to project probable events. Literature is an old and very sophisticated science; we don't know how old. We're aware that the art of painting developed its skills over 30,000 years at least. Surely it's likely that when our Cro-Magnon ancestors conducted ceremonies before the great painted bison, mammoth and reindeer of the vaults of Altamira or Lascaux, they addressed them with verbal formulas and chants; and that, perhaps, their Neanderthal predecessors muttered some rude spells over the bones of the dead as they embellished them with red ocher before interring them in corners of their caves. In any case, literature has had a long time in which to refine its analytic and expressive powers.

Interestingly enough, however, when we ask it about the family in America, it has little to say. This is a strange aberration, for family relations, good, bad or indifferent, manifest themselves profusely in the literatures of our European cousins. Jane Austen, Dickens, George Eliot, Trollope, Flaubert, Balzac, Turgenev, Tolstoi, Chekhov—how often we find ourselves *at home* with them, in the literal sense of the term. From the kin of Lampedusa's Sicilian Prince in the south to the Vita-Conzini's in the north, Italians have families. Thomas Mann pondered the institution from *Buddenbrooks* to *Joseph and His Brothers.* But when we come to our native land, we find ourselves in the position of Sherlock Holmes—explaining that the vital clue to the mystery is that the dog *didn't* bark in the night.

For the one universal and easily stated judgment on the family to be found among serious American writers is—get out! The family is a trap or a cage. Escape as fast as you can. Light out for the territory. Take off on a whaling voyage, shouting "Call me Ishmael" over your shoulder as you leave. Ship out for two years before the mast, missionize China, settle in Japan to practice aesthetics, but shake the dust of Nebraska or Kentucky or Minnesota off your feet and flee! Go to Paris, go to Rome, go to New York at least, go to Los Angeles at even leaster—but go!

This is disturbing news, I realize, to bring to a conference on kin and community. I feel a little like the Bad Fairy at the christening party. But there you are. Families in American literature are not happy places to be; at least in writing aimed at an adult audience. Beyond *The Little House on the Prairie* and its sequels, happy families hardly exist. J. D. Salinger's Glass Menagerie? Too close for comfort, surely, bound in an intimacy that approaches spiritual incest, as was Tennessee Williams's original. Of course Louisa May Alcott and the March girls are part of our heritage; but if you reread Alcott in later life, you find that her families do not come easily by their togetherness. They have to work for it. Mrs. March contrived to raise a happy family by an astonishing tour de force of moral might and private public relations; and remember, that all through the first volume of *Little Women,* Father March was off attending the Civil War. He survived and returned for the second volume, but if anyone present can recall one significant act or statement emanating from the paterfamilias of the March household—please arise and share it with me; for I can remember none.

I might add that Alcott's other books abound in orphans or deserving young people taken in by families other than their own and that her heroines often looked forward, astonishingly for the times, toward pursuing a remunerative vocation when they were grown. Jo March and her husband ran a school; Polly in *An Old-Fashioned Girl* taught music, not out of the parlor of her family home but in a strange city to which she had moved; and the serious stories for adults that Alcott published under her own name bear the title *Work.* She was not at all persuaded in fact that retirement into family life and nothing else would supply a happy ending for her heroines. She herself, of course, never married, worked all her life, and the family she began to support at an early age was the one she was born into, where Father March's model, Bronson Alcott, proved rather a failure at breadwinning.

Now there are, certainly, families to be found in American literature; but they are almost always either vestigial takeoff points for individual adventures or else they are simply terrible. In a few, rare, cases where happiness breaks in, remembered scenes shine through a golden haze of nostalgia. Such, for example, is the family Eudora Welty creates in *Delta Wedding*: A book laid a generation in time before it was written, located on a great plantation whose operation casts back to a pre–Civil War South. It's a lovely read, but it tells us little about any contemporary family situation. Welty is celebrating a golden past, and the character who represents the author is just nine years old.

In contrast, Faulkner's families of the delta, haunted by the past but confronting a real present, offer a decidedly unattractive vista. The Compsons struggle under a burden of history that crushes them. The horrible Snopeses owe their ratlike vitality to their unwillingness to accept such a burden. They're not a family at all, just a litter. The theme of illegitimate descent, often mingled with racial interbreeding —it would have been called miscegenation when Faulkner was writing —runs through his work and signifies not relationship but an abyss of guilt. These kinships are antifamilies, crying out for moral resolution, but not in an intimate setting.

What in our past can account for this American deviance from the European norm where family connections figure so often? Why do so many American families stagger under a burden of history instead of marching forward behind a flag of pride? Why do life histories open with the protagonist struggling free from a snare of kinship, before the tale can properly begin? I do not wish to repeat the work of the historians who are here, but perhaps it is not out of place to recall that all of us who arrived in America came from somewhere else, leaving settled patterns of life behind, and also that most of us came as single individuals. True, many immigrants managed later to bring other family members across the Atlantic to join them; but even this often disrupted expected family status, since it was usually the young who came first, gained a foothold, and then brought parents after them. In any case, the immigrating Europeans found themselves forced first to create and later to conform to new ways of living.

Though we know this from our own experience or family history, our mental picture of America's first colonists, influenced by the culture of our elementary schools, is generally that of the Pilgrim fathers leading their wives and children into a comfortable sort of wilderness and settling down to worship God and cultivate the land with the help and guidance of their Indian neighbors, who are frequently presented as forerunners of the Welcome Wagon. Indeed, New England did receive many intact families in the early days of settlement; but New England was unique. Elsewhere the peopling of America was often in the hands of recruiters who rounded up unattached and hungry young men, and young women too, though in lesser numbers, and dispatched them to plant the colonies. Sometimes they enlisted on their own, but quite often they mortgaged themselves to pay for the journey, promising to work off the price over a span of years. Some were all but kidnapped, were held under restraint till they could be put aboard ship and, on landing, were sold off to work out their term of indenture. Their condition was not as hopeless or horrible as that which Alex Haley's black ancestors faced, but they were gathered up for money and shipped as cargo, as lucrative merchandise, so that the whole enterprise might be seen as a dry run for the slave trade from Africa, which succeeded it.

The Puritan families who came to New England, then, were not typical of the single adventurers who first crossed the Atlantic, willingly or not; one of my own ancestors, who refused to pay Charles I's taxes, found himself bound for a penal colony. Even for the Puritans, it was not as families alone that these colonists set sail. In the majority of cases, they left their native shores in groups, with a religious purpose and a spiritual mentor at their head; or, coming later, they set out to join such a colony. Their purpose, that is, was not to establish cosy households, to take up land and pass it to their descendants; or at any rate, this was not their sole, or main, purpose. They moved west as members of a community larger than the family, and—to their minds—more significant, a community that stretched beyond the life span of one human creature and beyond the limits of the physical world. Their concerns took less account of the family than of the obligations that lay between an individual and a society that was a bit less theocratic than that of the Zuni, but not much. Protestantism demands, and always has, that the individual labor to gain his or her personal salvation. This emphasis on single striving lies deep in our cultural past, and it affects even those who came later and who professed a different faith or no faith at all. So here, I think, in the *single journey* to America and in the *single duty* to God, we have two clues to the reason why Americans and their literature tend to fight free of family connections.

There is another. I touched on it when I said that in Faulkner's work the family often carried a burden of history. From our earliest days we in America have been trying to put that burden down. We can see how the theocratic regimes of New England drew their strength from eternal verities, from sources outside time. But they were not alone in seeing America as a New World: a world free of the weight of the past, free of feudal duties, of subservience to rank, or tyrannical obligations to the state; a world that offered a New Eden in which Adam was being granted another chance. In a cartoon by Whitney Darrow that appeared in *The New Yorker* at the time when our space program was getting under way, a newly landed astronaut finds that he has invaded a re-enactment of the Primal Scene—not as described by Freud but the one recorded in Genesis. A charming Eve, differing from humankind only in boasting a modest pair of antennae growing out of her temples, is offering a good-natured bumpkin of an Adam the fatal apple. The astronaut's cry is given in the caption: "Oh Miss, please Miss, stop!"

Four centuries ago, a habitable New Found Land offered itself to sinners as the possible scene for an actual new beginning. A sinless Adam, whose later incarnation as the Noble Savage only strengthened the appeal of the idea, was miraculously given the opportunity to shrug off the weight of history and start anew. It is a seductive theme and one that has been worked and reworked in American literature from the time of Cooper on. But we must realize that there is no place in it for a *family*. Eve and her apple must be forsworn, and if they are—well, I'm afraid that so are Cain and Abel; and all those generations of begats, beginning with Enoch and trundling on through Irad and Mehujael and Methusael and Lamech, not to forget Seth and all his line, whom I shall, unlike Genesis, pass over in silence. In another happier Eden, Eve must know her place and avoid converse with serpents. Oh Miss, please Miss, stop!

In American literature, then, it is the romantic myth of brotherhood as the foundation of a new Utopian society, free of a sinful past, that holds a central place. I imagine we have all read Leslie Fiedler's thoughts on the matter in *Love and Death in the American Novel*: how love in America was sanitized of the great theme of sexual passion by some dreary alliance of Puritan pastors, schoolmarms and "damned female scribblers"—I am quoting Fiedler quoting Hawthorne here, which he does every twenty pages or so through the 591 he devotes to the topic. Passion between man and woman having been censored out of literary consideration, says Fiedler, it was replaced by a semidisguised obsession with passionate fraternal love between white and colored males: Natty Bumppo and Chingachgook, Ishmael and Queequeg, Huck and Nigger Jim.

There's a good deal to what Fiedler says; and if we enlarge his range, we see that the absence of mature heterosexual passion also denies, by extension, an interest in other mature ongoing relations in which those of settled and powerful families would have a place. Fiedler's concentration on male bonding ignores what serious women writers have to say. But if he had stopped admiring Hawthorne's terse condemnation long enough to look, he would have observed that the family has been no more popular with them than with their brothers of the pen; though perhaps for different reasons. Reading Fiedler, one would expect to find his female scribblers bent on making a case for eating the apple and settling down. They don't, as we shall see. The difference between male and female writing lies not in approving families; no one likes them much. The question is rather whether they are mentioned at all.

Male writers tend to ignore the institution and concentrate on the hero—the historyless hero—and his confrontation with society and/or nature. What Cooper or Melville has to say of the family is—damn all. If Arthur Dimmesdale had settled down with Hester to raise their daughter, Pearl, in loving togetherness, Hawthorne would have turned his back. Where families exist in Mark Twain, they commingle with a larger society and are not separated from it. Tom revolts against Aunt Polly, Huck flees from the Widow, because these good women wish to tame and civilize them. It is not family ties they reject, it is the whole process of socialization. The fact that socialization is usually conducted by a female relative or connection certainly colors the attitude of the heroes. But as Fiedler notes, and as is brilliantly analyzed in Ann Douglas's new study, *The Feminization of American Culture,* the absence of fathers from American families is a rather special phenomenon, which happened to coincide with the development of American literature. During the nineteenth century, the father became an absent breadwinner instead of an active parent. The center of gravity of the American family shifted, as it did not till later in the settled and stable communities of Europe. For American writers the family is a place where "you hang your childhood"; and once you've moved on, "You can't go home again."

Thomas Wolfe told us so. Dreiser saw families as hindrances to his driving men intent on carving out a career. We know that Hemingway's Nick Adams had a doctor father because he took the boy to an Indian camp, to witness a birth so difficult that the father of the child cut his throat. But when Nick came back from war, he sought solace not from his nearest and dearest but from the wilderness where the Big Two-Hearted River ran. Fitzgerald? Even a damned female scribbler would not call Tom and Daisy Buchanan a family, while the first feat of Jay Gatsby was to depart forever from his native heath, changing his name as he did so. I suppose that the only operative family relation to be found in Fitzgerald is the father-daughter incest that sets Nicole Diver on the road to madness, in *Tender Is the Night.* Henry Miller, Norman Mailer—if they mention families it is as a sort of reverse grace note; could that be a *disgrace* note? Philip Roth does indeed involve us with families, as do some other Jewish writers whose cultural background is closer to European roots than that of the Puritan tradition; and James Farrell has worked the same vein among the Irish, as did Edwin O'Connor. But these families are, again, traps to be got out of; and if they are not, their denizens grow strange beyond the limitations of realistic fiction. They become caricatures or—like Mrs. Portnoy, for example—some kind of antigoddess.

We do find a real exception to the rule that male writers ignore families in Henry James; but James, after all, crossed the Atlantic back to the continent, though not the ambience, of his forefathers, at a period when the literatures of France and England were still much involved with a family setting. Even so, the myth of an American Eden and the special innocence of its inhabitants is a recurrent theme with James. If we see it as weaving a counterpoint with family concerns, it helps to explain the richness of James's work, a richness greater and more mature than any of his American contemporaries. When in 1905 he confronted *The American Scene* for the first time in many years, his original impression was of a lack of human figures in the landscape and of European social depth. To James, the orphan hero of American literature exposed himself perilously to the disease of moral irresponsibility when he tried to lay down the burden of history.

John Cheever and John Updike seem to be the most obvious heirs to James's ability to use both the themes of American innocence and that of family matters; and both come from old and relatively stable areas of the East where some degree of social depth has developed. Even so, their use of family settings often hails back to the protagonist's childhood, as in *The Wapshot Chronicle* of Cheever and Updike's *Of the Farm* and *The Centaur.* The family that Updike's Rabbit contrives for himself is, once again, a trap; while Cheever's view of contemporary families grows increasingly strained and bitter. The tension in the household of *Bullet Park* is painful, and the echoes of family life in *Falconer* are discords. Recently Updike's families have begun to come apart into single searchers, a congeries of questing isolates recalling the dream of past intimacy and driven by its loss. At a higher social level, their plight recalls Mick Jagger's bitter complaint of getting no satisfaction. Rabbit's third installment of accommodation to a continuing household is not a happy ending but an acceptance of compromise as moral degradation due to loss of hope, of *any* familyness as better than isolation and a continual hunt rising not from expected joy but from its remembrance.

Turning now to American women writers, we find them dealing more extensively with family situations—but no more cheerfully. For them too families are traps; but traps that are harder to struggle out of. Again, this is a reflection of the historical situation. American women writers born in the nineteenth century or soon thereafter carried over to their work their own experience: which was both of a great need to escape from the orthodox feminine role that confined them forever to a family setting and of the difficulties they lived through in getting out. If they did get out. Emily Dickinson did not. For her, the American myth of innocence could only work its way out in a secret garden, a private Eden, whose mental boundaries were impregnable to family, friend or foe. Kate Chopin's heroine in *The Awakening,* Edna Pontellier, moved out of her interior world and found that active intervention with real relationships revealed her to herself as—a family prisoner. Nineteenth-century American literature offered little place for a female rebel, and Edna went to seek her Eden in death by drowning.

The next generation of women writers found no greater solace in family ties. In Ellen Glasgow's fine novel *Barren Ground,* her heroine Dorinda, seduced and abandoned as so many heroines have been through the centuries, staggers home after discovering that her lover has married another; only to ask herself "Why had she come back? It was worse here . . . her suffering was more intolerable . . . she dreaded her mother more than anything . . . Yes. She had made a mistake to come home." And so, pulling herself together, she packs her possessions and boards a train north, for New York. Unlike Edna Pontellier, Dorinda is a survivor who can, in the end, manipulate life and people her way. But though she finally marries, this family, of a faithful hardworking but unloved widower and his children, is an

accommodation to reality, not a happy ending. The closest we come
to this is when Dorinda finds her own ability to "face the future
without romantic glamour, but with . . . integrity of vision." It is her
own strength, not family support, that sees her through. In her posthumous memoir, *The Woman Within,* Glasgow recalled her own
family strains and conflicts that forced her, when hardly more than
a child, to set herself against the rulings of her parents and declare:
"If I won nothing else, I had won liberty." Like Dorinda, she had
stamina and knew when to ignore orthodox counsel like that of the
editor who assured her that "The best advice I can give you is to stop
writing and go back to the South and have some babies." Presumably
he meant her to marry first. She did neither.

Willa Cather, an almost exact contemporary of Glasgow's, knew
both the pull of the New Eden and the struggle exacted of women who
tried to reach it. In her preface to the revised edition of *The Song of
the Lark,* she wrote, "What I cared about and still care about is the
girl's escape." It was no quick flitting but a matter of dedicated work
and grinding determination that allowed Thea Kronborg to shake the
dust of Moonstone, Colorado, off her feet and set out on the road to
an operatic career. In Cather's best book (or so I think), *The Professor's House,* the hero's family is, perhaps, more of a drain than a trap;
but Professor St. Peter's ability to survive derives from the spiritual
double life he has led. The first component of this interior Eden has
been the writing of a long and demanding—as well as rewarding—
history of the Spanish conquistadors and explorers in America. The
second was his association with Tom Outland, the orphan hero who
walked into his life and changed its inner structure forever, supplying
an emotional fraternity similar to that which Fiedler celebrates.

Another generational step brings us to a writer who created perhaps the most horrible household in literature since that of Jason and
Medea: the one of Sam and Henny Pollit in Christina Stead's *The Man
Who Loved Children.* At home, the Pollits act out a devilish drama
of hate, spite and malicious fury. Henny rejects her children, Sam
plays on their sympathies with maudlin self-pity in equally maudlin
baby talk. He likes to tell them of his wife's "vicious upbringing, that
of a rich wastrel." He confides "to a great many of his bosom friends
. . . that never was a more faithful, long-suffering husband than he
(joined to) a lighter-headed, vainer, more pernicious woman." To his
oldest daughter, Louisa, whom he calls Looloo, he suggests that
Henny is capable of criminal activity: "Many is the time I have gone

(to work) not knowing whether I would come home to find you butchered."

As for Henny, she acts on the same unfortunate child to create an emanation of feminine fury. The role of woman that is being transmitted from mother to daughter bristles with inevitable, fated frustration, as if female existence were enclosed under a reverberant iron sky, which neither hope nor prayer could pierce. Escape and revenge come together as a way out, but it is not an escape into salvation but into guilt and an eternal denial of guilt. The effect of living with a blood-sucking hypocrite of a father and a gorgon of a mother drive Louisa to escape by revenge. Like Edna Pontellier, Louisa kills to get away: Not herself, but her mother is the victim.

Stead's contemporary, Louise Bogan, recalled her own feelings when young, not in a poem but in a letter to fellow-poet Theodore Roethke. The means of her escape were not as drastic as those of Louisa Pollit, but the emotions came close.

> I, too, have been imprisoned by a family, who held out the bait of a nice hot cup of tea and a nice clean bed and no questions asked, until the mould starts effacing the last noble lineaments of the soul . . . And let me tell you right now, the only way to get away is to get away: pack up and go. Anywhere. I had a child, from the age of twenty, remember that, to hold me back, but I got up and went just the same, and I was, God help us, a woman. I took the first job that came along. And there was a depression on, as there is now, not quite so bad (she was writing in 1935), but still pretty poor, and I lived on eighteen bucks a week and spent a winter in a thin suit and muffler. But I was free. And when this last time I couldn't free myself by my own will, because my will was suffering from a disease peculiar to it, I went to the mad-house for six months, under my own steam, mind you, for no one sent me there, and I got free . . . When one isn't free, one is a *thing,* the *thing* of others, and the only point, in this rotten world, is to be your own, to hold the scepter and mitre over yourself, in the immortal words of Dante.
>
> . . . Believe me, I saw my brother, from the age of twenty-six to thirty-three, when death providentially took him (in the First World War), and he stayed home and didn't put up a fight except towards the last when he used to knock down doors and smash windows with chairs, and be brought home, beaten to a pulp, and I tell you, anything in God's world is better than that . . .
>
> . . . Take the word of one who has lain on the icy floor of the ninth circle of hell, without speech and will and hope, it's the self that must

do it. You, Ted Roethke for Ted Roethke, I Louise Bogan for Louise Bogan.

Are we to conclude that these exacerbated judgments on the family are fated to endure forever among American writers? Or even the more moderate view of another poet, who wrote: "One would be in less danger / From the wiles of the stranger / If one's own kin and kith / Were more fun to be with."? Interestingly enough, the new feminist movement appears to be gentling the rage of the female of the species as expressed in literature; no doubt because she is no longer, necessarily, the "house-jailed and child-chained" creature that she used to be. The introduction of real choices in women's lives, of respectable alternatives to imprisonment by a family, has in itself made possible a more objective look at family relations. If a door is left open, after all, a cage ceases to be a cage, and what happens inside can be thought about with ordinary rational curiosity instead of egotistic terror. Women's literature is now able to revalue relationships because they are no longer inevitable, no longer dictated from outside, to be evaded only by furious flight.

The marital relationship was the first to be examined. The sixties saw a spate of novels about wives who left their husbands—for flings with other men, for careers or attempts at them, for lesbian relationships, or lonely desperation, or attempts at political action. None of these offered any easy solution, no immediate triumph; indeed, no approach to Eden. The fantasy of a happy ending to flight was fading away. Women who left husbands found their lives fragmented and full of struggle. Yet as the years pass and the volumes accumulate, as "romantic glamour"—in the words Ellen Glasgow used half a century ago—is replaced by "integrity of vision," the tone of this writing steadies and toughens; grows comic, as in Grace Paley's cheerful, satiric mockery, or laughs at the Gothic terrors—some of them real— that surround such a stubbornly independent young woman as the heroine of Diane Johnson's novel *The Shadow Knows*. Raising three children alone, after a divorce, she fends off anonymous phone calls and ambiguous friendships but refuses to close her mind to a world where affection and respect may be possible.

The judgment on marriage as it has been practiced, however, does not much soften. Instead of the diatribes of a Henny Pollit, we have wives who have judged their situations—and voted with their feet, the feet that carried them out the door. Few, if any, go back; and if they do, it is with the feeling that flight has effected some interior change.

They are not the same women who left. They do not intend to renew old relationships but to find out what, if anything, can be salvaged on which to build a new relationship.

Building new connections involves more than the one between husband and wife. As the sixties turned to the seventies, women's fiction, poetry, and nonfiction too have begun to consider the possibility of revaluing the relationships between parents and children. Let us go back for a moment to those orphan heroes—or would-be orphans —who were rejecting the "civilizing" of the Aunt Pollys because they saw the civilization offered them as castrating. And now let us try to enter the minds of the women who have been expected to carry out this process of civilizing, or socializing, children. What is it they have been asked to do? Nothing less than pass on to the next generation the norms of behavior, the social myth and the explanatory structure of belief that shapes our society. And where do they, themselves, stand within that society? In woman's place—or so they had done. In a place that both degraded and trivialized the image of their abilities; that put an impenetrable ceiling on their aspirations; that set them against each other because, if one cannot respect oneself, how can one respect the others of one's class?

How can these people easily, happily teach the norms and standards that they are forbidden to share? How can they not rage against the falseness and the hypocrisy of such demands unless they are talked into the "Aunt Polly" image, which could be taken as that of a WASP Aunt Jemima? How can those who are completely domesticated take seriously the pompous creatures who fail to see the implicit incongruity of the situation? Is it not possible that children felt, however obscurely, the blind submerged anger that lived in their mothers' breasts; that might never surface but that nonetheless shadowed the purity of the mother-child bond? Perhaps the message that civilization by women threatened castration was true. True, that is, as long as women could sit and think about themselves and their condition as analogous to that of slaves; an analogy that was noted and spoken by many a female abolitionist.

Today, however, American women writers, beginning with the poets, have begun to think their way to a new understanding of what one generation owes another and to purify the connections between them by finding and destroying the sources of anger and mistrust that have lain there in the past. That is, of course, an enormous task; and yet if we are to talk to each other honestly we must undertake it, even though perfect success is surely as unlikely as any Utopian dream. Anne Sexton writes to her daughter:

> What I want to say, Linda
> is that there is nothing in your body that lies.
> All that is new is telling the truth.
> I'm here, that somebody else,
> an old tree in the background.
>
> Darling,
> stand still at your door,
> sure of yourself, a white stone, a good stone—
> as exceptional as laughter
> you will strike fire,
> that new thing!

Here is something new and strongly affirmative, a mother message intended to nourish the faculties that are necessary if women are to survive our own mistakes; honesty, courage, joy are a few of them. We can be especially grateful to black women writers for their sense of a past reality that illuminates the passage of knowledge to their children in today's world. Gwendolyn Brooks, Toni Morrison, Toni Cade Bambara and Nikki Giovanni re-create in their books childhoods lived on an edge of daring, where tales of ancestral prowess, whether male or female, could help a child to stand his or her ground and refuse to "take low," even though the outer society continued to demand subservience. In such a world links to the past feed into one's own identity, as Alex Haley has demonstrated so clearly. But he is not alone. Lucille Clifton, in *Generations,* recalls the legend of her great-great-grandmother, captured in Dahomey by slavers when she was eight years old, brought to New Orleans and marched to Virginia for sale. This Caroline lived to raise her great-grandson and die once more free. Nikki Giovanni takes pride in her proud grandmother. Maya Angelou finds that in time of need she can go home again. Lineage, memory and support from kinfolk join in these novels and memoirs from black women writers to illustrate a sort of family that is not just a cage but a fortress against a hostile world.

Analogously, Maxine Kingston learns from her Chinese-American mother not just the expected rules of submissive behavior that daughters are expected to follow but also the legends of women warriors who defy the rules.

The revaluation of family relationships that we find as a central theme in contemporary writing by women might just point to new ways of living together as well as new ways of writing about living together. Let the Bad Fairy end on an admittedly Utopian note. The American need to create a new world and a new society out of a new Eden has foundered on the rocks of human limitations. We can't remove those rocks, but we certainly can make ourselves more aware of them. When our writers tell us that American families as experienced by individuals are too small and too confining; when they see them as cut off from the ongoing process of social interaction between the individual and the wider community—then I think we should listen. What we want to bring out of the past and hold onto as we invent a future is perhaps *not* the family but the other element we are discussing at this conference: the community. Can we make it a community of shared participation, where fewer stereotypes of sex or race or age divide us and force a retreat to isolated life, either as a single alienated ego or in a grasping, frightened, too-tight familial relationship? Kin and community, yes; but space within them for human growth and human aspiration where each of us can move and act and aspire, following our own dreams.

Lolita (Review)

THE FIRST TIME I READ *Lolita* I
thought it was one of the funniest books I'd ever come on. (This was
the abbreviated version published in the Anchor Review last year.)
The second time I read it, uncut, I thought it was one of the saddest.
I mention this personal reaction only because Lolita is one of those
occasional books that arrive swishing behind them a long tail of
opinion and reputation that can knock the unwary reader off his feet.
It is shocking; is it pornographic, is it immoral? Is its reading to be
undertaken not as simple experience but as a conscious action that will
place one on this or that side of a critical dividing line? What does the
Watch and Ward Society say of it? What does Sartre, Graham Greene
or *Partisan Review*?

This is hard on any book. *Lolita* stands up to it wonderfully well,
though even its author has felt it necessary to contribute an epilogue
on his intentions. This, by the way, seems to me quite as misleading
as the purposely absurd (and very funny) prologue by "John Ray, Jr.,
Ph.D.," who is a beautifully constructed character of American Academic Bumbledom. But in providing a series of trompe-l'oeil frames
for the action of his book, Vladimir Nabokov has undoubtedly been
acting with intent: They are screens as well as frames. He is not writing
for the ardent and simple-minded civil libertarian anymore than he is
writing for the private libertine; he is writing for readers, and those
who can read him simply will be well rewarded.

He is fond of frames and their effects. A final one is provided
within the book itself by the personality of the narrator, Humbert
Humbert ("an assumed name"). Humbert is a close-to-forty European, a spoiled poet turned dilettante critic, the possessor of a small
but adequate private income and an enormous and agonizing private
problem: He is aroused to erotic desire only by girls on the edge of

puberty, nine-to-fourteen-year-old "nymphets." Juliet, Dante's Beatrice and Petrarch's Laura all fell within this age range, but to poor panting Humbert Humbert, the twentieth century denies the only female things he really desires.

Then, as in a fairy tale, his wish comes true. Lolita is its fulfillment. She is the quintessence of the nymphet, discovered by total accident in an Eastern American small town. To get her, Humbert puts himself through a pattern of erotic choreography that would shame a bower-bird. He is grotesque and horrible and unbearably funny, and he knows it. He will settle for anything and does. The "anything" involves marrying Lolita's widowed mother, Charlotte, with all the lies and swallowing of distaste that this implies. Charlotte promptly arranges to send the child away so that the two "lovers" can be alone together, and Humbert begins to consider the distasteful lies necessitated by murder.

Fate, however, intervenes (McFate, Humbert calls him, envisioning him as an old, lavish and absent-minded friend addicted to making ambiguous gifts, a sort of deified Bernard Goldfine). Charlotte is killed in an accident. Dream come true! With his little step-daughter (he drops the "step" to strangers), Humbert sets out on an odyssey of lechery that approaches the flights and "fugues" of schizophrenia.

It turns into a nightmare. Through two years and two lengthy circuits of the American scene, Humbert spirals down the levels of his inferno. Possessed, insatiable, he can never stop wanting Lolita because he never really has her—he has only her body. In the end, his punishment matches his crime. Lolita runs off with a monster; Humbert attempts to track them (giving a hilarious impersonation of a Thurber bloodhound as he does), bounces into a sanitorium, bounces out and lives in despair until Dolly, who used to be Lolita, finds him. She is now an entirely different person, a triumph for the vital force that has managed to make a life out of the rubble that Humbert's passion created and the monster's mindless activity merely confirmed. For a moment Humbert stands revealed to himself as her destroyer. But this confrontation does him no good. He sheers off into action again and rushes away to find and murder the monster in a long tragi-farcical shambles that somehow combines the chase scene from *Charley's Aunt* with the denouement of *Titus Andronicus.*

In his epilogue, Mr. Nabokov informs us that *Lolita* has no moral. I can only say that Humbert's fate seems to me classically tragic, a most perfectly realized expression of the moral truth that Shakespeare summed up in the sonnet that begins: "The expense of spirit in a waste of shame/ Is lust in action": right down to the detailed working out of Shakespeare's adjectives, "perjur'd, murderous, bloody, full of blame." Humbert is the hero with the tragic flaw. Humbert is every man who is driven by desire, wanting his Lolita so badly that it never occurs to him to consider her as a human being or as anything but a dream figment made of flesh—which is the eternal and universal nature of passion.

The author, that is, is writing about all lust. He has afflicted poor Humbert with a special and taboo variety for a couple of contradictory reasons. In the first place, its illicit nature will both shock the reader into paying attention and prevent sentimentally false sympathy from distorting his judgment. Contrariwise, I believe, Mr. Nabokov is slyly exploiting the American emphasis on the attraction of youth and the importance devoted to the "teenager" in order to promote an unconscious identification with Humbert's agonies. Both techniques are entirely valid. But neither, I hope, will obscure the purpose of the device: namely, to underline the essential, inefficient, painstaking and pain-giving selfishness of all passion, all greed—of all urges, whatever they may be, that insist on being satisfied without regard to the effect their satisfaction has upon the outside world. Humbert is all of us.

So much for the moral of this book, which is not supposed to have one. Technically it is brilliant, Peter-De-Vries humor in a major key, combined with an eye for the revealing, clinching detail of social behavior. If there is one fault to find, it is that in making his hero his narrator, Mr. Nabokov has given him a task that is almost too big for a fictional character. Humbert tends to run over into a figure of allegory, of Everyman. When this happens it unbalances the book, for every other character belongs in a novel and is real as real can be. Humbert alone runs over at the edges, as if in painting him Mr. Nabokov had just a little too much color on his brush; which color is, I suppose, the moral that poor Humbert is carrying for his creator.

Never mind. This is still one of the funniest books that will be published this year. As for its pornographic content, I can think of few volumes more likely to quench the flames of lust than this exact and immediate description of its consequences.

Nabokov
the Magician

VLADIMIR VLADIMIROVICH NA-
BOKOV, aged sixty-eight, best known as the author of *Lolita,* has this
year become the object of scholarly study. Two book-length evalua-
tions have appeared, *Escape Into Aesthetics* by Page Stegner, and
Nabokov: His Life in Art by Andrew Field, while the University of
Wisconsin devoted the spring issue of its *Studies in Contemporary
Literature* to his work.

Ordinary readers are likely to be taken aback when this metamor-
phosis transforms a writer they have been following with interest and
pleasure into the subject of analysis and argument. The minutiae of
scholarship often seem irritating or grotesque. My father, in his latter
years, maintained that he had always read the novels of Melville and
Conrad as "good yarns," and he had no intention of changing his
mind because these familiar authors were suddenly being plumbed for
symbols. I must confess that the same sort of philistine cramp assailed
me when I came on Alfred Appel's remark (in Wisconsin *Studies*) that
"careful readers should be able to identify (the butterfly motif) for
many of the lepidopteral descriptions of Lolita are explicit, and a
familiarity with Nabokov's other books, especially *Speak, Memory,*
should alert one to this possibility"; or when Andrew Field advises us
that *The Defense* "is an ornament and perhaps even a cornerstone to
Nabokov's art, but one does not feel a need or compulsion to read it
more than twice." Gentle scholars! The plain reader confronted with
such dicta is almost bound to declare that he will read *The Defense*
four times or not at all, and that the metamorphoses of Lolita may be
intellectually interesting but add no emotional weight to the book.

Yet the plain reader is wrong. Philistinism is a much more dangerous disease (as Nabokov himself has shown—none better!) than even
that aberrant form of scholarship, Kinbotism, which our author de-

scribed so hilariously in *Pale Fire*. Appel and Field are excellent critics of Nabokov's work, and they have a great deal to tell us about it that we will be the better to know. Appel, who was Nabokov's student at Cornell, contributes to Wisconsin *Studies* an interesting, if rather reverential, interview with him and a most perceptive article on *Lolita* that can only enlarge one's vision of the book. As for Field, his painstaking survey of Nabokov's whole production in Russian and in English—novels, stories, poems, criticism, translations, and plays—will be indispensable for future students. It is a truly remarkable feat of analysis and integration.

Of course, scholarship has its failures. Claire Rosenfield, who writes on *Despair* in Wisconsin *Studies,* and Page Stegner, when he is discussing *The Real Life of Sebastian Knight* in his book, seem to have the sort of tin ear that can't detect irony. This is a truly disabling fault in reading Nabokov, who likes to let his characters convict and condemn themselves out of their own mouths. But the virtues of close and serious study are clear. Whether the plain reader cares or not, the effect of scholarly inquiry is to extend the context of a piece of work and deepen its resonance, to free it from its mold of "everydayness" and invite a more general as well as a closer view.

The one thing scholarship can't do is decide whether or not the piece of work is worth the effort. That job is for readers, contemporary and to come. It is the "one big thing" that the hedgehog knows and the fox does not. Criticism won't keep a work alive; only a continuing and living connection between a writer and his public will do that. Contemporary readers begin the connection, but none of them, alas, can really judge how long it will last.

Heaven knows whether Nabokov "is worth it" or whether he "will live." He writes magnificently, but then so did Swinburne. But whether or not his themes will attract readers in the future, they are profoundly a part of our world—exile from a lost and loved past; unprovoked violence; the uncertainty of one's identity, which sprinkles doubles and mirrors through his books; the equivalent questioning of the world outside oneself in an effort to understand what is really there; what art achieves and how it differs from the acting out of fantasy.

His method—tricks, puns, parody, and surprises, the coincidences that suggest a secret pattern, the stroke of McFate, the writer's face perceived behind the actions of his characters: all this is marvelously suited to his material. His technique in itself expresses and comments on his themes, and by so doing raises that very contemporary question:

control. How much of my life do I control, and if not I, then who? What? Which comes around again to the sense of identity and the value and function of art.

Nabokov's material affects his technique at another level. Much of it is taken from his own life: childhood happiness, exile in a strange land, the effort and rapture of creation, the father lost or killed, the grim absurd horrors of the police state, lepidoptery, teaching. Episodes from his past, reworked to varying degrees, have been bestowed on a number of his characters. Author-heroes, like Sebastian Knight and Fyodor Godunov-Cherdyntsev (in *The Gift*), have received the largest bequests, but many others, like Humbert Humbert, are also inheritors of Nabokov's memories.

To translate one's own life into fiction is extremely difficult to do. The fact that it's done all the time, badly and wrong, sentimentally, tendentiously, and that a vulgar interpretation of Freud's theories suggests it is always done—this makes doing it right all the harder. To do it right, an author must distance himself as creator from himself as character, step back to see himself in perspective, and drop, or cut, the emotional link of his self-justifying me-ness. Nabokov has been called cold. It is rather, I think, this distancing that produces that impression.

All fiction, of course, involves the use of one's own experience in the sense that one must find there analogies to the events one creates. But if the experience has *in fact* been lived through and felt strongly, the effort to cut it off from one's private (and therefore misleading) emotions is so much the greater. What is astonishing about Nabokov's use of his past is not that it occasionally seems cold but that so often it does not; and yet the tenderness and joy of memories given—for instance, to Fyodor, in *The Gift*—are totally unsentimental.

How much the experience of Vladimir Nabokov the individual, plunged from riches to poverty and driven from his home, influences Vladimir Nabokov the writer is an obvious question but not, I think, a profitable one. What happens to a writer is certainly important to his work, but the connection is labyrinthine, and trying to trace correspondences is a misinterpretation of art. I suppose one could make a case for the hypothesis that Nabokov's exile, which took from him a place in a wealthy and influential family, cost him the opportunity of following his father, a dedicated liberal statesman, into the arena of political action. Result: Nabokov's heroes are patients, not agents;

acted upon rather than acting. But so are the heroes of most serious
novels today.

Perhaps, to follow the argument around its circle, one should
conclude that we are most of us exiles from power; which at once does
away with the whole question of how Nabokov's individual experience
shapes his work, by sinking him back into a general situation. The
most one can say is that an exile's rootlessness probably forces the use
of his own experiences rather than more general social material, and
at the same time makes easier the "distancing" that allows such
intimate experience to be turned into art. But searching a man's life
as a way of understanding his books is a blunder based on a fallacy.
It ignores the creative act, by which alone experience and fantasy are
fused and raised into a work of art. It is the public work of art that
is the business of the critic, even when that work of art is a memoir.

In *Speak, Memory* Nabokov has written a classic of reminiscence.
But his younger self, whose life he is describing, mutters no secrets,
nor does he try to persuade his readers to this or that opinion, even
when the opinions are strongly held. He and his parents, his cousins,
his governesses and tutors and early loves are there to show us a
vanished way of life, a family-sized segment of the Golden Age. The
book is at once intimate and impersonal. If Chekhov had made himself
a character in *The Cherry Orchard,* the effect would be rather the
same.

Nabokov's art is full of tricks, sleight of hand and puzzles. He likes
to compose chess problems in which the purpose is to mislead, not the
innocent but the semi-informed. In somewhat the same way, his books
tend to lure the unwary into concentrating on the puzzles and ignoring
the total effect. (Here the plain reader who decides the puzzles are over
his head may initially be better off.) But the point of the puzzles is
what they do and how they work within the whole area of the book.

Often the overall statement that the book illustrates can be
summed up (though inadequately) by a simple phrase. As Field points
out, *Laughter in the Dark* is an enactment of the statement that love
is blind; and *Invitation to a Beheading,* that life is a dream. The book
then sets up a situation that both parallels and parodies the proposi-
tion. The parody and the jokes supply a running commentary interwoven with the action.

These propositions can be highly moral. The fate of Albinus, hero
of *Laughter in the Dark,* is announced by the author at the opening
of the book in terms that are naïve even for soap opera. Albinus is a
wealthy man with a wife and child who is infatuated by a greedy

young tart, leaves his family for her (the little daughter dies of pneumonia, and he does not attend the funeral), and in consequence comes to a very bad end, blinded, cuckolded and mocked. He sets out to shoot his mistress and kills himself by accident.

Thank heaven, says the plain reader at this denouement, with almost as much relief as when Little Nell finally breathes her last. But even in this quite straightforward book, irony and melodrama combine to question and judge the drama of the narrative. This apparently sentimental tale becomes suspenseful and funny, a result that eliminates the sentimentality and refreshes the banality of the situation. Albinus, the bewildered villain, becomes a sympathetic character; more so, in fact, than Humbert Humbert, whose moralizing over the wrong he did Lolita I find distasteful. Albinus simply is, does, and suffers. He is contained within his book as a parable is contained in a stained-glass window.

Thus the distance that Nabokov maintains by means of his tricks between his work and the world, and his work and his readers, permits the work to complete itself. His novels illustrate life while standing apart from it. Nabokov's books are not abstracts of reality, but constructs that mimic and perfect it. Sebastian Knight, his only novelist-hero, is discovered once lying on his back on the floor. "No, I'm not dead," he says to an intruder. "I have finished building a world, and this is my Sabbath rest." The novelist, that is, does not interpret an existing world. He creates another; which would be worthless if it were simply a mirror reflection, useless unless it were finer and more complete.

Another effect of the puzzle element in Nabokov's work may be the feeling, which he shares with Sebastian Knight, that his books exist before they are written, waiting to be discovered. In his interview with Appel he puts it this way: "I do think that in my case it is true that the entire book, before it is written, seems to be ready ideally in some other, now transparent, now dimming, dimension, and my job is to take down as much of it as I can make out and as precisely as I am humanly able to."

This is a hallucination that has haunted other artists and that seems to have a subterranean connection with the idea of puzzle-solving. Thus, in his latest collection of essays, *Norm and Form,* Professor E. H. Gombrich comes, by way of puzzle-solving, to a discussion of the feeling "expressed by Schiller that somewhere, in a Platonic heaven, the solution [the artist] gropes for is already prefigured—that once it is found it is inevitable and right. . . . Wherever you set yourself the task of combining a number of orders," he goes on, "the number of possible solutions will decrease with the richness of the order you aim at."

Clearly, Nabokov's work is "rich" in this sense; it combines layer after layer of intent, until it approaches that ideal point where there can really be only one "right" way of interpreting it. Taken in this light, the puzzle element in Nabokov's novels and stories is not an overlay put there to irritate the reader and entice him from the point. It is rather a way of defining the central mystery and directing him toward the solution.

Return for a moment to Sebastian Knight, spread-eagled on the floor. The incident illustrates just how Nabokov does use his memories. In *Speak, Memory* it was his mother's brother, Uncle Ruka, who lay on his back on the floor after dinner. "He insisted that he had an incurable heart ailment and that, when the seizures came, he could obtain relief only by lying supine on the floor. Nobody took him seriously, and after he died of angina pectoris, all alone, in Paris, at the end of 1916, aged forty-five, it was with a quite special pang that one recalled those after-dinner incidents in the drawing room."

After Sebastian dies, young and alone, of Uncle Ruka's heart ailment, this pang creates the book in which Sebastian appears, for it impels his younger brother, V., to search out *The Real Life of Sebastian Knight* in order to write his brother's biography. Yet to imagine that Sebastian is Uncle Ruka in any useful sense is absurd (though I suspect that Uncle Ruka turns up in other guises). A particle of memory has simply served as a magnetic point to attract layer upon layer of diverse material, which then becomes a created character-and-situation. To this point, Nabokov says in his interview with Appel, "Imagination is a form of memory. An image depends on the power of association, and association is supplied and prompted by memory. In this sense, both memory and imagination are a negation of time."

"I confess I don't believe in time," Nabokov writes in *Speak, Memory.* But in the same book he also records his first consciousness (at four) of "the radiant and mobile medium that was none other than the pure element of time"; and postulates that "the beginning of reflexive consciousness in the brain of our remotest ancestor must surely have coincided with the dawning of the sense of time." Time, for this nonbeliever, is not something to be ignored but to be met actively—challenged, tricked, perhaps turned inside out. His new novel, Field tells us, "is to be in large degree an artistic expression and exploration of the exact meaning of time." But as Field also points out,

"Time has held an important place in almost all Nabokov's major fiction."

The perception of time is one way of ordering the world, and it is intimately connected with other kinds of ordering. Jean Piaget and Bruno Bettelheim, in separate studies of children, have found evidence that the ability to predict what will happen (and memory comes in here, for one can predict only if one can recognize a pattern) precedes an understanding of causality. Without such an understanding, meaningful action is impossible; and the ability to predict, understand, and act to control one's environments is basic to the growth of personality. I apologize for this shockingly oversimplified summation of complicated theory based on long observation; but these themes chime together at the heart of Nabokov's work. It is therefore important to suggest that he is handling a complex of material that has turned up in quite another context as being related and as being central to the formation of identity: memory involving prediction, understanding that permits action and leads to control. Without these props, children retreat into violence, schizophrenia and autism; into fantasy, repetitive ritual, useless action and withdrawal. The insane have a great deal to tell the normal about how the world works.

Nabokov's exploration of time is much closer to such psychological studies of time-perception than it is to Proust's search for things past and lost time. It is in a way more mechanical, just as Nabokov's use of his own experience is more objective; but it is also more complex and more inventive.

For a sketch of how he handles these themes, we might glance at *Pale Fire,* that trap, that puzzle-novel par excellence. Like all Nabokov's books it is a construct, but this one lacks the usual outer layer of plausibility. There is no sensible narrative, no real-seeming hero, no story. Only a madman and a poet exist, plus the creations of each—the poet's autobiographical poem, "Pale Fire," and the madman's commentary on it, which turns out apparently to have nothing to do with the poem.

Now a great deal of research has been done to discover how these two creations are in fact related: strange voices speak through each, ghosts knock, mirrors shine, and the verses that the poet John Shade has discarded are closer to mad Dr. Kinbote's commentary than the ones that make up the poem. But I would like to step back from this intimate inquiry—"distance" the book—and try to see what sort of

shadow this construct throws if one looks at it from the right angle
and asks it the right question; or rather, *a* right question. Perhaps
there are many.

A useful question, perhaps a right question, is, Who is the Red
King? Who is dreaming whom? Has Shade created Kinbote, or Kin-
bote Shade? Let us, that is, approach *Pale Fire* through the Looking
Glass.

> I was the shadow of the waxwing, slain
> By the false azure of the windowpane.

So begins John Shade's poem. The windowpane has become a
mirror, reflecting the bird it kills. Alice, dreaming before the fire, saw
the mirror over the mantel fade and become a window through which
she could climb into another world, paralleling and parodying ours.
Descending, she discovered she had landed on a chessboard and was
involved in a game whether she liked it or not. All this, of course, is
familiar Nabokov symbology. So are the characters Alice met—a
couple of lunatics of varying charm, the White Knight and the Mad
Hatter, now transformed into Hatta the Anglo-Saxon messenger,
Tweedledum and Tweedledee, the twins and doubles who engage in
fake combat, Humpty-Dumpty, whose words mean whatever he tells
them to, the White Queen, who reversed time and lived backward, and
the above-mentioned Red King, asleep and snoring, who, Tweedledee
assured Alice, was not only dreaming, but dreaming *her.* "If he left
off dreaming about you . . . you'd be nowhere. Why, you're only a sort
of thing in his dream." To which Tweedledum adds, "If that there
King was to wake, you'd go out—bang!—just like a candle!"

Among the chores that Nabokov did as a young exile in Berlin was
to translate *Alice in Wonderland* into Russian. Perhaps his next inter-
viewer will undertake to ask him whether he also translated its sequel,
Alice Through the Looking Glass; but really, it hardly matters. No one
who knows Alice well enough to translate the first volume is going to
be ignorant of the second. The young Nabokovs, growing up in an
Anglophile household at the turn of the century, must certainly have
had Alice read to them. Indeed, when Appel in his interview spoke
of Lewis Carroll in another context, Nabokov replied, "In common
with many other English children (I was an English child) I have
always been very fond of Carroll." To anyone exposed to them in
childhood, the Carroll books become a lingua franca. Leaving the

theater recently, after seeing a Pinter play, I heard myself asking exactly this question, Who was the Red King?

Andrew Field arrives at the same question by another route (his discussion of *Pale Fire* is very interesting, though not, I think, complete), and his answer is that Shade creates Kinbote, not Kinbote Shade. His argument is that a sane poet can create a madman, but not the other way around, which is persuasive. I agree, but on other grounds as well, that Shade is the primary character, who in a sense creates Kinbote, while Kinbote creates the third person who is present, Gradus, the murderer. (Field maintains that the third member of the trilogy is Nabokov himself, creating them all. But I believe Gradus must be included to understand the pattern of the book.)

The sequence then runs, Shade creates Kinbote, who creates Gradus, who murders Shade. And at once it becomes impossible, a vicious circle. For how can already-murdered Shade create the Kinbote who writes the commentary to Shade's poem, which he sees only *after* Shade has been shot down by the creature Gradus, who first appears in the commentary? But the impossibility of an answer is no reason for discarding the question, as a friend from *Alice Through the Looking Glass* will remind us—the White Queen, who practiced believing impossible things before breakfast. An apparent impossibility is a signal that one is looking at something in a wrong or superficial way. If we again "distance" the problem presented by this apparently impossible situation, we can arrive at an answer; and one that is entirely consonant with Nabokov's experiments in time. For what is impossible *in reality* becomes possible when taken out of time and placed in the world of art; and because it *is* impossible in reality, it *must* be so taken. Then the vicious circle—but let Nabokov himself explain:

> The spiral is a spiritualized circle. In the spiral form, the circle, uncoiled, unwound, has ceased to be vicious; it has been set free. I thought this up when I was a schoolboy, and I also discovered that Hegel's triadic series (so popular in old Russia) expressed merely the essential spirality of all things in their relation to time. Twirl follows twirl, and every synthesis is the thesis of the next series.

Art is the home of the impossible, in which time is suspended. The wandering madman who shoots Shade in the real world (a world which is absent in *Pale Fire*) is accidental. He has mistaken Shade for the Judge who sentenced him. But in art there can be no accidents.

Take time away, and the murderer becomes a purposeful figure who tracks down the banished King of Zembla, mad Kinbote, in a world that is ordered by causality, not mere prediction. So art and reality confront each other, mirror images and doubles that illuminate each other by their differences. The book is like a top, spun by the bullet out of "real" time, but whirling through another dimension.

Why should Nabokov do this? Or, to put it differently, what is the book about? Field says—and Field is intelligent as well as hardworking—that it is about death, and indeed, as many deaths occur, at least, as in *Hamlet.* But death in Nabokov's work is curiously unfinal. Smurov in *The Eye,* Cincinnatus in *Invitation to a Beheading* may or may not die. If they do, they continue in some other time element. In *The Gift* a father sees his son's ghost and a son feels the living presence of a dead father. Sebastian Knight's brother attempts to resurrect him in a biography. In *Pale Fire* Shade's daughter Hazel talks with ghosts, and the poet himself experiences (he believes) death, a vision of the hereafter, and immediate resurrection.

Pale Fire, then, is as much about survival as it is about death. The shadow of the waxwing, slain in the first line of the poem, "lived on, flew on, in the reflected sky." As a boy, Shade had wondered how one

> ". . . could . . . live without
> Knowing for sure what dawn, what death, what doom
> Awaited consciousness beyond the tomb,"

and decided to "explore and fight / The foul, the inadmissible abyss, / Devoting all my twisted life to this / One task." If we live on, he wonders, how do we live on?

> What if you are tossed [he asks]
> Into a boundless void, your bearings lost
> Your spirit stripped and utterly alone,
> Your task unfinished, your despair unknown. . . .
>
> A wrench, a rift—that is all one can foresee.
> Maybe one finds *le grand néant;* maybe
> Again one spirals from the tuber's eye.

His experience of death and resurrection convinces him that something survives, but "that the sense behind / The scene was not our sense." In fact, to one's present self, one's ghost might well appear mad.

The clues point in one direction. Kinbote is Shade's mad ghost, attempting in his commentary to carry on the unfinished task and write the last line of Shade's poem; to express the simplicity of the expected repetition, "I was the shadow of the waxwing, slain," in his grotesque autobiography.

The impression is reinforced by the possibility that Hazel, Shade's daughter, may be a reincarnation of Aunt Maude, who brought him up. Hazel is odd and unfitted for life, perhaps because she is close to the ghost world with its sense-not-our-sense. In fact, once one sees that the true relationships in the book can exist only outside normal time, and actually counter to it, the problems start to unravel. And this, finally, is why there is no "real story" in *Pale Fire*: It is a work of art that can exist and be understood *only* outside the time-tied world of reality.

Under the guise of a study of death and immortality, it is an inquiry into identity. Who are we? it asks. What is that "I" that each of us feels to endure through the passage of time and of change? The study of this problem has been a lifelong task not only for Shade but for Nabokov himself. "Over and over again," he writes in *Speak, Memory,* "my mind has made colossal efforts to distinguish the faintest of personal glimmers in the impersonal darkness on both sides of my life. That this darkness is caused merely by the walls of time separating me and my bruised fists from the free world of timelessness is a belief I gladly share with the most gaudily painted savage." But, he adds, "I groped for some secret outlet only to discover that the prison of time is spherical and has no outlets."

It is in his books that Nabokov breaks through the prison wall. His art is not, as Stegner suggests, "an escape into aesthetics." It is an instrument of inquiry into reality, into the nature of the prison that holds us and of the creature that bruises its fists against those prison walls. His tricks are not an attempt to obscure reality but to determine its nature by imitating it.

In the fall of 1939, in Paris (Field tells us), Nabokov wrote a story that was a first version and false start of *Lolita.* It was called, in Russian, "Volshebnik," which Field translates as "The Conjuror"; and indeed, the unfortunate middle-aged hero who falls in love with a twelve-year-old nymphet was a conjuror. But the straightforward translation of *"volshebnik"* is rather magician or enchanter, a larger and more ambiguous term that admits the possibility that the magic may work, or be real. This minor fact seems to me a pointer. Nabokov is a magician who at times calls himself a conjuror, but he is fooling. His magic works, and its purpose is to understand reality through creation.

Witches and
Witch-hunts

A NUMBER OF SERIOUS studies of witchcraft and witch-hunting have appeared in the last few years. British historians have been especially active in the field. Keith Thomas and H. R. Trevor-Roper, for example, have considered in some detail the Grandmama of all witch-hunts, the one that swept through Europe in the fifteenth, sixteenth, and seventeenth centuries, and touched down at Salem as it drew to a close. Now Professor Norman Cohn, of England's University of Sussex, has written a documented and highly readable survey of the evolving social forces that produced these three centuries of murderous witch craze, when tens of thousands of victims were tortured in the name of religious zeal.

Europe's Inner Demons is not Dr. Cohn's first exploration of deviant countercultures of the Middle Ages. In *The Pursuit of the Millennium,* which over the past twenty years has achieved the position of a classic, Cohn investigated the appearance and development of those End-of-the-World sects that sprang up in northern Europe in the shadow of the high culture of the twelfth century and after. In this new book, Cohn discusses the further reaches of aberrant reactions to medieval orthodoxy; but not simply as aberrations.

For the witch craze was invented and given its form, Cohn believes, by orthodoxy itself. Medieval culture, that is, constructed its own opponent counterculture as a scapegoat and handy whipping boy for its own errors and failures. This was largely an unconscious process, but when it had gone far enough, the Establishment looked, like Frankenstein, at its own creation and beheld a monster. Terrified of the demons it had dreamed up, it attacked them in paranoid panic as a hideous conspiracy of Satan himself.

The materials that went to make up the nightmare myth of a witch conspiracy were not new. They had been floating about for centuries and were attached from time to time to any unpopular group. Rumors of incestuous orgies, ritual child murder followed by cannibalism, and worship of a god who bore an animal form had been trotted out and pinned on the Jews by some Romans, on early Christians by other Romans, and on various heretical sects by later Christians. It took a while, however, before they were applied to witches.

Perhaps this is because the idea that witches exist is so common. Anthropologists note it round the world. The early Middle Ages believed in witches, so had classical antiquity, but what they believed was rather humdrum. Witches operated by occult means, it's true, but at low voltage. The technique of ill-wishing was used to afflict an enemy or his livestock with illness, to raise a storm that would damage his crops, or to render a faithless lover impotent. The Church didn't approve of such goings-on, but it wasn't in a panic over them. The basis of its dislike was that ill-wishing one's neighbors implied an appeal to occult powers outside the Church and smelled of a relapse toward paganism. The thought that such an appeal might work challenged the Church's control of supernatural power, and it therefore played the practice down as superstition.

Up to roughly the year 1000, Cohn suggests, the Western Church and the civilization that it structured and expressed had little occasion for self-doubt. The Moslems had been thrown back beyond the Pyrenees, the pagans to the north and east were progressively accepting the new faith, and the subtle heresies that beset the Byzantine Empire found little fertile ground in the West. But with the consolidation of its position, the Church found itself facing challenges from, so to speak, the Left: at any rate, from the pious and scrupulous. At Orléans in 1022, a group of learned and devout men and women, canons of the church, nuns, and aristocratic laypeople, were brought to trial for questioning both dogma and practice. They wanted to purify and simplify the Church and reform the life of clergy and laity.

Now, the Church was not simply the religious but also the intellectual Establishment of its time. To dispute any part of its system of belief was to attack it all. Those who deplored laxity and luxury on the part of the clergy, for instance, might all too easily be accused of attacking the legitimate order of society. Those who wished to reform it were accused of wishing to destroy it. Those who joined together for any purpose, but especially for any spiritual purpose, were denounced for challenging the One True Faith. The intellectual Establishment perceived itself as being surrounded by enemies and persecutors. It proceeded to persecute *them.*

By the thirteenth century it had a new judicial procedure at hand for its defense. Earlier on, most lawsuits had been brought by individuals in rather the way that civil suits are today. The plaintiff laid his charge and was expected to sustain it. The process was essentially accusatory, fought out between the two parties involved.

In 1231, a papal bull authorized a different procedure in cases where heresy was charged. The authorities were to take over the inquiry, which could not go against the accused unless he confessed. "How civilized!" one might say; but the use of torture to procure confession was permitted. What we have arrived at is the Inquisition.

But we haven't quite arrived at the witch craze. Heretical sects and such closed secret societies as the Templars, which frightened the Church by demonstrating an autonomous structure of power or of independent thought, could be accused of conspiracy. But witches and warlocks were small-time, self-employed entrepreneurs; at the most they were family businesses. The *"maleficium"* they worked was directed at neighbors in the village, not against the authorities. It was not their ill-wishing that finally put them at risk; that happened because the ruling power structure scared itself into a state where witches began to be thought of as conspirators, as a cult with fixed meetings where the Devil was worshipped. Instead of merely calling on heterodox sources of power, they had entered into a pact with Satan and become his minions.

This transformation of your run-of-the-mill ague-bestower into an agent of evil was not simple. Cohn's exposition of the social and psychological forces involved is illuminating—and disturbing. Our contemporary idea of a witch-hunt, which is generally based on the well-remembered activities of Joe McCarthy, goes astray. We tend to see it as constructed by conscious policy for individually selfish ends. Ambitious men, greedy for power, discredit their opponents by associating them with some recognized, pre-existent menace. If this were true, the witch-hunters would be acting rationally, if immorally, and should be reachable by reason, if only by money-reason. They could be bought off. That idea is the basis of all appeasement policy, and it is the reason for its frequent failure. For witch-hunters are not just manipulating popular fears, they share them. When "dealing" works, we're in a political area. Both sides stand on some common ground of reality even though they disagree. But if that common ground splits and shatters, there's no use trying to deal. The sense of a shared reality and a comprehensible causality is gone.

At the start of his book, Dr. Cohn remarks that his topic proved to be wider than he had thought. In fact, he's writing not just about witch-hunts but about delusionary thinking and the power such thinking can exercise over the minds of the great and learned as well as the simple. When things go wrong within a society, as Arnold Toynbee pointed out long ago, that society starts to lose confidence in itself. If actions don't produce expected results, those who undertake them begin to doubt the old laws of cause and effect. Challenges from without can be fought off, but how does one deal with one's own growing distrust of traditional explanations? One attempts to incorporate the anomalies into the theory, making whatever small adjustments are necessary. Ptolemaic astronomy preserved itself by introducing epicycle upon epicycle to explain the wandering planets. The medieval structure of thought preserved itself by attributing its misfortunes to demons.

The Middle Ages didn't invent demons; everyone knew they existed, just as angels did. But at some time in the twelfth or thirteenth century they, like heretics, began to proliferate. A swarm was said to attach itself to every human soul, tempting it to vice and distracting it from all that was holy. Compendia were written to warn the faithful against diabolic intrusion: seduction, possession, lustful dreams, cold hands, fits of the yawns, flatulence and untimely naps. By this time, writes Cohn, "demons have come to represent desires that individual Christians have but that they dare not acknowledge"; irruptions from the id. But they did more than represent such desires, they explained them. In a world that was becoming unpredictable, uncontrollable, demonolatry provided a new causality. One's faults could be attributed to this outside force, and one's guilt removed.

All very well. But if one attributes to demons the power to make things go wrong and things do go wrong, the power of the demons will appear to grow. They had become omnipresent, now they seemed on the way to becoming omnipotent. At first ritual gestures, like the sign of the cross, held them off, or increased prayer and strict devotion armored the soul. But if the demons did not flee, if lustful dreams and cold hands and unexpected events continued, new countermeasures were needed. How could the demons be reached and made to desist? Why, by means of those evil humans who had entered into an antihuman conspiracy with them, and that meant the witches. Slovenly old Meg, looking askance at her neighbors, was promoted from village nuisance to enemy of society.

Cohn tells us, and serious historians agree, that the old peasant accusations of *maleficium* had never alleged the elements of conspiracy, of devil worship and pacts, Sabbat gatherings, ritual murder, and incestuous orgies. It was organized, frightened society looking for a scapegoat that produced an organized, frightening enemy. Intellectually the process was convincing. Since what was known about a witch cult was what the Inquisitors racked out of accused witches, it agreed with itself in a most impressive way. If one witch came up with a new wrinkle, the next was sure to be asked about it, and to confirm it for the same reason she had confessed in the first place. (Increasingly it was a she.) Had she rubbed a stool with black-magical ointment and taken off by air to meet with her neighbors and worship a huge toad? Yes. Had she kissed the creature on arrival? Yes. Had she had intercourse with the Devil? Yes, and it was extremely unpleasant since his member was ice-cold. Had she murdered children? Yes indeed, including her own. And so on and so forth.

By the end of the fourteenth century, that cycle of catastrophe (Templars' Trial, kidnapping of the Papacy, Great Schism, Black Plague, Hundred Years' War, peasant risings, Turkish invasion), the stereotype was complete. In the 1390s two women were burned in Milan for joining a demon-worshipping cult; one of them had had intercourse (she said) with a creature named Lucifels. It was another hundred years before the handbook of witch-hunters, *Malleus Maleficarum* or *The Hammer of Witches,* appeared, and still another before the full tide of the witch craze swept across Europe, but the image of the witch conspirator had been drawn and the social implement for making her bear testimony against herself had been proved. Henceforth the powerful could point to a reason for the recurrent difficulties of life, for bad crops, the disasters of war, for illness, misery and early death. Power could name its enemies and at once discredit them by showing, out of their own mouths, that they were agents of Satan.

On the face of it, this might seem advantageous for the powerful, inasmuch as any opposition could be smeared with the taint of demonism. Moreover, this "bent" causality could be used to direct the anger and discontent of the common folk away from those in charge. It was a mighty weapon; but we would go wrong, I think, if we assumed that it was one the powerful enjoyed using. They too were terrified. Were they not engaged in battle with superhuman powers of darkness? The special horror of the witch craze was that it was created not by greed and trickery but by a paranoia that dehumanized one's enemies, a paranoia that spread through the central structure of society and became epidemic. It was a disorder not of politics but of philosophy.

Can that happen again? Does the current tide of interest in the occult portend the onset of that sleep of reason in which monsters are born? It's hard to discuss this question without appearing to take seriously what is intellectually ridiculous. But though the content of present-day occultism is certainly ridiculous, the extraordinary range and the rank, continuing growth of these phenomena suggest that there's something going on we should pay attention to.

A cursory glance at the popular press turns up an embarrassment of examples. Round the corner from where I was born on respectable Brooklyn Heights, for example, there's a dealer in magic and spells who boasts of supplying hundreds of witch covens with the materials and implements they require for their sacramental rites. Naturally he ships to dear old loopy Los Angeles, but he also has clients in Middle-American St. Louis and Cincinnati. A lecturer at Notre Dame, discussing the literary topic of "Witchcraft in Shakespeare," was thanked by a young listener "for taking us witches seriously." The 1970 graduating class at Berkeley included the world's first B.A. in magical studies—except, I suppose, for Faust. Courses are now being offered at accredited institutions on Satanism (in Boston), vampirism (in San Francisco), and witchcraft (in Wisconsin). On the nonfiction bestseller list for six months, and leading it as I write, is a volume advancing the idea that a large area of the Atlantic Ocean is hexed by supernatural forces. Some of us sing to our plants, some of us photograph auras. More people turned out to see a movie in which the Devil was exorcised from the body of a tormented child than usually go to church; and some churchmen said they thought that this was a good way to attract religious dropouts back to the faith of their fathers.

The Air Force spent months and millions investigating reports of Unidentified Flying Objects, and the public credulity that instigated the inquiry was not for one moment appeased by negative official findings. ESP and telepathy, psychic energy that acts on material objects apparently without using material means, the recollection of incidents from earlier lives—reports of all these activities generate litters of guests for late-night talk shows. All we are missing at the moment are a rain of frogs and the telekinesis of some astonished peasant from Novosibirsk to Madison Square Garden, and it's entirely possible that these events will transpire before my words see print.

Does this matter? Isn't it simply up-to-date evidence of that eternal human desire to be fooled that filled the pockets of P. T. Barnum and supplied H. L. Mencken with matter for columns of amusing copy? I want, with Cohn's book as my text, to consider why it might matter. For what we are witnessing today is not just superstition, but a strong growth in delusionary thinking, delusions that are being chosen by an awful lot of people in preference to standard, orthodox explanations of cause and effect in the world around us. This suggests that traditional patterns of causality are felt to be insufficient. They are. For example, it's clear that the actual scientific and technological working of our society isn't understood by most of its members, and that they aren't interested in understanding it. Jacob Bronowski remarked on this with sorrow at the end of the television series in which he did his Herculean and charismatic best to enlighten us about just this scientific basis of social reality. "I am infinitely saddened," he said, "to find myself suddenly surrounded . . . by a sense of terrible loss of nerve, a retreat into . . . Zen Buddhism; into falsely profound questions about Are we not just animals at bottom; into ESP and mystery. . . . We are a scientific civilization: that means, a civilization in which knowledge and its integrity are crucial."

Bronowski was not declaring that scientific knowledge is complete. A wilderness of unexplained events lies about us, pointing to unused energies. For all we know, our grandchildren will gossip with each other by ESP as easily as we do by that unknown-to-our-ancestors instrument, the telephone; an instrument whose workings are, incidently, incomprehensible to most of us who use it. The body of knowledge changes but, as Bronowski said, its integrity must remain: the sense that a fact is testable, a hypothesis capable of being sustained or disproved on exact grounds that can be replicated in different laboratories by different individuals at different times. It is this integrity that guarantees our shared reality, our common understanding of cause and effect—and it is failing. Said Herman Slater, proprietor of The Warlock Shop on Brooklyn Heights, "When you buy an airplane ticket, you're putting faith in someone's power to fly you somewhere. Why shouldn't a love philter give you the confidence that you're going to get where you want with your love object?"

Mr. Slater is obviously the victim of a confusion about what goes on inside his head and what goes on outside. And he isn't the only one. Now, it may be that Western science has not paid enough attention to the inside of our heads, that is, to the emotional and relational context of human life. Cohn suggests that the rigorous demands of medieval Christianity may also have been too difficult for the average man, just as scientific knowledge as it is communicated or not communicated today is too difficult.

Of course the experts know how to fix things when they go wrong, how to repeat the experiments that told us DNA is structured in a double helix, or that muons and pions peel off from the nucleus in different directions. (If they don't, please write.) But experts hesitate to talk to the laity. What they know is so complex, the laity is so ignorant! So the split grows, as it was already doing when C. P. Snow bemoaned the lack of communication between the Two Cultures. The experts get more expert, the laity becomes more dependent on them as it becomes less capable of valuing their work.

The human psyche needs explanations. Children ask Why? as soon as they know what the word means. Explanations tell us how to behave, how things connect, what to expect. If the experts can't elucidate their explanation to our satisfaction, we look for another. Cohn shows us how swarms of demons and evil-working witches "explained" the misfortunes of earlier times. These were false causalities. They didn't work. But—as Cohn also shows—*they were not therefore abandoned.* Let us not, consequently, suppose that contemporary occultism will be abandoned because it is false and doesn't work. On the contrary, it may grow, as the witch craze grew. Its prevalence has increased, its power may also, just as did the power attributed to demons and their witch agents, for if occult practices are held (inside our heads) to explain and direct events in the external world, if they can be seen as the cause of misfortune and misfortune happens, then many of us will "know" that occult practices are powerful. We will fear them. We will try appeasement and it will fail. We will project our fears onto the world outside our heads, looking for scapegoats to focus on, constructing enemies lists. Surely our recent history makes it hard to deny that power and paranoia can exist together. Power and paranoia, in combination, produced the great witch-hunt.

What can protect us from such a grotesque potentiality? Not reason alone, for reason can't answer emotional needs. The great witch-hunt was not a phenomenon of the Dark Ages; it coincided with Renaissance, Reformation, the age of discovery, the birth of the Royal Society, the bursting energy of a rising middle class—with the founding of modern times. Protection has to be sought, rather, in a shared understanding of the workings of the world outside our heads. When that once more prevailed, the witch-hunt ended. So, though it's a mistake, I think, to condemn the rise of occultism in our society as evil, or even as merely silly, it is not wrong to see it as a symptom of possible irrationality that can breed evil. It can do that if it splits us off from each other and permits some of us to devalue others until they become not merely subhuman but so alien to us that we feel no connection at all.

Modern technological society is no more immune to that disease than were our superstitious forebears.

DAILYNESS

"**D**AILYNESS" can be defined in many ways. It's the data base of existence, what happens that we all confidently and indifferently expect to happen, boring and repetitious, but disturbing when it isn't there. It's the homely details of ordinary life, from one tooth brushing to the next. "You'll know you need a psychoanalyst," a friend once explained to me, "when you get out of bed, look down at your feet, and can't decide which shoe to put on first, left or right." Dailyness is immediate, the grid we walk on. It's lack comes up over us in a whelming wave when links of habit dissolve, when continuity dims to nothing, when management of the physical world requires a nagging infinity of decisions. Dailyness lies in the minutiae of relationships, in *Encounters, The Presentation of the Self,* and *Relations in Public,* to borrow the titles of works by an eminent observer, Erving Goffman. Or, to recall the mission of the Collège de Sociologie, born in France in the 1930s and strangled in the cradle by war, it is "the ethnology of the quotidian," whose pursuit involves a search for the subterranean rules of the game that are knowable only by tracking back from the taken-for-granted actions and reactions that are shared and accepted by any society or social group. If poetry is what gets left out in translation, dailyness is what falls through the sieve of history, the unnoticed background radiation against which Notable Events are recorded, in whose light they are interpreted. Reverse it, and we are "through the looking-glass," in a world of antimatter and contradictory connections. Wipe it out, and the terrified isolate will try to remake reality in his or her own image; or so doctors who have worked with schizophrenic patients say. Dailyness is the social frame of reference present immediately, pervasively, in each individual life. Because it is social, and therefore shared, it creates and expresses the community that holds humankind together.

I guess that means that it might cover any kind of doing or being, and so it might. But it is the fact of there being any continuing processes of recognized doing and being, acted out all the time at simple and at grand levels, that is significant: the dynamic, shaping structure rather than the content. And yet the content can't be ignored. Change it, and the overall structure must eventually adjust, or it will deny the cumulative shifts that affect real action in real situations. Today, changes in women's lives and, surrounding this central group, in the lives of others among the governed majority of human beings, have begun to alter the ways in which we see each other, act toward each other, and look into the future. At first glance these differences in experience seem tiny and inconsequential, a matter of simple, almost physical reflexes in reaction to random events. But as time passes they and their inescapable influences come together. They testify to the existence of a different system of operations in the external world, and their impact grows greater year by year, week by week, day by day.

I close this book with two papers written five years apart and addressed to different audiences but both concerned essentially with interpreting and responding to the lumpy, unromantic, intrusive substance of existence. The first deals with "midlife crisis." The phrase will date it, though the experience continues to be common. It was given at a conference of middle-aged, middle-class women, conscientious, public spirited, responsible, and uncertain about the nature of their proper obligations to community, family and themselves; and who isn't? Like dailyness itself, that description applies across the boards. In this case it refers specifically to people who are involved with, and indispensable to, the implementation at everyday level of large-scale social purposes and processes, the folk who accept the rules of the game and labor to carry them out in order to keep families and communities in healthy being. Historically it is women in such positions who see themselves as healers of crisis, upholders of order. What does it say about the deep and spreading disorders of our times that these women now find themselves becoming aware of personal dilemmas, of immediate crisis, continuing disruption, in the daily course of their own lives?

The second paper is a recent contribution to an academic seminar, which I now think was inappropriate for that purpose. The seminar and I were somewhat at cross-purposes, I guess. My own was really to survey in a preliminary way the subject of a future but soon to be written book, a topic that has been cropping up in these essays and articles fairly often: the power to define. I suspect that for many writers future books are more absorbing than those that have been finished, if only because they promise surprises and revelations. Seldom, however, are books that are envisaged entirely new. They will have roots in previous work in which issues are broached but not really dealt with, issues that continue to surface and demand attention. The earlier book wants a successor in which the surprise packages that didn't get unwrapped are opened, in which surface solutions are pursued. Not to finality, of course, but further and deeper.

In my own case I am certainly not finished thinking about processes of power relationships just because, in a recent book, *Powers of the Weak,* I tried to work out some of the means of interaction between rulers and ruled that are serviceable to the ruled for survival and beneficial to rulers too, because interaction stabilizes political community. Great and small hear each other, and that promotes social coherence. Under the surface of that book there ran a continuing consideration of what I called the power to define: the unspoken forces that set up the rules of the game, the process by which any establishment builds a related system of ideas, myth, scientific paradigm and customary behavior into, first, an explanation of the world-as-it-appears-to-be and then a code of action suited for managing such a world.

The power to define involves more than naming or labeling. It distinguishes lumps of perception, or happenings, as events that can be named; it relates them to each other; and one of the pre-eminent relationships is by rank within a hierarchy. The power to define identifies an idea or a person or a problem and then assigns priority to it by saying, "Pay attention! Deal with me first." Then the whole network of relationships is defined, and part of this definition is a designation of how to handle events, what set of concepts and techniques to use in classifying this obtrusive bit of existence that has forced its way into our daily routine and gained our notice. How shall we look at this question? Do we address it by political methods, is it a question of economics, is it a moral dilemma or a pragmatic hang-up? A problem for our ancestors ran thus: Is it more important to abolish slavery on the grounds of its immorality than it is to suffer the disruptive economic effects that will be caused by the accompanying changes in the base of agricultural production? The Civil War, that is, can be defined as a clash between two differing views of an important element in the human condition.

We ourselves are looking at an attempt to present abortion as nothing but a moral question, without considering the existential, personal, social relationships that tie it into the fabric of life at other levels. What happens if these matters are ignored can be seen by the decision to outlaw the consumption of liquor on moral grounds without giving pragmatic support, in the everyday world, to this high-minded edict. The power to define, it would appear, can overreach itself when it fails to take account of other networks and systems of explanation and action that affect the matter under consideration.

But we need definitions and explanations. What is public and political, we ask ourselves, what is private and psychological? Where we get into trouble is the point where we allow that only one definition is valid. We need to go on asking questions—which description should take precedence? In this particular case, and not in that? If we sacrifice personal passion and need to public demands, what energy, what possible assets are lost to the very public sphere that requires our sacrifice?

Most important of all (or so it seems to me now—that may change), the power to define goes on to establish the structure of causality that we agree on as being operative in our world. In theory, our society pays tribute to science and the scientific method and has done so pretty much since the time of the Enlightenment of the eighteenth century; our own founding documents are written in that spirit. In practice, however, we deal much in magic and the sacred. Cognitive observation gives way to emotional pressure. The rules of causation, which are supposed to be governed by reason, are fundamentally a way of explaining the sequence of events in our human world, and so they cannot ignore desire and will. Those emotional forces light up rational explanations with personal feelings and thus enlist drive and creativity. But, reciprocally, in order to act on our feelings in a sustained way, we need a system that tells us that this event results from that operation not by happenstance but by strong determined and reasonable links that our minds can follow and understand. These connections give us a place to stand, from which to act. Without such orderings of the phenomena of existence, we wouldn't be able to place ourselves, we would whirl out of dailyness into the void. The crises we live with arise when we don't know quite what to make of the things that are going on or how to fit them into the ordinary context of time and process.

Given time and a hold on process, I hope to creep up on one corner of this question and do what I can to define its own defining potency. Meanwhile, the paper "Are Women's Rights Human Rights?" can stand as a tentative attempt at defining the significance of gender difference. As background, the series of seminars where it was given was devoted to human rights, and a decision had been made by its organizers to take up the topic of women's rights over the course of an academic year. That is certainly to be welcomed, but it does lead a woman to wonder how she and her kind came to fall out of consideration under the general heading and it does raise some immediate questions. What does it mean that we have been put aside as separate from humanity at large? What follows from this strange tendency of the rules of the game to split the species in such a fashion? Should we see this as the primal split, from which other dichotomies follow? How does the habit of dichotomizing as a way of defining operate to control both judgment and behavior?

Thinking it over, I wonder now whether my unscholarly approach to a scholarly gathering was not an unconscious, rather prickly response to another sort of dichotomy, that between academics and laity. The paper I gave originally has since been rewritten and somewhat enlarged for this book, but not enough to transform it into the kind of academic hypothesis that would have been really appropriate at its first presentation. It is still brash, argumentative and unfootnoted. I am sorry that I was not more aware of my underground resistance to playing the game by the rules, for I probably could have addressed the question better if I'd been more conscious of the atmosphere inside my own head. Let it stand now to illustrate a fairly common human huffiness about being defined by others and the general urge that we all feel at times toward changing the rules of the game in a sly, nonverbal, low-level way—by "the presentation of the self" during "encounters" and within "relations in public"; by bringing the homely details of diurnal existence into the Platonic realm of ideas.

Midlife Crisis

If you're anything like me, you get awfully tired of being told that crises are good for you; that they are really opportunities for growth, challenges to new life, and should be welcomed with open arms. And I who say this, remember, am in the fortunate position of being able to *do something* with the confounded things: I can write a book incorporating the experience and expressing sagacious ideas for dealing with it. But, to tell you the truth, I have quite enough subject matter lying around already to keep me busy far past our natural span of years. And if offered another crisis that supplied rich literary material, I would definitely reply— Thank you, but No. I've had an elegant sufficiency, any more would be a superfluity.

The trouble is—and well you know it, well I know it—we don't get offered crises, they arrive. It is no use saying, Please go next door. There the bloody thing is, with its head in your lap, displaying the boundless energy and enthusiasm of an English sheepdog that thinks it's a Yorkie. There's no use welcoming it or not welcoming it, it has moved in; sometimes literally, like arthritis, a parent-in-law, or your younger daughter's gentleman friend; and sometimes only figuratively as a sense of something lost, a purpose gone. Well, I am not going to tell you to welcome it. But I am going to tell you, I guess, to cope with it. And you, I daresay, would like to know how.

That's something we shall have to work at, together and alone. After all you know a lot already. You have coped with crisis before; and you know that when you manage to do it, you feel an access of strength, and validation of your capability. That is a profoundly good thing, and I don't mean to mock it. What I'm trying to say, when I laugh a little at positive thinking about crisis, is not intended as a putdown to positive thinking—I value it. But I want to be sure that

294

we are really defining it right, that we understand what we're looking for.

To say it as simply as I can, I think that what we should look for when we face a crisis in life is not success but survival. That sounds bleak, doesn't it? Well, here is where positive thinking comes in. If it is true and sound, it is based on the sense of there being an inherent, intrinsic value in life itself; in human interaction; in the multiplicity of experience; in the infinite possibility of a future that is not closed off to participation by the self. That sense persists whether or not one's efforts in meeting a crisis are crowned with what is defined as success or whether nothing so clear and immediate can be made out of what happens. Success can be a very sometime thing. Personally, I like it very much when I run into it; but just because it's around today, the law of averages warns us not to count on it's being around tomorrow. Life doesn't stop because success arrives; it trots right along, keeping in step, still carrying its full load of problematic events, asking for resolutions of critical situations. Also bearing its everyday rewards and compensations, what we get from each other, what we give to each other.

Midlife crisis is no stranger to either sex, but since human experience of life still varies according to gender, the crises that plague women differ from those that confront our husbands and brothers. They come in many guises, but most of their elements derive from the social mythology of our time and our place. They arrive with a personal label on them, that is, but they are posted out there, in the cultural context of life. That doesn't make them much easier to deal with, it's true. And the fact that social change, affecting attitudes and patterns of life, has been very rapid during the last generation means that we don't have a long experience, mediated by our mothers and grandmothers, to call on when we face its effects. It may help, however, to examine the provenance, in social change, of these elements that are to be found in the midlife crises of today. If we see where they come from, it can be easier to understand them; and understanding a situation is the first step to coping with it.

First a whole redefinition of the label, female, is under way. Begin with what women do at home, in that area known as woman's place because all of us do some of it whatever else we do. It's very different from what it was a generation ago; and even more different from what it was in the era when most families lived on farms and worked the farms together; and when urban living still had room for a lot of small family businesses, so that making a living and being a family were intimately connected. Over the last two centuries, from the time of the industrial revolution, making material goods to use and to sell in the marketplace has moved steadily and relentlessly away from the household and into industrial and commercial institutions.

So has the education of children. A lot of that used to be done by the family itself, not only formal education in the Three R's, as our grandparents called them, but even more in craft-skills, ways to make a living and, for girls, ways to run the kind of productive home that accompanied and accommodated the making of goods. Even when I was a girl, a lot of clothes were still made at home, and all the cooking and preserving was done there. No convenience foods. No take-out meals. No laundromats. No television to provide entertainment from outside, we all learned a great repertory of parlor games, we sang around the piano, popped corn, made fudge, told ghost stories, read aloud.

Well, even then the major enterprise of the family at home was raising children. Already women had all but lost the continuing economic work that had routinely been part of a functioning household. And therefore, when the children left home, mothers did face a critical change in their lives. But this was lessened in practice by several factors. First, children didn't leave as early as they do now; and usually there were more of them, so that the youngest child left later in the mother's life. Second, they didn't go as far away but tended to stay in the same area, if not in the same neighborhood; and third, the neighborhood itself was more stable. A mother would be in closer touch with a married daughter than she is now, most of the time; and she would have her own old friends closer by and quite possibly some of her own sisters and brothers. Life didn't change as fast; people didn't move around to the extent they do today. All this combined to prevent the sudden drastic isolation that many women feel when the "empty-nest syndrome" hits them. The major change that occurs when children leave home is not as critical if other relationships and activities continue. And small towns and stable neighborhoods preserve friendships more than big cities do. By the way, they preserve enmities and rivalries too; and those can be highly enlivening. They are also relationships!

Another possible element in the midlife crises in women's lives is the high valuation we place on youth. Again, that hits us all, working women or "home bodies." That was not absent from our attitudes in the past, but it worked a little differently. It was, so to speak, spread over a longer period of time. If you didn't get married, you turned into an old maid at a relatively young age. That bit of crisis took place well ahead of midlife. Moreover, in a certain number of women, it encouraged a revaluation of themselves and their activities at a time when they had a lot of energy to use. Some of them did undertake careers, got themselves into law school or medical school. Some of them—Jane Addams is the prize example—launched themselves on unpaid but enormously valuable work. Some of them—Gertrude Stein —went to Paris and wrote.

Those were extraordinary women, but school teachers and missionaries, social workers and unpaid campaigners for reform, from abolition to temperance to women's rights, kept a grip on the world outside the homes that were supposed to contain and focus the labor of the female sex. For poor women, staying home was often an unaffordable luxury; or else the home became a scene of sweated labor. For them, life was one long crisis. For the old maids of the middle class, the confrontation that we now name "midlife crisis" made little difference. They might be making do with second-best, by the standards of their time, but those who had gone through the crunch of not marrying and survived it twenty years before had had time to come to other accommodations with existence. Some of them, especially the daring and active, lived lives that were neither lonely nor unfulfilled nor unproductive.

The impact of aging today is also increased by the present emphasis on sexuality. Our grandmothers mostly settled down for life when they had got their man, or he had got them. Or they had settled on spinsterhood. Now, a lot of them did infinitely more than sit on a cushion and sew a fine seam in a lovely middle-class home; but at least most of them felt no need whatsoever to compound their activities by coming on like the Cosmopolitan Girl all through their thirties and forties and into their fifties. They relaxed and got fat, if they felt like it. They may have been wrong, but they expected marriage to last. They were consequently spared a lot of anxiety. True, when they reached menopausal age—the Change, they would have said—they reached the end of what was supposed to be woman's great function, bearing children. But let me tell you a secret—probably a rather well known one; a lot of them were absolutely delighted. Quite a lot of women, in the last century, spent most of their fertile married life pregnant or nursing babies. Now, some women feel great at these times; others don't; but the others didn't have much choice. And it's also true that feeling great gets to be less likely in your eighth pregnancy than it does, say, in your second or third. Today a lot of women regard menopause as symbolic of the loss of youth. A century ago a lot of them sighed with relief when it happened.

The appearance of youth is also more important to us today than it used to be; we read and see those ads that demonstrate how youthful grandmothers can be—and we turn that into "should be." If we don't reach the Oil of Olay advertisement standard for looking twenty-five when we're forty-two, we get another anxiety cramp.

And it isn't silly. It's no secret to you or to me that middle-aged women are not the first people to be waited on in restaurants, stores or on airplanes. We get to be kind of unseeable—aunts to Ralph Ellison's Invisible Man. It is not ridiculous, in a youth-oriented society, to try to look normal—which means young or youngish. Too often women are ridiculed for trying to disguise their age; who wouldn't disguise an aspect of oneself that is reckoned as a deficit by other people and sometimes even scares them? Dressing young, dying your hair, is much more frequently a method of achieving social normality than it is a way of presenting yourself as something you're not or as looking for sex. That is the construction that is put on it at times, and it's a nasty one, hostile and unfair. You know, feminists get reproved, over and over, for being hostile to men. I waked up the other night wondering why more men did not get reproved for being hostile to women.

The kind of hostility I'm talking about contributes in a very negative way to the midlife crisis of women. It tells us that we have lost value by aging, it demonstrates it, and we tend to agree. Not only do we get the message from the structure of our own social mythology, interpreted by the behavior of those around us, this bad news is reinforced by something rather more inward: a sense that we have somehow wasted our time in the living that took place before we reached this middle stage. Successful there or not, the past doesn't seem to count for anything when we look ahead. It doesn't appear to have taught us what we need to know. Many of us stand here puzzled and frightened, uncertain, wondering, wanting to move on to a new stage but unable to figure out what that stage is, let alone how to get there.

That's the real midlife crisis, the heart and center of it. It's a crisis of values and of meaning. And it is especially corroding because it does feel as if it came from inside, from the intimate self. We feel as if we wouldn't know what to do with life even if we could get a grip on it. The things we managed to do well in the past we did, so to speak, as someone else, someone young, someone who fitted a desired and approved pattern—but not the person we are now; and therefore we doubt the wisdom we gained in the past from our experience of life, even when it was good. We feel we've lost identity. Our new lodger is named Self-doubt.

How to cope with that? How to survive? First by understanding that this is not a personal, individual situation. It often feels that way, I know; but in fact, a major contributing factor comes from outside. There's a bad match between our surrounding social myth and the reality of the last half of our lives. In the past there was an approved pattern of living that was close enough to reality to be acceptable. Maturity offered substantial rewards of power and knowledge and place in a community—it was something to aspire to. Youth had certain restrictions placed on it—it wasn't something to cling to. Beyond maturity, there was a vision of a mellow age of wisdom, when the aging withdrew from active participation in events but were still valued for their experience and judgment and consulted for guidance. Each age led on to the next, and though each age focused on different activities—learning, acting, teaching—they were part of the same process. One lived in the midst of family and friends, once one had settled down and found one's place, and it was expected to be the same place into the years when grandchildren clustered round and the old people told them the folktales and fairy tales, legends and family history, that made up a useful store of knowledge. This vision may itself have been something of a fairy tale, but it existed, and it described what was held to be good and desirable. It provided goals and standards.

We don't have them now. There does not exist a convincing pattern for an approved way to live out the second half of life. That is a social problem, and it is—paradoxically but precisely—why we feel the crises of midlife as *not* being social. There isn't any structure of support, and because there isn't, each of us has this terrible feeling of being caught alone in an individual dilemma. But it isn't an individual dilemma, it is the product of changes in the base of everyday life that we see and accept in their material effects—but that we have not examined for their spiritual, emotional and intellectual effects. We know that families are small, that we move around the country in unprecedented fashion, that grandparents are more apt to be a thousand miles away from their grandchildren than within walking distance, that marriages break up and it's normal for mothers to work—but we have not even begun to try to rethink the ways to adjust our behavior and our ideas to these events.

I would like to think—indeed, I dream—that women facing the midlife crisis were going to supply the energy and imagination to see past the personal dimension toward social solutions, toward a redefinition of maturity and the creation of new social networks of friendship and affectionate interaction that would be both satisfying and realistically functional in our world. If we did that, we would not only succeed, we would survive. I throw in that bit of positive thinking here because I am now going to be rather negative, and I want you to know that what I say is said in the service of a positive goal.

My criticism is directed at solutions to crises in midlife that are purely personal, and stop there, and there have been a lot around recently. These sloganized solutions—Be active! Learn something new! Seek self-awareness!—are contained within no frame of meaning, no system of values. Now that's understandable. I've just got through telling you that the old system has lost its validity; but what disturbs me is that these solutions posit no *new* social system, they float in a vacuum, inviting obvious questions that they don't answer. Where shall I be active? What should I undertake to learn? If I find self-awareness, what shall I do with it? The usual answers to our uncertainties, it seems to me, are small and trivial. They aren't wrong answers—I too believe that it is important to be active, that there is great profit and pleasure in continuing to learn throughout one's life, that blindness to the needs and desires of the self invites disaster. What I am saying is that these answers are insufficient if we see them as personal, as merely individual. Doing your own thing can be a great relief from restrictions; but it doesn't bring us together. And we humans are social animals, as well as individuals. We don't thrive alone. If the world needs changing, we don't do that alone, either, by changing the inside of our heads.

Sure, that's a first step. But changing the inside of your head *without regard* to the world around is not an answer to the crisis we face today or to any crisis. It may be a beginning, it may be an opening door, but it isn't an end. The door will shut again, unless you go through. If you want a slogan to suit what I'm saying, I'll give you one. Revelation must be followed by revolution.

Take a familiar example. When St. Paul got knocked off his donkey by a blinding light on the road to Damascus, he didn't sit there congratulating himself on having a peak experience and then go on about the business of Saul of Tarsus. He had been converted, yes indeed, and the search for conversion is not only familiar today, it's a very old part of the American pattern and the Protestant pattern before it. Today, when customary religious frameworks have weakened, conversion is often sought elsewhere, but it is basically the same sort of psychological event whether you find it at a camp meeting or an est session. Speaking functionally, much of its value lies in the way it breaks old bonds of thought and shakes people out of ruts of feeling. The burst of illumination it produces also provides an access of strength and a feeling of wholeness.

But it is, by definition, momentary; its immediate effect is temporary. It can be remembered but not re-experienced at will. What Paul did was to go through the opened door and begin a hard, demanding, rewarding life work; he became active, all right—but he became purposively active. He had learned something new—and he did not hug it to himself, he went out and preached it. His awareness of self showed him how to use himself and his knowledge to illustrate his experience and communicate it to others. His mind changed, and he changed the world because he acted.

I don't suggest that we here are saints who can change the world today by our missionizing. I am saying that interior solutions to crises will fade unless they are validated and supported by interaction, by taking them outside the psyche. In other more fortunate times—not the times of St. Paul, those are useful to us just because that period, like our own, was also one of disruption and violent change—but in other times, a stable society has usually supplied the visionary with a mythology that interprets the vision, places it, says it means this or that. Today we do not have these resources. Indeed, the context of life in which we live, the orthodox interpretation of the world around us, is part of the problem, not part of the solution. When we go looking for personal revelations, when we try to understand what has happened to us to leave us, in midlife, uncertain and distressed, it is often the regular rules of the game that we are rebelling against. We want something new, new interpretations, new awareness. We look for the peak experience, just because it opens the door to new perceptions—a new heaven, a new earth.

And I don't for a minute deny that we need new perceptions, I just repeat, What do you do then? Believe me, those perceptions will lose their value, even for you, if you keep them to yourself as a solution in themselves. Human thought, human feeling, are funny things. They don't work by ordinary arithmetic. What we share grows, what we keep for ourselves and to ourselves dwindles away. It is our relationships with other people, our shared knowledge, our caring for each other that give reality and significance to ourselves and our own experience. I've had to do quite a lot of reading in very early childhood psychology for the book I'm writing now—and it is the consensus of the explorers in this vital and still rather mysterious field of preverbal learning and growth that all later understanding of the world, all our later ability to deal with it, comes from the early relationships of affection and learning and valuating in which every child grows up. Without caring adults—please note that plural, I advocate more than one loving person rearing and caring for little ones—babies don't grow, they don't even live. And those first experiences shape the way we exist in the world for all the rest of our lives. We live in relationships, in groups, in communities; and the value of our interior lives derives from those relationships. The psychiatrists have a phrase to express the desolation of the lonely and isolated individual who can't connect with others—"very flat affect," they say. It's expressive, isn't it? Such a life has lost its color and its warmth and its excitement. I guess you could be self-aware, in such a state, but I don't see it as being much of a deal. A person in such a condition needs more than to be told: You're OK, I'm OK. He or she needs to find that out for her or himself, by involvement in activities that affect the real world. Interaction, influence, control of a bit of life—these are the mirrors that reflect a healthy self; though a healthy self is usually too busy to look.

Let me see if I can sum up what I've been saying. The crises of middle life are perfectly real. Women in their middle years find themselves looking at a problematic future, with no approved paths, or roles, to follow. This is particularly true for women who have not found or established a continuing career or work role that is less apt to suffer sudden change and that involves one with people in work relationships that may shift, of course, but do not usually crest at the same time that life at home is shifting. I know that feminists are accused of downgrading the orthodox feminine role of wife, mother and housewife; frankly, I think it's not feminists who do that, it's our society that tends to judge people by the money they earn and the noise they make in the outer world. But I am willing to say that it is an advantage, a real one, to have a role, to have activities and work and a set of connections outside the home that give one a sense of continuity. God knows, there are disadvantages to running a home, raising kids, and holding down a job too—like missing out on sleep and fun; there is also the danger of accepting unthinkingly a macho mystique, as the price of rejecting the feminine mystique. No, making a career is no bed of roses, and it's no guarantee of eternal happiness. But don't overlook the value it provides by the relationships it sets up and by the opportunities it offers to prove one's own value in a world that isn't isolated in the way that family life is today.

Incidentally, I don't think it's impossible to find these advantages in civic or community work, or in political involvement, or in work for a cause you care about. There's an awful lot of work that needs doing. I warn, however, that it is at least as easy to be co-opted by unquestioned orthodox assumptions in the realm of volunteerism as it is in pursuit of a career in management. Honest work for human betterment is going to land you in a place, quite often, where you will honestly have to oppose the Establishment. Some friends of mine in a middle-western city, for example, have been running a center for battered wives for some years. What they know about opposing the Establishment, including established Do-Gooders in churches, at the Y, and so on, would fill a number of volumes. They are still working; and I think they'd tell you, as I have, that what they're aiming at isn't success, it's survival.

In any case, a career is certainly not going to guarantee immunity to midlife crisis, because so many influences that combine to produce it hit all of us—the current value placed on youth affects us all, and so does the underlying male image of women as being less capable, less decisive, less enduring, less imaginative than men. A midlife crisis for a woman with a job can damn well mean getting a deserved promotion —or achieving tenure at a university. All of us, at home and at work, fight the stereotype of femininity that stamps us as passive, needing to be taken care of, and better off in a subordinate, adjunct position than in charge of an enterprise—any enterprise. This devaluation of women's abilities is an element in midlife crisis because we accept it too readily. It's part of the message society still gives us—and we do not question it enough. We don't ask questions, you see, because we think that, being women, we don't have a right to, don't know enough, won't understand the answers, have no way to act on them or in opposition to them—and there we are, chasing our tails round and round in a vicious circle.

Here's a simple suggestion for a start on coping with the lack of self-valuation that's part of a midlife crisis: Ask some questions. Ask them at meetings or organizations. Ask them at social gatherings. Ask them at conferences like this. Don't take things for granted. In fact, doing a little homework on what's happening in any organization, or just in your town, can make the questions you ask really valuable contributions to knowledge and to planning. A lot of us still sit around and let the men do the talking. Why? Because they know more than we do? Sure they do, about some things; so why don't we go and find out? Every time you raise a feminine voice in an open meeting, or in general conversation, and ask something sensible, you are making it easier for another woman to do the same thing, and you are establishing a sense of yourself as a capable person. Society needs capable people, and it's been depending on one sex only for too long. There's a great reservoir of talent and energy available right here among us, the other sex, who needn't put up with the label "second" anymore—if we get going.

The crisis of middle life confronts us with a need to change our lives, but it does not invite us toward any pattern of changes; and thus it is a source of personal dilemma. It's as if we had to invent the rest of our lives, and we don't believe we know how to do that. Well, I suspect it may be true that we have to invent the rest of our lives; and there certainly aren't many rules around for doing that which bring satisfying results. I began by saying that the usual answers were too small, too trivial—too personal, unaware of the need for a social context. But I also affirm that we are embedded in a social context, that we cannot succeed and survive alone; and that survival means interaction with others in a continuing process. A resolution of crisis does not come by a single act or a single experience. Integration of the self, getting your head together, is not an end but a beginning. Success is only the start of survival.

For survival is what happens afterward in the life we are inventing. It means continuing existence in an ongoing world, where we have some idea of what's happening and why. Where we judge events and our potential influence on them and direct our activity toward certain ends that we believe to be better than others. We are not active simply because activity is healthy, as if we were galvanized into mindless, conditioned reflexes; we act purposively in order to have a hand in—shall we say—the stream of politics, or to create something that we see to be needed in our social setting, or to make a work of art that will communicate some kind of truth we've stumbled on. This sort of action is really interaction, aware not just of self but of others, aware of life as a process from past to future, and of thought as a product of experience. It provides a continuity; it tells us that what we learned in the years that are past has value in the present, gives us a handle on what's to come. Activity for activity's sake is isolating, and because it is, it returns us to the isolated confusion we started from. Purposive activity not only involves us in events, it gives meaning to them, it deepens experience.

What can you do to find such purposive activity? You can look around you, beginning with a sense of the value of your own interests and knowledge. What is happening in your town to battered wives and battered children? What day-care facilities exist for mothers who have to, or want to, work? What's the condition of women prisoners in the penal institutions in your state? Many of them are mothers, you know, and very few penal systems take any account of that simple fact. Their children are fostered out, sometimes they don't know where, often even if they know, they aren't allowed to see them, or they're housed so far away they literally can't see them. Yet keeping family connections alive is one of the major means of preventing recidivism—that is, renewed criminal activity.

You don't have to get into that kind of crusade—I'm just noting a few places where crusading is badly wanted. Maybe you have talents and skills you haven't developed fully. Try a course or two that will help you brush up on them and try out your abilities; the availability of higher education of all sorts to people in middle life is a new force in society and a revivifying factor in a lot of colleges and universities. Once you've developed a skill, use it. Take it seriously enough to consider that it may be more than a hobby; perhaps it isn't, but perhaps it is. You won't know if you don't try.

Don't forget about asking those questions. They may lead you straight to an area of involvement. If there are political causes you care about, learn how to lobby. It's a universal skill, usable most anywhere. If you're shy about talking, begin by writing letters. That will show you how to organize your ideas and make it easier to talk when and if you want to. And so on. Yes, do your own thing—but do it with other people. When you do, it becomes larger than yourself and your own will; it takes on a life of its own, and it gives you a direction in which to go.

All those directions, all those roads we take, all those ways we invent to survive—they are going to come together, bit by bit, to overlap or to run side by side. As they do that, they will slowly create a new pattern for the middle and later years that is more than personal. When social mythology gets out of whack with reality, it has to be created again. I believe we are going to be making it, just by the interaction, the learning and the awareness of ourselves as individuals who have a vital role in society that we have to undertake to survive. No, I don't welcome crisis—but if it's there, it's there; and it speaks of wide human needs because it hits so many of us. In closing let me give you one little phrase that I've found awfully useful when I faced decisions that didn't look very cheerful. I don't much want to do that, I say to myself but—consider the alternative. OK. Surviving may be hard work—but consider the alternative.

Are Women's Rights
Human Rights?:
The Power to Define

ALL OF US HUMANS, whatever our sex, our race, our religion, our previous or present condition of servitude, are embedded in society. The question of our rights is consequently a social question, not just an individual, personal matter. When we ask what entitlement we should properly be granted, what rights we can claim, we are also asking, "How does society see us?"

How *does* society see women? Ambiguously. Part of the time we are included in the species as the female pronoun *her* is included, we are told, in an overall *him.* But part of the time we are set off from the human norm as a subset of creatures called "women" who are understood to differ somehow from the generic masculine. Societies and cultures, so far as we know, have always taken their references, their ideals and their prescriptions for behavior from masculine experience, and women have always presented a variant that is easily exaggerated into an anomaly. If men's lives set the pattern, then, how do women fit in? If we are both like and unlike men, is the difference more important than the likeness, or vice versa? Should women's problems be taken seriously by nonfemales? Are women's rights human rights?

Unless the cultural power structure can agree that they are, women's entitlement to social status and political space is going to be smaller than that of the other sex. Existing data from life and from scholarship suggests that, yes indeed, men are regarded as being more human than women. It's the masculine reactions, the male approach to goals, and the techniques worked out by men for reaching them that furnish the standards for human norms.

By contrast, the importance women are granted is simply as part of the machinery of existence. Our activities are not causal but derived, dependent on the ways that we support what the men are doing socially, economically, politically. That has precluded many direct woman-to-woman links in the past. Our heritage has seldom been handed down from mother to daughter but has tended to run outside our control, so that connections are made via others, at the pleasure of others. The inner significance of women's lives is not considered for its own sake. History as it's taught and politics as it's practiced deal with important people and the matters that concern them, and that's a group that has never included women. The *power to define* pays attention to these more obvious kinds of power. As long as society takes seriously only what's important to important people, any group that needs help in defending its rights is just not going to be taken as seriously as those who can hold their own. The weak are not only weak, they are uninteresting; and if they are anomalous too, their problems become still less pressing. Human wrongs are obviously more prevalent among marginal people than in the power elite; that's why these people are marginal. But righting their wrongs demands less commitment and receives no priority, at least until the marginals begin to make trouble for the powerfuls. Putting women's rights in a separate area, then, implies that these rights needn't be taken as seriously as the entitlements of other human beings. Which means that the first right that women need to assert is that our rights should be considered human rights, important not only to women but actually, factually, of grave significance to the rest of the human race; and not out of charity or altruism or because the rest of the race has wives, mothers and daughters for whom they care, but because these issues, being *human* issues, impinge on them personally.

The idea that feminism will produce benefits for men has been stated often and has received some agreement, though not much, and generally less comprehension. One large reason is exactly the separation of women's interests from the central significant processes of any society rooted in male interests. If we are not important, what useful help or support could we bring to their concerns? And why should they turn aside to support ours? If we are more unlike than like, how could they share our feelings? Sympathy, yes—but comradeship, empathetic understanding? It's very rare. And so the statement that "feminism will in the end benefit men" is generally discounted as meaningless, even if it's thought to be well intentioned and courteous, a friendly gesture; though of course it may also be taken as an effort to manipulate men by sweet talk. In neither case is it taken seriously.

It should be. Not only is it perfectly possible for felt alliance to exist between men and women; women clothe themselves in male

concerns all the time. Also available and offering immediate benefit to
men are the human resources they can reach and the comrades and
colleagues they can find in such *ententes cordiales.* But until femaleness fades into humanness more than it yet has done, women will not
be taken seriously enough for our public support to seem valuable.
Now as ever, our ability to enter vicariously but enthusiastically into
male interests follows from the importance that we grant to men and
their activities. We've been taught that masculine doings and think-
ings and sayings symbolize the noblest *human* capacities. Our womanhood may deny us the chance to represent such ideals ourselves, but
they are (we understand and agree) worthy of being honored by all
humans—a category in which we are included for the purpose of
honoring.

Now it isn't the fault of any male individual if he can't manage to
reciprocate—can't comprehend personally, for example, that a vote
against the Equal Rights Amendment is a vote for inequity because
it's a vote to repress half the species to which he belongs. How can
he really feel that when, forever and a day, the magisterial system of
concepts and premises by which patriarchy rules has been busy teaching him that women's difference from men is more important than our
likeness to them? We, of course, have learned that too, but since in
our case difference means male superiority, we are ready to make the
effort of thinking and feeling our way into man's world and male
habits of thought. For us, it's important. But as long as women are
felt to be different and consequently ranked as inferior, men have little
reason for learning the way into our thoughts.

Indeed most men still tend to assume that women acquiesce in the
doctrine of difference and the doctrine of ranking too. Didn't they
learn these things from their mothers, weren't their mothers women?
Why should women teach, and act out, a condition of inferiority if
they don't think it's true?

Because unlikeness and ranking are the way of the world, and
what loving mothers must teach their children is how to survive, how
to get on, and one doesn't survive by being ignorant of the rules. And
yet consciously or unconsciously, the women who handed on the rules
of male dominance must have hated it. I don't know how else we can
explain the multitude of furious goddesses who hold a place in every
pantheon one can think of: Hecate, Kali, Medusa and the Eskimo sea
creature who waits for the drowned hunters to circle down through
the freezing waters to her lair, Grendel's mother, and all the ogresses
of fairy tales. They surely represent human counterparts whose rage

vibrated in every nerve. But angry women still had to teach the brutal facts of survival and, once learned, the rules helped to anchor girls in place, for no successful rebellion will be mounted by those who don't believe in their right to rebel, nor in their chance of winning. Yet life in the routine of dailyness meant learning the game and handing on its rules to the next generation of daughters, who would, like their mothers before them, feel themselves betrayed by those who had given them life and then forbidden them to use it. No doubt the break between daughters and mothers was deeper sometimes than at others, but could it ever have been absent? How could girls who were told of humanity's highest virtues and then denied the right to aspire to them trust their teachers? If they accepted the ideals, how could they accept their likeness to the timid betrayers, their mothers, who spoke with such double-mindedness: Honor these goals, but never try to reach them? If you honored the rules you could not honor the teacher; and so women learned isolation too and dependence on more trustworthy (it seemed) male authority. They learned not to act for themselves.

But action is vital to rights. If you possess them you are surely entitled to fight for them. When we ask, Are women's rights human rights? we are asking about channels for action. Are women's issues women's business alone? Do they affect only women's lives? Should they, consequently, be dealt with by women in the sphere reserved for female action? Or are the causes of women's difficulties broadly social, political, economic, common to general conditions of existence? If that's the case, they point to something rotten in the human universe and not just in woman's place. But in order for society to accept that conclusion, and to act on it, standard thinking has to accept the premise that women are human beings first and female creatures afterwards, for only then will our experience be taken as a useful tool for interpretation of events and problems in the world at large. Some male minds are ready to do that, but it isn't yet a "normal" response. The instinctive reaction is to see difference first. Freud's famous question not only despairs of male knowledge of women's purposes but it also assumes we don't and can't know ourselves, while rational men are fully aware of their goals; a very iffy assumption, in fact. But as long as mystery surrounds the desires and goals of women, any issues that do concern us will appear to be private. Until we can articulate them clearly, no one else can understand them, and so they will continue to belong to a realm where masculine angels fear to tread.

In short, what we need is a handhold on the power to define, to group events according to our priorities, to relate them to each other by a system of cause and effect that we put together out of our own lives. Until we can say what it is that we want, women's issues will seem to men to be special and peripheral to the central human matters that have real weight. Now, the weight assigned to any phenomenon is of great importance to the way we think about it. No one is going to work hard in order to figure out how to deal with a problem unless the problem *matters.* Long ago it was borne in on me that the most important question in the world is not "What is good or what is bad?" or "What is right and what is wrong?" or even "What is true and what is false?" Weighty and substantial as all these queries are, the most important question in the world is "What's important? What must we pay attention to, first of all?"

If women's issues can be defined as important only to women, they don't have a high priority for action in the world at large. The consensus view today, I would say, judges women's rights as being a bit more important than they were considered a decade or so ago. We can see the change in the fact that by the late seventies the Equal Rights Amendment had become worth defeating, while it had previously slid through a lot of state legislatures defined as an unimportant sop to womenfolk. There's not much real joy to be wrung from this rise in the significance of ERA, but it does indicate that the presence of women in man's world of action has become evident enough to provoke counteraction. It can't be denied that we are functioning as agents of change, and the perception has raised our status. We are now no longer a joke; we are a threat, which I guess means we are getting somewhere.

We haven't got far. The tactic of insisting on our difference as being more significant than our human likeness is very destructive here, for it pushes us out of the central arena of politics, where issues that society must deal with in a practical way are handled. If women's issues can be assigned to another area of attention, they can be bundled out of politics, labeled moral, religious, psychological, personal— above all, *private.* Make abortion a moral issue, and talking about it as a political matter becomes immoral and shocking. Every feminist speaker who has traveled the Bible Belt knows that God in all His Fatherhood is going to manifest himself along the way and that St. Paul's injunction to the women of Ephesus to obey their husbands will be raised by a gentleman caller-in to a broadcast talk show; that makes equality a religious matter, to be advocated by secular humanists only. If you can get "traditional family values" colored by dreams of a Golden Age into a condition of sacredness, you will remove them from discussion by people who have in fact studied the diverse and changing history of the family in Western culture. These are all efforts to keep women's issues out of the political arena, where they can be addressed in terms of their public causes and consequences and dealt with in the same way as tax reform or immigration policy or funding mass transit. Woman's otherness may put her on a pedestal or in purdah but, practically speaking, its effect is always to keep her out of politics.

In deconstructing Johnson's Great Society and Roosevelt's New Deal, the aim of the Right Wing has been to return women to the domestic sphere and bring back a comfortable-for-others past, when women's issues were indeed consigned to female territory, where they were to be handled without bothering men. If occasionally one of these problems escaped the bounds of woman's place and found its way into the political mainstream, the very fact of its intrusion was cause for resentment and disgust. The women who had let such a thing happen were blamed and shamed. Sexual difference has often been expressed in terms of female uncleanness, and spreading female problems out in public has been as shocking as the violation of the taboo that once isolated menstruating females in a secret and distant spot. In the ancient division of labor by sex, men did what they had to do to run and rule the world, and women picked up the pieces or dusted them away—at least, that was expected of them! If some remnant of these expectations are still with us, we may not be pleased, but we can't be astonished. Short of genocide, or genderocide, habits are hard to kill off. We've all been socialized into the old myth and even when we want to learn differently, we don't do it quickly, we don't do it fully. It is naïve to imagine that the segment of the human race that isn't female could agree easily that women's rights are really human rights; as naïve as to imagine that the feminine mystique is dead and gone.

Still, a start has been made. An increasing number of women know personally that *their* rights are human rights. Some of them certainly don't think of themselves as part of any "women's liberation movement," but what liberation has managed to win for them has come to seem part of a righteous entitlement. At the level of action, not thought, this reaction is an assertion of full humanness, and it is political whether she who feels it knows that or not. She very well may not, for we are not rid of our double-mindedness yet. But our growing participation in mainstream action, the growing number of women at home out there in the public world, inevitably produces a sense of likeness—at least *for us.* To put it simply, women think women are human first, before being female, more than we ever before have done.

This willingness to act for one's motivated self is enormously important, but it isn't enough. We need theory too, if only as a means for holding ourselves together as a group. No matter how motivated an individual may be, an isolated self can forget the past and imagine that a personal step forward means that the future is secure. But classes, races, ranks, estates do not advance in single file. Individual success disproves the old rules that say it can't be done; but until each success is added to a growing heap, real social change is not spelled out, not easily seen as a more-than-personal phenomenon. A changed-status person has grown in courage and a sense of her potential reach; but as an isolated individual, she has no protection against co-option. Women moving into the world of business and the professions are bedrenched and belabored by advice on how to get on there through learning how to behave like men. That's a mistake. What we need, all of us, men and women too, is to learn and invent and discover ways of behaving like human beings.

Easily said, harder to do. But if we can see that women's issues are human issues, we are on our way to understanding how the gender split has acted as a social control on both sexes, just as racism has bound whites as well as blacks into crippling and distorting behavior. Such behavior has been prescribed by whites just as a female behavior has been directed by patriarchy, but it binds white males into abnormality as thoroughly as it oppresses and represses those whom they see as enemies and inferiors and bogeys.

By these standards, abnormality becomes the norm. A man who refuses to accept them is subjected to peer pressure and shaming, bound to expected brutality as completely as the "others" are committed to victimization. At many times and in many places, and one of these times is now, young men who are seeking to place themselves in an amorphous world are invited to join defined action groups where they will be granted an identity as a member of—an age grade, a college generation, an army-service class, a gang, the Klan, or what have you. In order to become part of this comradeship, the novice will be put through a violent rite of passage—"blooded" in a most realistic way. Violence against blacks, against Jews, against immigrant East Asians, is generally seen as a means of keeping those attacked in their place, and of course it is. But the new boys are also kept in line by their participation in such an act at the behest of the old boys. Law-breaking makes them vulnerable to blackmail if they should later defect, but that's the least of it. More forceful is the violation they have had to make of their own consciences. The pain of facing what one has done, many veterans of Vietnam testify, is paralyzing.

In order to survive such knowledge, the easy way out involves a psychic path that runs something like this: If you are going to live as a normal person, you have to deny what you did, and if you can't manage that, then *you must deny that it was important*. How to do that? By denying that the person you lynched or burned or tortured or raped was really a person; she or he wasn't fully human, wasn't sentient and rational, like you. The creature you violated was different, other; more animal and primitive in the case of blacks or innately masochistic in the case of women. That's a denial of reality and a choice of fantasy, but once made it's terribly hard to get out; it takes, I think, a real conversion experience to do so, and those are rare, in spite of all the mechanical, ritualistic birthing-again we have been hearing about lately.

To accept the violation of others as a normal act forces an equally violent split in the self, a substitution of fantasy for reality in the internal being as well as in the outer world. The need to repress guilt becomes obsessive, and often the method chosen is the acting out again and again of the guilty action, in order to validate it as normal and acceptable. Over and over the victim is established as different, the likeness between humans is denied. The split in the human mind is magnified and reflected in the social split; and the primary division by gender reproduces itself in division by class, race, nation, language, religion—add any other prejudice you wish.

Patriarchal power (I called it The Thing in the introduction to this book, picking up William Cobbett's name for the mindless, pitiless aristocratic establishment of the eighteenth and nineteenth centuries in England) forces society toward this kind of splitting, and consequently it destroys community. In order to identify ourselves as individuals, we find it necessary to congeal into separate and hostile segments. Undervalue one segment and division becomes the choice because one dare not link oneself with the stigmatized group. Deny them the right to full humanity, and you deny it to yourself. It seems as if the powerful can never be secure in power because they fear the powerless—as if weakness were an infectious disease and the only protection a kind of social quarantine.

These are rooted impulses and they can't be changed by logical arguments. Logical arguments, however—theory—can contribute to sensible action. Women who work for women's rights know that they are human rights, and the knowledge contributes to a growth of community and a future healing of division. Future, not present, for our impulses are still bound by axioms of the old social mythology that was rooted in division, and learning demands that we be able to unlearn those lessons. Practical action, however, is a fine instrument for learning. One immediate advance comes as we begin to link together the various concerns of women that have been split off from each other and presented as diverse. For it grows clearer every day that demands for equal wages raise the question of equal opportunities for training and of equal pay for work of comparable value. As economic issues begin to come together, they point toward important social questions.

Sometimes that importance can be rather overwhelming. Tell a woman intent on gaining an immediate goal that she is actually attacking the whole complicated structure of society, and she may perhaps say, "OK, then society has had it!" On the other hand, she may be more likely to respond, "Dear me, then perhaps I'd better sit quiet and fan myself instead." Not everyone is stimulated by the prospect of making a revolution. But that's not the whole story, for a sense of challenging work to be done can evoke courage and endurance and direct frustration into productive channels. Women entering the world of work discover that change is possible, and they shrug off passivity. To the extent that the incapacity expected of them is replaced by ordinary human reactions to intrusion or to menace, the image of a special feminine nature is denied by daily experience, their own and that of the men who work with them.

As many people have said before me, the ancient otherness ascribed to the female sex grows out of the old habit by which the definition of woman is centered on that of mother; current feminine analysis pays great attention to this coalescence of social definitions, and its consequences. But pragmatic politics is heavily affected by the axiom that woman equals mother too. Ramifications of this equation stretch across the whole area of existence. Indeed, they present us with some of the very rights that we have to fight for as women's issues: maternity benefits, child support, child-care programs, these are seen as concerns for women and women alone, not of the whole society, which children will in fact inherit and have to manage.

Our right to equality in employment is of course deeply shadowed by the "woman equals mother" definition. In a happier world, the idea that adult human beings have important work to do in both private and public spheres of existence might operate to heal the split between these two areas of life. But our world is dedicated to division. If reproduction is taken to be a female obligation, it's also taken to be our primary job and if any group of creatures is held to have a primary job, all other activities will equally be counted as secondary in their lives. If they can do them well, it will be astonishing and unexpected.

Now women certainly do bear children, and we're not likely to give place to test tubes soon, if only for economic reasons. But when social mythology shuts its eyes and slides immediately from the physical phenomenon of bearing children to the social task of raising them, it's taking too much for granted. It isn't mothers alone who raise children—adults do, other older children do, the community as a whole has a hand in the task whether it knows it or not; and for a superior result, the more adults engaged in formal and informal education and the wider and more diverse the social involvement the better. Children and young people profit from finding many channels to the outside world. It brings them news of possibilities and increases opportunities to look ahead and choose work and friends and styles of living. In addition, it's good for young people of both sexes to know that their mothers are capable human beings both inside the house and out and that the matters that concern them are important human concerns too.

If we are to affirm these principles, it's time we took the power to define into our own hands. The place to begin is with the self-images that reflect our identities from warped and twisted mirrors. Not just women, but women always among the great majority of humankind, have been labeled by the powerful as weak, as less able than our masters, less linked with reality, less persistent in action, childishly inattentive to our own best interests, in real need of good counsel and a helping hand from on high, necessarily led and directed because we don't know how to help ourselves; but that description has been laid on many minority groups that included males. As long as the governed accept such a judgment as legitimate, this long shall we continue in subjugation; but in recent years, this acceptance has at last begun to break down. Women and minority groups are indeed on the road to redefining ourselves for ourselves.

What I mean by redefinition is easily illustrated. Let us, for simplicity's sake stay with the topic of women's rights, but let us think about our entitlement in broad human terms that put likeness before difference, terms based on a profound conviction that women's rights are human rights. Suppose we stop asking what women want, or even what women need as women, and pick up the question at the other end, asking instead, "What does society need in order to take the first steps toward the end of polarization and the building of real human community? How can it release, and profit from, the overlooked abilities of half the human race, which has never yet had a chance to use them in full? How can it relieve the other half from locking itself into reciprocal repression, devoting so much of its time and energy to keeping the lid down on the people it declares are powerless and on its own potential too? How can we best refresh mainstream life by cutting the dams that have held back all these streams of creativity at the cost of desperate anxiety?"

If we looked at gender division with some such questions in mind, we would of course see women as childbearers, but we wouldn't go on to declare that this female function made women so special that they had to be kept away from other activities, fenced in with their children in a separate, private area of existence. We wouldn't hand to one sex the community's job of raising and educating the next generation. We would redistribute that task and that opportunity for influencing the future, both because we wouldn't want to lose other contributions that the mothers of these children could make and because we would want to feed into education contributions that their fathers could make, both as males and as individuals. But beyond the joint obligations of parents, we would also see to it that all sorts of other adults and all sorts of social institutions took a hand. Those who had a gift for education, of either sex, might want to make it a life work. Others with special skills—musicians, storytellers, artists, people in love with hobbies—could come and go. Many roads to the adult world would open, where very few are now available.

At once other related questions would swing into perspective as the opaque curtain that now shrouds child raising in family privacy lifted. Society would be in a better position to deal with the half-glimpsed terrors we know are there and turn away from—abuse of children by violence or for adult sexual ends, by deprivation and neglect, by distracted or helpless single parents who have no larger network to which they can turn. Less extreme but more pervasive problems could be better handled, problems that may in fact take a greater toll overall. Most children now grow up with almost no firsthand knowledge of life in the adult world as it is, instead of as it's presented on the television screen where it's distorted, intensified, sentimentalized, and trivialized as entertainment; where human processes of interaction appear to be resolved in the hour's time allowed a program. When news programs show public events they are often sensationalized and may awake painful anxiety in children who feel them as immediate and personal threats. Schools and homes and peer-shared activities lie a world away, it seems, from the politics and economics of the mainstream. Formal education is nowhere near adequate to introduce the next generation, any next generation, to the interrelated conditions, the processes and obligations and consequences of action where adults do the work that earns their livings, and undertake the obligations of citizenship.

Once any sensible community turned its attentions to the education needed by the adults-to-be who will one day replace those now in charge, it would, sensibly, consider redefining proper preparation for the job. I hope it would be willing to try mingling liberal education with vocational and professional training, so that apprenticeship and schooling went on at the same time in a fashion that could build bridges across another split in our lives. Continuing education for adults has already done a good deal to bring the traditional academy back into closer touch with the dailyness of life in spite of resistance from the elite schools. The same approach to teaching the young by bringing in everyday skills that are no longer taught informally shouldn't be seen as "degrading" the curriculum. Instead it could create a curriculum that would be both wider and more connected.

Until recently, girls have learned more by such informal education than have boys. That, of course, was because feminine skills, suitable to those who were expected to get married, have babies, and spend their lives in the domestic sphere, were too mundane for the academy. We don't want to revive and perpetuate a vision of inescapable gender difference consonant with such education, but the usefulness of informal learning by doing should not be forgotten. To define equality of education for women as equal access to the current curriculum is not adequate, unless you happen to agree that preparation for life under patriarchy is not only the be-all and end-all for humankind but is also now conducted in an absolutely perfect fashion. In fact, adolescents of both sexes are probably less well prepared today for coping with adult existence as it is than are those of almost any other society that history records. Like the gender division, the age split takes its toll in many ways. It has been named "the generation gap" by adults, when they felt hostility from the young; but the desperation of the young, which can be traced in drug abuse, in the shocking rise of teenage suicide, and in recurrent waves of dropping out, is surely a more extreme problem. More "normal" reactions of apathy and narrow ambition speak of incomprehension and lack of control vis-à-vis the world at large, endemic to young people today.

As it is, we can almost diagram the dismal effects of basing education for life on norms derived from the experience of dominant males,
who make up so small a proportion of the total population. Because
orthodox definitions say that raising children is a job reserved for
mothers; because the sphere where mothers are expected to carry on
this labor is "woman's place," set off from public life, children are
placed in the same segregated area and left ignorant of what's going
on everywhere else. And because they are reared by women and only
by women, it's women alone who are supposed to worry about them.
By a kind of backward logic, other human beings, active in man's
public world, do not need to worry about them.

So the effort to keep women isolated from the mainstream works
to keep children isolated too and thus to separate them from opportunities for learning about adult activities through taking part in them
or indeed from even watching them in process. Craft-skills and hand-
work, so common up to a century ago, have been replaced by the
mysterious functioning of machinery and the even more mysterious
shuffling of paper or manipulating of computers that controls work
today. Physical work could not only be seen, it could be understood.
If your father was a blacksmith, you knew what he did all day. But
suppose your father is an insurance executive or a clerk in personnel
records? In an urbanized, industrialized community, introducing the
young to the daily data of adult life doesn't happen easily and almost
automatically, as it did when small-town doings took place under their
eyes. In the city neighborhoods that Jane Jacobs celebrated a generation ago, in *The Death and Life of Great American Cities,* a fair
amount of adult existence and street life was part of everyday knowledge. It isn't now, and the split between home and the world of work,
still largely separated by gender, contributes to the divisions of our
time.

Should we see the task of healing this division as another "woman's issue"? It's a problem for all women, whether they have an
outside job or not. If they don't, they are without current information
of the work world. If they do, they are in the first place pressed for
time, and they are also invited by the continuing force of orthodox
gender roles to blame themselves if anything goes wrong in the growing up of their children. It absolves a patriarchal society from blame
if bad mothering is made the standard reason for juvenile delinquency;
and bad mothering is quickly equated with holding down a job for pay
along with one done at home for free. The effect of the "woman equals
mother" definition first hampers women in doing anything else; it goes

on to weaken their desire to do anything else by handing out a plentiful portion of guilt for less-than-perfect children if they do enlarge their lives. And by providing a scapegoat for mishaps, it lets the rest of the world ignore any obligations to take a hand in educating and training the next generation.

Women's rights, human rights. The consequences of separating them are many, and I don't believe that we are yet close to seeing them all. Division by two creates otherness, for it sets up an "us" and a "them." Then, since the normal powerful "us" half of society naturally assumes precedence, division by two produces ranking. It cuts off the range of thought, so that we fail to see connections between actions in one area and results in another. Most insidious of all, it suggests that polarization is the proper approach to analysis. Defining an entity by what it isn't draws attention from what it is and what it might become. By emphasizing difference, it obscures identity.

What do we lose by opting for polarization and dichotomy, for beginning any definition or any process of reasoning with the question "either—or"? What happens to all the gradations and possibilities that lie between the two opposing ends of that question? It seems to me that we lose not only enriching diversity, but also a sense of becoming. We are afraid to live with the ambiguities of change and process, and we choose the sharp outlines of what can really be said to be there, right now—absolutely there and irredeemably static. Even when the need for becoming makes itself felt, when process is introduced by way of thesis, antithesis and synthesis, we fail to ask "What got left out in the first place, was never included in thesis nor countered in antithesis, and must still be lying around somewhere in the dark of reality?"

So much of what women have lived and known has been forgotten there in the dark! And it is human experience that has got lost. What we find as we search the world outside the spotlight of orthodox concerns and traditional knowledge is matter pertaining to the whole species, matter that is valuable for interpreting the past, explaining the present and pointing toward new ways of imagining the future. Women's issues are human issues, and human rights can never be won in full until we understand from the bottom of our brains and our hearts that they involve all of us humans, our needs and our capacities, across the boards.